The
Creative
Community
College:

Leading Change Through Innovation

The
Creative
Community
College:

Leading Change Through Innovation

Edited by John E. Roueche,
M. Melissa Richardson,
Phillip W. Neal, and
Suanne D. Roueche

The American Association of Community Colleges (AACC) is the primary advocacy organization for the nation's community colleges. The association represents more than 1,200
two-year, associate degree–granting institutions and more than 11 million students. AACC
promotes community colleges through five strategic action areas: recognition and advocacy
for community colleges; student access, learning, and success; community college leadership
development; economic and workforce development; and global and intercultural education.
Information about AACC and community colleges may be found at www.aacc.nche.edu.

Design: Gratzer Graphics LLC
Editor: Deanna D'Errico
Printer: Kirby Lithographic Company, Inc.

Community College Press
American Association of Community Colleges
One Dupont Circle, NW
Suite 410
Washington, DC 20036

Printed in the United States of America.

Library of Congress Cataloging-in-Publication Data

  The creative community college : leading change through innovation / edited by John E.
Roueche ... [et al.].
     p. cm.
  Summary: "Provides 14 profiles of innovative and transformational leadership at community colleges. The experience and knowledge shared by the contributors demonstrate how
community colleges are adapting creatively to rapidly changing economies, technologies, and
education standards"—Provided by publisher.
  Includes bibliographical references and index.
  ISBN 978-0-87117-385-0
  1. Community colleges—United States—Administration. I. Roueche, John E.

LB2328.C77 2008
378.1'010973—dc22

Contents

Foreword

O F ALL OF THE SEGMENTS of American higher education, community
colleges have been the most flexible, the most responsive to the educational needs of communities, and the most resourceful, taking calculated
risks and leveraging scarce resources to accomplish their educational missions. The
innovative and creative spirit of these unique institutions is captured well by the
authors of *The Creative Community College: Leading Change Through Innovation.* The
colleges and systems that are profiled in this volume are exemplary of what is won-
derful about community colleges and how they can turn adversity into success.

But this book is really about leadership: creative and transformational leadership. Each of the chapters tells a story of unique challenges and equally unique
responses by community college leaders who built alliances, systems, and programs, often facing significant obstacles and even active resistance. In *The Creative
Community College,* these leaders share their success, their failures, and the risks they
took to strengthen their institutions, to build alliances, and to create new systems.

While each of the authors tells a distinct story, there are some common leadership characteristics that emerge. For the most part, these leaders had been with
their institutions for some time, providing consistent and committed leadership.
They built a trusting environment, sometimes where one had not existed before.
They engaged in purposeful environmental scanning, looking for opportunities
and potential for improvement. They determined what was most important for the
future of their institutions or systems and focused on those priorities. They were
clear about their goals and communicated them effectively, securing the necessary
support from others. They focused the resources of the institution or system on

students and their learning and success. They provided professional development for their people. They were persistent, realizing that progress can be slow even in today's fast-paced world. They worked on building supportive relationships with individuals, with business and industry, with area schools, and with universities. They were able to make unpopular decisions when necessary.

These leaders created a culture of evidence, using data and establishing performance indicators to determine whether changes were producing the results they and their leadership teams expected. They nurtured and developed the future leaders of their institutions and systems. They made appropriate use of modern technology to support student learning and institutional processes. They gave credit to others: faculty, staff members, trustees, school leaders, and other partners.

The stories that the leaders tell in *The Creative Community College* give life to the leadership competencies that were developed through the Kellogg Foundation–funded Leading Forward project and approved by the AACC Board of Directors in 2005. The six competencies identified in *Competencies for Community College Leaders* (go to www.ccleadership.org/resource_center/competencies.htm to view the complete document) are as follows.

Organizational Strategy. An effective community college leader strategically improves the quality of the institution, protects the long-term health of the organization, promotes the success of all students, and sustains the community college mission, based on knowledge of the organization, its environment, and future trends.

Resource Management. An effective community college leader equitably and ethically sustains people, processes, and information as well as physical and financial assets to fulfill the mission, vision, and goals of the community college.

Communication. An effective community college leader uses clear listening, speaking, and writing skills to engage in honest, open dialogue at all levels of the college and its surrounding community, to promote the success of all students, and to sustain the community college mission.

Collaboration. An effective community college leader develops and maintains responsive, cooperative, mutually beneficial, and ethical internal and external relationships that nurture diversity, promote the success of all students, and sustain the community college mission.

Community College Advocacy. An effective community college leader understands, commits to, and advocates for the mission, vision, and goals of the community college.

Professionalism. An effective community college leader works ethically to set high standards for self and others, continuously improve self and surroundings, demonstrate accountability to and for the institution, and ensure the long-term viability of the college and community.

Among the challenges that our society faces today are shortages of nurses, which threaten the quality of health care, and shortages of teachers, which threaten the education of our children; a growing skills shortage that threatens our nation's productivity and standard of living; a stubborn equity gap when we need all of our people to be educated and productive; and concerns about preparation in science, technology, engineering, and mathematics in a globally competitive economy and with a planet that seems more fragile than ever before. We will need a higher education system that is willing and able to move beyond tradition and to be creative in meeting these challenges and others not yet apparent.

Historically, creativity comes from people who are not bound by tradition but people who are willing to take risks, to think new thoughts, and to do things differently. "Necessity is the mother of invention," is a saying that certainly applies to community colleges. Their leaders have often had to be inventive and creative to strengthen and sometimes even save their institutions. This is the environment in which new ideas emerge. For example, today's focus on student learning and student learning outcomes that is sweeping across American higher education started in the community college, where leaders dared to say that our true mission was student learning rather than providing instruction—that we should measure institutional success by the success of our students rather than by our resources.

Creativity also requires transparency. Innovative leaders must be honest and open with their goals and the degree to which they are achieved. In this regard, community colleges are again leading the way. Community colleges currently participating in the Community College Survey of Student Engagement and the Achieving the Dream: Community Colleges Count initiative openly share their data and use benchmarks to motivate their teams to develop strategies that improve student engagement and student success.

One other uniqueness of community college leaders is that they are willing to share ideas and to "steal" good ideas that they can adapt to meet the needs of their institutions. The authors of *The Creative Community College* openly share their strategies and their successes and failures in this volume. Readers are invited to learn from the experiences of these leaders and to take the kinds of calculated risks that will make their community colleges even more creative.

George R. Boggs
President and CEO
American Association of Community Colleges

Acknowledgments

We acknowledge and forever will appreciate the contributions of the amazing corps of leaders who contributed to this book. The tireless efforts in writing their stories amidst hectic schedules and never-ending demands demonstrate their commitment to sharing their insights about leading creatively. In the same way these leaders use team approaches within their institutions, many called on the collective genius of staff members to craft their message. A special thank you is extended to all who assisted in telling the inspiring stories of their colleges.

Introduction

John E. Roueche, M. Melissa Richardson, Phillip W. Neal, and Suanne D. Roueche

IN 1961, EDMUND GLEAZER, THEN of the American Association for Community Colleges (AACC), predicted the issues community colleges would face in the future—changing demographics, a global economy, and technological advancements. Today, colleges grapple with issues envisioned almost 50 years ago, many of which are addressed in the following chapters. The pace and complexity of life create enormous challenges. As an economic futurist, Ed Barlow (2007), warned, "The key to success in the 21st century is alignment—staying in alignment with a world that will be characterized by complexity, diversity, and pace of change." To align with this century, community colleges must adapt, forecast changes, and be creative with their solutions to higher education in an incongruous world. Our history of flexibility and innovation tells us we *can* and we *will;* stories of success, showcased in this collection of contributed chapters, provide perspectives of *how.*

TRACKING THE CLIMATE OF HIGHER EDUCATION

Educational Testing Service's 2007 policy paper, *America's Perfect Storm: Three Forces Changing Our Nation's Future* (Kirsch, Braun, Yamamoto, & Sum, 2007), described the confluence of demographic changes, global economy, and education failures. Our education system needs major disaster management before our students become its future victims or survivors, rather than its champions. So how do today's leaders transform campuses into cultures in which lifelong learning can begin and the U.S. economic health be secure? We believe leaders must value creativity and allow each facet of the college to feel supported and willing to move beyond the status quo. College leaders must take every opportunity to create meaning and purpose for students, faculty, staff, and the college community—using all the tools available to them.

Policymakers and agenda-setters are recognizing and acting on the need for change in higher education, and community colleges are involved whether they wish to be or not. According to a 2006 survey of registered voters, "92% agree that actions taken today on higher education policy will be critical to U.S. competitive leadership in the world 25 years from now" (American Council on Education, 2006, p. 1). More than a decade ago, the League for Innovation in the Community College asked, "For *what* are we educating people?" Answers included "for happiness, a fulfilled life, opportunity, and physical and spiritual survival" (LeCroy, 1993, p. v). Gleazer (1980) believed in the work of educating people for lifelong learning. For all of these reasons, leaders and educators must ensure that community college education remains a long-lasting and compelling argument for improving quality of life.

Much is being made about creativity in the workplace, about the creative economy—a motif that inspires urban growth and champions a diverse, talented workforce (Florida, 2003). Creative economies thrive in cities known for higher education, where innovative ideas are nurtured and encouraged. Creativity is the new buzzword in the corporate world out of necessity. As education guru Sir Ken Robinson observed, "The world is changing so quickly that promoting the ability for creative thinking and promoting cultural adaptability is essential"; creativity is "applied imagination," using the imagination to solve problems (cited in Scanlon, 2006). Creativity is defined by more traditional definitions of art, music, theater, or dance. Community colleges with thriving arts programs often have strong relationships with their communities. These definitions of creativity are both appropriate here because they promote the unions between concepts of critical thinking, new vision, and community spirit. Of particular value on any community college campus is the willingness to engage in new and courageous combinations and to trust moments of great creativity.

Creativity thrives in paradox. Creativity encourages innovation outside traditional boundaries and yet is made possible by relying on unwavering values, for example, integrity, vision, and community. Valuing relationships and the whole person, striving for innovative yet disciplined decision making and having the courage to change are qualities that provide the foundation on which creative cultures can flourish.

Proactive and creative leadership can support and inspire a college to new levels of success. For example, consider Greek architecture, particularly the keyhole arches. Greek artisans cut the marble so perfectly that each piece placed the exact pressure necessary to the next piece—keeping both in place and supporting all pieces on all sides. No hardware is needed to adhere one stone to another. The result is an archway that is functional, beautiful, enduring, and deceptively simple. This is the tension and the outcome a great leader respects: each piece is integral to the whole.

DEVELOPMENT OF THE BOOK

Successful leaders are proactive in the midst of 21st-century challenges. We invited community college leaders of selected benchmark institutions to discuss their creative solutions to change at their colleges and in their communities. Many community colleges are demonstrating extraordinary feats of purpose and success. The colleges featured here share a blend of useful information by which they serve as role models and benchmark institutions in a unique fashion, contributing to a growing body of usable tools and information about creativity at work. Authors were asked to provide a quote that showcases the primary values they embrace in their creative solutions and singles out lessons learned. The following leaders have contributed their stories, describing challenges and creative solutions.

- Don Cameron, Guilford Technical College (NC), explains that partnerships with public schools and area businesses enabled the college to establish new early college and TechPrep programs. Guilford's pioneering programs are considered best-practice models and have inspired changes in North Carolina's community college system.
- Marie Kane, Chaffey College (CA), writes about an innovative program to ensure the success of basic skills students with new Success Centers for math, reading, writing, and ESL. Success rates of all students, not just basic skills students, have improved: a remarkable feat considering the current crisis in underprepared students.
- Bob Paxton, Iowa Central Community College, ushered in a "Student First" culture to create an environment in which students are excited to enroll. New partnerships, new dormitories, and new programs thrive in this culture of team spirit.
- Brent Knight, Morton College (IL), answered a call for change by modernizing an outdated physical structure into a vibrant, interactive learning

environment. Knight describes the reconstruction and how it revitalized the college culture.

- Stephen Mittelstet, Richland College (TX), emphasizes the importance of authenticity in action and enjoying one's work and learning. The college business profits by a systematic evaluation process that has garnered acclaim and national awards.

- Richard Rhodes, El Paso Community College (TX), explores the spirit of the college and the community, symbolized by renowned artist Amado Peña's prominent mural on the wall of a major building on campus. El Paso Community College has embarked on a bold and important path toward becoming a learning college and has implemented data collection and evaluation measures to transform student outcomes.

- Richard Carpenter, formerly of the College of Southern Nevada, discusses the college's critical challenges that required immediate creative responses. Today, the college is financially healthy, organized, and positively driven; it delivers high-quality education across all its programs.

- Jerry Sue Thornton, Cuyahoga Community College (OH), leads the college into the 21st century as a strategically technological institution. "Second-generation technology" offers unifying, flexible tools that make this large multicampus institution successful as "one college."

- Christine Johnson, formerly of Community College of Denver (CO), discusses challenges that became positive realities for the college. Traditional high-risk factors such as a majority-minority population, inner-city incomes, and high enrollments in developmental education are no longer predicting factors for attrition, and partnerships in the community support the college so that low state funding does not limit its effectiveness.

- Steven Wallace, Florida Community College at Jacksonville, presents many innovative programs that illustrate the creative spirit of this institution. The college undertakes change at the organizational, mission, and macro-strategic levels to blanket the institution with solutions that address 21st-century challenges.

- Michael McCall, Kentucky Community and Technical College System, discusses the history and mission behind the founding of this state system in the mid-1990s. With strong, deliberate leadership and emphasis on important partnerships, 16 colleges emerged to serve their communities and be accountable to student needs.

- Walter Bumphus, president emeritus of Louisiana Community and Technical College System, details how the state's disparate community and technical colleges were united into one system and how a new leadership institute strengthened the new system's future. The system's unity was demonstrated by its extraordinary reconstruction efforts in the aftermath of Hurricane Katrina.

- William Law, Tallahassee Community College (FL), explains his community college's creative information center with student portals that track college data and empower students to be in charge of their own learning goals.

Today's community college leaders must seek creative options; work to free their teams to discover how to generate, support, and sustain new practices; consider options for how best to live up to the promise that *community* implies; engage in the deliberate practice of positive, vital, lasting change; and keep America's promise to offer opportunity and equity for every individual. Answers abound; many are addressed here.

REFERENCES

American Council on Education. (2006, Fall). *Poll reveals eight in ten voters believe vitality of America's colleges and universities critical to future economic success.* Retrieved August 12, 2007, from www.acenet.edu/solutions/media/Microsoft_Word_-_Poll_results_Narrative_Graphs.pdf

Barlow, E. (2007). *Creating the future with Ed Barlow.* Retrieved January 25, 2008, from www.creatingthefuture.com.

Florida, R. (2003). *The rise of the creative class: And how it's transforming work, leisure, community and everyday life.* New York: Basic Books.

Gleazer, E. J. (1980). *The community college: Values, vision, and vitality.* Washington, DC: American Association of Community and Junior Colleges.

Kirsch, I., Braun H., Yamamoto, K., & Sum, A. (2007). *America's perfect storm: Three forces changing our nation's future.* Princeton, NJ: Educational Testing Service.

LeCroy, N. (1993). *Catalyst for community change: Guidelines for community colleges to conduct community forums.* Phoenix, AZ: League for Innovation in the Community College.

Scanlon, J. (2006, February 23). *Reading, writing, and creativity.* Retrieved October 1, 2007, from www.businessweek.com/innovate/content/feb2006/id20060223_167340.htm

1

From Challenges to Opportunities

John E. Roueche, M. Melissa Richardson,
Phillip W. Neal, and Suanne D. Roueche

"**M**AGIC MIRROR ON THE WALL, what are the opportunities for us all?" It is a common question asked by community colleges across the land. Forecasting both trends and challenges is as much a part of being a leader as attending committee meetings is. Yet, how are creative community college leaders successful at availing themselves of opportunities? They build relationships with others who research, create, and shape trends—with local, state, national, and international leaders who bring new information about how the world is changing; with our new generation of students who bring insights to learning styles of lives already engaged with technology; with business and industry providing valuable feedback about workforce needs; and with school districts who share the challenges in K–12 education.

So what do these diverse relationships tell us about tomorrow's challenges? They forecast that the waves of change will grow larger, reach globally, and impact colleges faster than ever before. In some cases, the waves look similar to what we have seen in past decades. In other cases, the waves have never been seen in the United States before, and they resonate throughout the world in many industries—not just in higher education. Trends in the commercial retail industry in Illinois mirror those being addressed halfway around the world in Australian e-government (Stanyon, 2004). Australia is using technology to expedite many government functions such as business registry, information dissemination, and public policy creation, which allows for a more efficient and effective government and generates greater interaction with its citizens. "The time saved converts into economic opportunity that leads to greater economic activity and commercial benefit accruing earlier and more quickly" (Institute of Public Administration Australia, 2004, p.1).

These challenges should not blindside U.S. schools. However, they should wake up politicians who want to prevent our nation's losing more ground in the global economy. Community colleges are poised to be a part of the solutions to these problems. Flexible in their identities, true to their missions, and accessible to millions of Americans, community colleges are reliable, responsible institutions ready to forecast the future and adapt to the country's needs. Community colleges can, have, and will continue to create, shape, and reshape these challenges into opportunities—if they choose to be creative. The following is a look at current and future issues with which leaders will live.

CHANGING FACES AND ISSUES: SOME OLD, SOME NEW

Changing Demographics

Students of tomorrow's community colleges will be demographically different from students at the turn of the century. There will be more of them, and minority students will increase as community colleges solidify their places as the primary points of entry into higher education. "The period from 2000 to 2015 will see the single largest growth in college enrollments in our nation's history: upwards of 2 million more students, or nearly 20 percent growth overall" (American Council on Education, 2006). More than 50% of minorities in higher education are enrolled currently at community colleges, and this number will increase. Latinos are fast becoming the largest minority group in the United States, and some states (e.g., California and Texas) now have "majority-minority" populations (U.S. Census Bureau, 2004). Arizona, Illinois, and several other states are predicted to follow. Unfortunately, the educational gaps between Whites and many minority groups continue to widen: "If these educational disparities are not addressed, anticipated demographic shifts will have a major impact on the educational attainment of the U.S. population" (Kelley, 2005, p. 6). By necessity, the socioeconomic needs of the Latino population will begin to dominate state policies:

> If we are unable to substantially close the existing skill gaps among racial/ethnic groups and substantially boost the literacy levels of the population as a whole, demographic forces will result in a U.S. population in 2030 with tens of millions of adults unable to meet the requirements of the new economy. (Kirsch, Braun, Yamamoto, & Sum, 2007, p. 24)

Minority groups traditionally report lower average household incomes; however, as the population increases, wages are not expected to keep pace. Therefore, as more Latino students attend college, and as the cost of education rises, they will need more financial aid. The increase in Latino students—and other minority groups—will create language barriers and demand that colleges offer more ESL programs. In a recent presentation to the United States Senate Finance Committee, Flathead Valley Community College President Jane Karas offered this analogy to illustrate the importance of 2-year colleges in the life of immigrants: "Community colleges have evolved from being the 'Ellis Island' of American higher education—providing higher education access to those who could not otherwise attain it—to serving as a linchpin of 21st-century prosperity for a broad swath of society" (Karas, 2007, p. 1).

Currently, millions of undocumented immigrants live in the United States. This population will need education and will have a significant impact on the United States economy. The challenge is enrolling and serving undocumented immigrants if federal regulations will not allow them to obtain financial aid. In some states, colleges are required to report immigrants to the federal government. For these potential students, the perceived risk of deportation outweighs the benefits of an education.

First-Generation Student Retention

The unique recruitment and retention issues of first-generation students are nothing new on the community college landscape. In fact, many colleges consider themselves uniquely positioned, ready, and proud to serve them. Community colleges have been the entry point for many first-generation students for decades and will continue to be. Because minority students are more likely to be the first members of their families to attend college, first-generation student challenges will be compounded as the minority population increases.

Relationships between students, faculty, and families will increase in importance. Students' support networks must learn about available resources to help with struggles ahead. Helping families and communities understand students' experiences can strengthen the support system. This one change can pay dividends to the college, family, and community. Providing a family with one successful college graduate creates new possibilities; parents, siblings, aunts, and uncles see that a college degree is possible. Bringing the family members to campus exposes them to students of all ages and nationalities. The realization that higher education is a possibility may help other family members seek it as well.

Developmental Education

Historically, community colleges have provided the only college access available for students with low academic skills. As the number of students increases, those students needing basic skill development will increase, as well. College-bound populations with the least access to a high-quality public K–12 education—that is, minorities—are most likely to feel the effects of this reality. "Historical data link minority groups to educational underpreparedness, with strong links to less-than-adequate facilities in the schools that serve them and the communities in which they live" (Roueche & Roueche, 1999, p. 3).

Regardless of race, there is growing evidence of the rising need for math, English, and reading skill development, as seen in the increasing number of developmental education courses offered in all college curricula. Challenges lie ahead in determining the priority levels assigned to these courses. Colleges who place developmental education at the center of their mission experience improved student retention (Kozeracki & Brooks, 2006). Developmental education has societal benefits as well. Spann (2000) suggested that remedial education is in everyone's best interest: "If just one in three developmental students taking at least one remedial course were to graduate with a bachelor's degree, they would reciprocally generate over $74 billion dollars in federal taxes as well as $13 billion in state and local taxes" (p. 2). The American Council on Education (2006) estimated that "increasing the country's average level of schooling by one year could increase economic growth by 6 to 15 percent, adding between [$]600 billion to [$]1.5 trillion to U.S. economic output." If this prediction is accurate, investing too little in developmental education will be detrimental to the United States's economic future.

Academic Advising

Today, few students seek advisors' help with course selection. Approximately 67% of all community college students view academic advising as important; yet, relaxed or nonexistent college policies allow 26% of developmental education students and 41% of the students enrolled in college-level courses to disregard the process (Ashburn, 2006). Colleges will be challenged to refocus efforts on creating advising programs that encourage what, in many cases, is the only on-going, one-on-one relationship students will have with a college official.

Replacing the Veterans: Retirement's Booming Effects on Leadership

Community college administrators face a convergence of sociological factors never seen before. The body of teaching and leadership talent, which helped create today's modern community college campuses, is retiring within a relatively short timeframe. The challenge is to fill the large number of vacancies. "With nearly half of community college CEOs expected to retire this decade, two-year colleges are looking at ways to encourage potential future leaders to consider becoming presidents and to get the education and experience needed to land those jobs" (Dembicki, 2006). This groundswell of retirements is happening at the presidential level and at instructional and staff levels, as well.

Colleges may use this opportunity to solve one of the longest-standing criticisms of higher education. For decades, leadership in the faculty and administrative ranks has not been representative demographically of the communities and student bodies it serves. As U.S. demographics shift, filling employment voids on college campuses will offer institutions opportunities to examine their own values regarding diversity. This opportunity will allow colleges to provide professional development and training for new hires. Mentoring will be a key ingredient to their long-term success. Colleges who take this opportunity to diversify themselves will need to use existing mentors to reach out to potential leaders who may not have had access, or given thought to, leadership roles. Providing role models and mentoring systems will help those in the leadership pipeline and guide those who seek entry.

Often, more than 75% of college budgets are dominated by salaries and benefits, and many educational leaders have chosen to curb personnel costs by shifting more of the teaching loads to part-time employees who do not require long-term contracts or benefits (Wallin, 2004). In many institutions, adjunct instructors teach more courses than do full-time faculty members teach. Vaughan (2005) found that 69% of community college courses are taught by part-time faculty members. Rarely do adjuncts provide one-on-one mentoring and academic advising—factors leading most significantly to improved student retention and achievement. These duties and college committee responsibilities shift to full-time faculty who rarely receive time or pay for their extra duties as assigned. Will full-time faculty members become academic coordinators while part-time instructors become the teaching corps? The leadership challenge is to balance the use of part-time instructors with budgetary needs while maintaining opportunities for students to become engaged at levels previously offered largely by full-time faculty.

TECHNOLOGY: THE SECOND GENERATION OF OPPORTUNITIES

Chalkboards: Ancient History

The first generation of Internet-related advancements has come and gone. We have assimilated computers and the Internet into our lives. A new generation of users is coming in with computers-in-hand and expecting information to be a few clicks away. Technology has great potential to help the United States respond to 21st-century challenges, but it has equal potential to become a problem unless properly planned for and implemented. It is the race without a finish line, and it is expensive. The second technological revolution is here and will "dwarf, in sheer transformational scope and power, anything we have yet experienced in the current information age" (Bement, 2007, p. B5). For students, technology is about mobility and access to resources, school, friends, recreation, work, travel, shopping, and entertainment. Technology is the mobility tool by which students will create and maintain.

With the information technology revolution, a second generation of challenges arrived for community colleges. In many ways, the Internet has created access as never before. Information about any college, in any country, can be accessed instantly. Now classrooms are smart, students conduct research on their cell phones, and professors converse in chat rooms with multiple students around the globe, simultaneously. Three-dimensional, interactive live images and sounds of a lecturer can be projected from a classroom in Cairo to students in El Paso. "And information technology may grow from a set of tools that help colleges do what they have always done to a set of systems that can transform the very nature of higher education itself" (Chronicle Review, 2004, p. B1).

This second technological revolution is about creating and sharing knowledge and maintaining it for application. According to Bement (2007), "It adds new dimensions that greatly increase transformational potential" (p. B5), forcing community colleges to rethink the way they do business. Creative leaders realize they cannot maintain the status quo. "Doing nothing or doing things as they have always been done, even if more quickly, efficiently, or with more technology, will prepare us for a world that no longer exists" (Milliron & de Los Santos, 2004, p. 105).

Digital Divide: Myth or Reality?

At a time when it appears obvious that every household should own a computer and have Internet access, the digital divide for those who do not becomes even more problematic. Although human computer proficiency is higher than ever, the rate of technological advancements may be outpacing the United States's ability to reach out and educate the have nots. "One in five American adults (22 percent) say they have never used the Internet or e-mail and do not live in Internet-connected households … Thirty-two percent of Americans do not use the Internet" (Fox, 2005, p. 1).

Increasing need for college survival skills accompanies the rising rates of first-generation minority students attending college. Using the Internet is one of those skills. Fox (2007) found that of Latinos who speak only Spanish, only one third use the Internet. Ironically, inside college walls, all students—regardless of ethnicity—find a plethora of computer-based resources and instruction. Cotton and Jelenewicz (2006) noted that ethnic differences disappeared when analyzing the type of Internet usage by college students. However, there is a different picture outside the college walls. "Minorities have lower regard for computer access and Internet use. This suggests that minority college students, especially Black students, continue to lag behind their White counterparts in use" (Cotton & Jelenewicz, 2006, p. 498).

Demographic, technological, and economic circumstances leave a large segment of society without home computers. Computer ownership and access to the Internet is tied to income levels (Madigan & Goodfellow, 2005): 86.3% of households earning more than $75,000 have access to a computer, and 77.7% have access to the Internet. By contrast, only 19.2% of households earning less than $15,000 own a computer, and 12.7% have access to the Internet. Obviously, significant numbers of students are not likely to have the tools necessary to complete their work at home.

Students without computer access and computer skills are challenges that can be met. However, meeting these challenges is not as easy as offering computers only. The challenges are psychological and economic. The intimidation first-generation college students experience will be stronger for those who live in a world saturated with technology and for those who cannot speak the language.

The Need for Nontraditional Teachers and Classrooms

For students who have grown up with computers—the Net Generation—learning styles have morphed into what looks like social entertainment (Oblinger & Oblinger, 2005). Learning platforms previously thought of as nontraditional—for example, instant access, social information sharing, and gaming—are available in many classrooms. For many students, faculty, and administrators, the concept of a traditional student will never be the same again. If faculty and administrators who are not part of the Net Generation do not reshape their thinking about students, education, and their teaching styles—based on the "sage on the stage" tradition—they may become the "nontraditional" component of the college family.

In addition to learning styles, communication tools have a new look. The iPod music craze that took the nation by storm in 2001, is now a new means of faculty–student interaction. More than 88 million iPods are in circulation according to Apple (2007). Nielsen Media Research (2006, p. 1) reported that more than one in four (26.7%) U.S. households use an MP3 device, and homes with children ages 12 to 17 are 250% more likely to own or rent one. Class presentations and lectures can be purchased commercially, and iPods are almost as standard as books. Lectures, which have been preloaded onto iPods and given to entering students, can be reviewed over breakfast or while jogging or driving to campus. iTunes U gives students and higher education the ability to share educational content 24/7. Many public K–12 education, homeschool agencies, community colleges, and universities are using this resource-sharing service (Apple, 2007).

Access to teachers has created a boundary issue between faculty and students. Students now contact professors via e-mail 24/7 and expect nearly immediate responses. Office hours are becoming virtual and can take place from the bus, office, or beach. According to the Community College Survey of Student Engagement (2007), "A quarter of students (25 percent) say they have never used e-mail to communicate with an instructor." This leaves 75% of students reporting they have used e-mails to contact faculty; 39% reported using e-mails often or very often. Creating behavioral expectations regarding e-mail contact at the beginning of class will require that both students and faculty have a firm understanding of the process. Short of cutting the e-mail umbilical cord—turning off devices—faculty who do not set strong boundaries will be inundated with inquiries. Leaving work at work has become a matter of just not logging in.

Maintaining the Human Factor

How do leaders maintain the human touch when around every corner is a new technology with claims to help you "reach out and touch someone?" The sign of advancement and transformation in the 1990s, "You've got mail," hardly begins to describe the connectivity leaders have in the early 2000s. With the onslaught of contact buzzing in pockets, purses, or laptops, communicating via the barrage of available communication tools today makes life and contact easier than ever. A mere tap on the wireless headset, and conversations can begin. Instant communication is giving way to mass communication. Group e-mailing provides a mechanism to communicate quickly with hundreds of people simultaneously and delete hundreds more. In an age when the importance of listening and relationships is the critical message, the challenge is finding ways to connect in a personal way through impersonal means.

Making the most of the human factor is a matter of being present—focusing on people and the issues before them is a challenge. With increasing accountability pressures, the challenge also becomes focusing on tomorrow while simultaneously concentrating on today. Being present and enjoying the moment will not only influence relationships but also determine the leader's quality of life. This same concern for personal interaction accompanies Internet-based instruction. As courses became hybridized, the potential for alternate forms of faceless interaction has increased. In a 2006 study of the 12- to 17-year-old crowd, 55% used social networking Web sites, and 48% interacted daily with friends via some faceless mechanism (Lenhart & Madden, 2007). Fully 91% of the teens in the study used the social networking sites to communicate with friends on a regular basis. Community colleges must address the reality of teens using other forms of communication in the same way telephones once revolutionized connections. We are moving from the Information Age to the Interaction Age. In education, "Applying the concept of interactivity to the real world means creating environments that will (1) preserve the richness of interactions that are not technology-mediated and (2) allow these interactions to co-exist with those that are technology-mediated" (Milne, 2007, p. 15).

BECOMING A FEDERAL PLAYER: FUNDING, ACCOUNTABILITY, AND NATIONAL SECURITY

Ebbs and Flows of Federal Funding

The vagaries of funding cycles—perennial issues in higher education—continue to challenge community colleges to seek partnerships and alternative resources for operating budgets, salaries, maintenance, renovation of aging facilities, and student financial aid. The percentage of funding per student has been decreasing steadily; larger shares of the educational costs are being transferred to students. Colleges raise tuition and fees to offset escalating costs, and students turn to more loans and more work (Field, 2005). Unfortunately, this downward spiral leads to lowered access for many people. "The rate of growth of private student loans was higher in 2004–2005 than the rate of growth of any type of student aid" (College Board, 2005, p. 5). From 1994–1995 to 2004–2005, unsubsidized loans increased 253%, and parent loans increased 358%—that is, more than $90 billion was handed out in loans (70%) and in grants (20%).

With tightened budgets, students turn to bargain shopping. The size of financial aid packages is influencing where students enroll and if they will succeed (Nora, Barlow, & Crisp, 2006). Nearly two thirds of community college students enroll part time and hold jobs to help pay for educational and living expenses. The irony is that financial aid formulas are designed for traditional-aged students, and federal regulations base aid packages on current wages. Therefore, students who work while attending school have their current wages count against their following year's financial aid allocation.

As funding decreases, community colleges seek alternative revenue streams. "Some leaders realize that as state support continues its precipitous decline, creative endeavors alone may not be enough to ensure continued vitality" (Roueche & Jones, 2005, p. 8). Increasingly, they turn to their communities and local businesses to raise additional funds for capital construction, scholarships, and endowments (Gose, 2006). Communities pass bonds as a political means of increasing money. "Friendraising" has entered into the lexicon of many educational leaders. Whether colleges are creating endowed chairs, seeking financial aid, or replacing an aging structure, strengthening relationships with individuals and groups who care about the college has never been more important.

Public and Government Demand for Accountability

In 2006, Secretary of Education Margaret Spellings echoed the accountability trend seen throughout the U.S. community college world. With increasingly restricted funds and worries that the United States is slipping as a world leader, parents, governing boards, accrediting agencies, legislators, and presidents want to know that community colleges are achieving their goals. Graduation rates are often remarkably disappointing and do not demonstrate acceptable levels of success. Documenting the reality that valuable resources being directed at programming are producing actual learning is the new reality and expectation. To demonstrate learning, standardized testing is being proposed at all levels of education. Recently, legislators in Texas battled over this issue. The question of exit exams has been debated (e.g., their effectiveness, cost, and value). Community colleges and universities foresee numerous testing requirements for each discipline, similar to those currently implemented in law, nursing, and accounting.

Data-informed decision making at the institutional level is crucial to this effort. Programs such as the Community College Survey of Student Engagement provide tools with which to measure institutional effectiveness. With nearly 250,000 students surveyed, this effort has amassed the largest database of community college data available to date. Although this is the largest repository of data, it is not the only tool—thus, the challenge. Leaders understand the importance of demonstrating effectiveness, using data-gathering software to manage the data and then comparing the data on a common platform.

The amount of information colleges will be handling is unimaginable. In *No Place to Hide*, O'Harrow (2006) asserted, "All the information collected by humanity through 1999 would more than double in the next several years… . That's approximately a dozen exabytes … Just five exabytes equals all the words ever spoken" (p. 43). The need for secure and accurate data storage systems will continue to accelerate, and managing bureaucracies so that apples are compared with apples will be a tremendous organizational and political struggle.

Securing a Nation

Today's security issues are another chapter in the United States' concerns about global relationships. Attacks on U.S. soil created a new determination to fight further threats and protect ourselves from terrorism. We face a paradox of problems related to wars fought in other lands but controlled here in our own. We face the task of preparing for natural disasters (Gose, 2005). Hurricane Katrina almost destroyed drowsy New Orleans and woke up a nation to disaster preparedness. Government inefficiencies in emergency response reminded people of their own responsibilities to help others and helped build a stronger sense of national citizenship.

Natural disaster planning became a deadly reality for Louisiana colleges after hurricanes Rita and Katrina. The destruction closed entire campuses; temporarily suspended classes; and relocated students, faculty, and staff. Throughout the next 4 months, the state system kept everyone on full salary and continued operations to rebuild itself while assessing the damage and loss of life. Although no one could have prepared for this worst natural disaster in U.S. history, the Herculean efforts of dealing with death and destruction will serve as a future model for disaster planning. "Hurricane Katrina taught us many things, one being that technology can be your lifeline during a time of crisis; it can also be the anchor that weighs you down" (Martin & Samels, 2007).

Security was not as common of a topic at community colleges a decade ago as it is today. September 11, 2001, and the war with Iraq have generated issues unimagined on campuses not so many years ago. Military training contracts, homeland security, and terrorist threats are new in the community college vocabulary. AACC recently emphasized the importance of our institutions in responding to these crises:

Thus, when the events of September 11, 2001, made ensuring the security of our communities and the nation a more urgent concern, the question became not if, but how and how broadly, community colleges would become engaged to meet this new and compelling need. (AACC, 2006, p. vii)

This new world made leaders rethink community colleges' roles.

Opportunities and challenges arose from this perceptual shift. International affairs are important issues on campus. Instructional divisions are developing programs to train homeland security officers. Student services are working to regain international students lost in the wake of the terrorist attacks when new policies prevented foreign students from entering the United States. Instructional technology departments are working with software manufacturers to increase Internet security to prevent cyberterrorism and file corruption.

Proudly, community colleges quickly moved to the forefront with first-responder training programs. Now, 80% of the first responders are trained on community college campuses. According to AACC (2006) data, the majority of nurses, police, firefighters, and emergency medical technicians are trained by community colleges.

MISSION MORPH: RECREATING, RETOOLING, AND RECRUITING

Recreating Boundaries

The topographical landscape of community college education continues to change. In the past, community colleges were assigned service districts on the basis of county lines, and they competed for students with the local universities; then came online education. The service district boundaries virtually disappeared, enrollments soared, and a new competitor emerged in the market.

The number of proprietary schools is on the rise, and a review of any city's *Yellow Pages* illuminates their presence in communities large and small. "There are thousands of proprietary institutions in the United States," in contrast to the nearly 1,200 community colleges (Kinser, 2007, p. B9). These for-profit institutions have given notice that they are here, they are competing for the same students as community colleges, and they promise business and technology a higher quality of education for students that is more responsive to their needs than not-for-profit institutions.

Community colleges are looking to recreate and change themselves to help their communities. The original junior college mission grew from a relationship with public school systems into a unique comprehensive mission, and now community colleges are being asked to return to serving high school students who need or want an opportunity to complete high school and begin college concurrently. They are opening charter schools and early colleges; they are going back to their roots. "Too few students earn a post-secondary degree, an increasingly important experience and credential for economic success and informed participation in American democracy" (Bill and Melinda Gates Foundation, 2007, p. 9). In many cases, students who need a different challenge are showing promise in this atmosphere, and success rates are surpassing those in traditional high school settings. Foundations are taking notice of community colleges to encourage innovative efforts to better educate today's youth. For example, the Bill and Melinda Gates Foundation has designed and funded programs to reach kids who otherwise would fall through public education's safety nets.

Retooling a Skilled Workforce

Jobs in the United States increasingly require higher-level degrees and creative capabilities. Tomorrow's workforce will harness the mind's creative potential. "The Bureau of Labor Statistics estimates that jobs requiring higher education will grow by 22 percent between 2002 and 2012—nearly double the rate of non-college jobs" (American Council on Education, 2006). Community colleges will be challenged further to put their energies into creating graduates who think creatively and are service minded.

The United States' powerful industrial workforce has lost steam to greater global powers: "If the recent meeting of world leaders at Davos is any indication, India is rapidly becoming an economic 'rock star.' If China is the world's factory, India's become the world's outsourcing centre" (Florida, 2006). Friedman's *The Lexus and the Olive Tree* (2000) and *The World is Flat* (2006) brought national attention to the benefits and challenges related to knowledge distribution across borders. Tapping into the unique potential of the United States' creative industries is proving to be difficult for businesses and industries that rely on old industrial models, and preparing young workers for the workforce is difficult for educators who are not able to see beyond the skill and drill competencies of the past. According to the National Association of Manufacturers' 2005 Skills Gap Report, "The vast majority of American manufacturers are experiencing a serious shortage of qualified employees, which in turn is causing significant impact to business and the ability of the country as a whole to compete in a global economy" (p. 1).

Creating intellectual capital in students has been the primary mission for community colleges since their inception. Imparting wisdom and honing skills are our responsibilities. The goal has been to create a productive workforce, taking the United States to the forefront of commerce. However, much of our workforce training is based on manufacturing as it was in the old industrial economy but at a time when industrial jobs are moving overseas. Florida (2006) warned that if we are not careful, the "creative class" will find most of its support beyond the borders of our nation.

Recruiting: Students Wanting to Shop

Recruitment has changed forever the manner in which community colleges reach potential students. Printed marketing material is complemented by constantly refreshed electronic billboards on every college's Web site. Effectively engaging potential students in the recruitment process will be critical in a future that will see the largest student growth in U.S. history.

Along with the Information Age comes the reality that students can sample classes from multiple institutions. A result of the "shopper" mentality, students can investigate the best courses from around the world and handpick their professors. Web sites such as Rate-a-Prof.com or Pick-a-Prof.com allow students to share insights into their perceived quality of faculty. In April 2007, Pick-A-Prof.com claimed to have more than 11 million ratings and reviews on more than 800,000 professors teaching 3.5 million classes.

Students shopping for the best professors, professors teaching across the Internet, and colleges relying heavily on part-time faculty offer new opportunities for growth. Colleges have access to virtually any professor on the globe. Strategic employment is now possible. Instead of teaching world history from a classroom in middle America, colleges can hire a part-time instructor who can teach the course from her office in Rome where she can transmit photos and video to students as she tours the Coliseum.

Retaining shopper students within the walls of one college is a concept under siege. The question becomes, Where is the student's home institution, and from whom will he or she receive financial aid? Policies governing fee structures and tuition will create points of discussion, particularly because shopper students are sensitive to cost and quality. Now states are creating consortiums of institutions from which students may enroll in courses through multiple institutions and earn degrees without regard to campus property and service lines. Institutions such as Western Governor's University and the Virtual College of Texas allow students to choose classes from diverse colleges while earning degrees and receiving financial aid. These partnerships have become so popular that, in 2006, Western Governor's University claimed to be the nation's largest provider of science and math teachers, "rapidly becoming one of the largest teacher education programs in the country," with 4,000 students enrolled in its Teacher's College (Western Governor's University, 2006).

CONCLUSION

In building relationships with business leaders, politicians, school officials, parents, and students, community colleges become part of the fabric of change. No longer are community colleges in the back seat of education, reacting to national and state policy. Community colleges are no longer reactionary agents: They create change. The following chapters provide creative examples of how leaders transformed programs and cultures within their institutions and positioned their colleges to better handle the challenges yet to come. All of these leaders support strong value systems, providing flexibility and plasticity within each college. Although not impervious to change and challenge, these value systems allow for enduring adaptation and adjustment; for shaping and reshaping institutional programs, behaviors, and efforts while maintaining the underlying focus on serving the community's needs.

Read about the challenges they face—their fears, hopes, and dreams—and the cultures that shape their communities. Each chapter highlights how and why these leaders and their institutions are looking to their collective creative spirits to save the day. Current and future community college leaders can glean from these stories a clearer perspective of the opportunities that await, the values that transcend challenges, and the institutional cultures that can mold and support the future.

These leaders have created institutional cultures that view the United States' challenges as opportunities for evolution, if not for positive revolution. By focusing on values, they have led colleges to shift perceptions about mission and helped free the colleges' transformational potential. Therefore, we begin this larger discussion of values, creativity, and opportunities that our authors have provided with a bird's-eye view of the challenges all colleges face. We begin with the positive: seeing challenges as opportunities.

REFERENCES

American Association of Community Colleges (AAAC). (2006). *First responders: Community colleges on the front line of security.* Washington, DC: Community College Press.

American Council on Education. (2006). *Enrollment changes: Demographics are shifting.* Retrieved April 10, 2007, from www.solutionsforourfuture. org/site/PageServer?pagename=enrollment_changes_r

Apple. (2007). *iTunes U: The campus that never sleeps.* Retrieved March 12, 2007, from www.apple.com/education/itunesu

Ashburn, E. (2006, December 1). 2-Year-college students rarely use advisers, survey shows. *The Chronicle of Higher Education, 53*(15), p. A1.

Bement, A. (2007). Cyberinfrastructure: The second revolution. *The Chronicle of Higher Education, 53*(18), p. B5.

Bill and Melinda Gates Foundation. (2007). *High schools for the new millennium: Imagine the possibilities.* Seattle, WA: Author.

Chronicle Review. (2004, January 30). 10 challenges for the next 10 years. *The Chronicle of Higher Education, 50*(21), p. B1.

College Board. (2005). *Trends in student aid: 2005. Trends in higher education series.* NewYork: College Board Publications.

Community College Survey of Student Engagement. (2007). *Survey results: Student–faculty interaction.* Retrieved February 10, 2007, from www.ccsse.org/survey/bench_sfi.cfm

Cotton, S., & Jelenewicz, S. (2006, Winter). A disappearing digital divide among college students? Peeling away the layers of the digital divide. *Social Science Computer Review, 24*(4), 497–506.

Dembicki, M. (2006, November 21). Taskforce grapples with recruiting college leaders. *Community College Times, 18*(23), p. 1.

Field, K. (2005, March 4). Change in the Pell-Grant formula is likely to drive up loans and work hours. *The Chronicle of Higher Education, 51*(26), p. A21.

Florida, R. (2006, February). Let's get creative. *The Times of India.* Retrieved from the Creative Class Group Web site: http://creativeclass.com/article_library/search.php

Fox, S. (2005). *Digital divisions: There are clear differences among those with broadband connections, dial-up connections, and no connections at all to the Internet.* Washington, DC: Pew Internet & American Life Project.

Fox, S. (2007). *Latinos online: Hispanics with lower levels of education and English proficiency remain largely disconnected from the Internet.* Washington, DC: Pew Internet & American Life Project.

Friedman, T. (2000). *The lexus and the olive tree.* New York: Random House.

Friedman, T. (2006). *The world is flat.* New York: Ferrar, Straus, and Giroux.

Gose, B. (2005, October 28). The front line in training for disasters. *The Chronicle of Higher Education, 52*(10), p. B1.

Gose, B. (2006, October 27). At a growing number of community colleges, fund raising is no longer optional, *The Chronicle of Higher Education, 53*(10), p. B5.

Institute of Public Administration Australia. (2004). *Future challenges for e-government* [Monograph]. Retrieved June 18, 2007, from www.agimo.gov.au/publications/2004/05/egovt_challenges

Karas, J. (2007, March 20). *Realizing a competitive education: Identifying needs, partnerships and resources* [U.S. Senate hearing transcript]. Retrieved from the U.S.

Senate Committee on Finance Web site: http://finance.senate.gov/sitepages/2007hearings.htm

Kelley, P. (2005). *As America becomes more diverse: The impact of state higher education inequality.* Boulder, CO: National Center of Higher Education Management Systems.

Kinser, K. (2007, March). For-profit institutions need to be classified, too. *The Chronicle Review, 53*(30), p. B9.

Kirsch, I., Braun H., Yamamoto, K., & Sum, A. (2007). *America's perfect storm: Three forces changing our nation's future.* Princeton, NJ: Educational Testing Service.

Kozeracki, C. A., & Brooks, J. B. (2006, Winter). Emerging institutional support for developmental education. *New Directions for Community Colleges, 2006*(136), 63–73. doi:10.1002/cc.260

Lenhart, A., & Madden, M. (2007). *Social networking websites and teens: An overview.* Washington, DC: Pew Internet & American Life Project.

Madigan, E., & Goodfellow, M. (2005). The influence of family income and parents education on digital access: Implications for first-year college students. *Sociological Viewpoints, 21.*

Martin, J., & Samels, J. E. (2007). 10 Trends to watch in campus technology—Plus 8 myths and 7 key skills for CIO's. *The Chronicle of Higher Education, 53*(18), p. B7.

Milliron, M. D., & de Los Santos, G. E. (2004, February). Making the most of community colleges on the road ahead. *Community College Journal of Research and Practice, 28*(2), 105–122. (ERIC # EJ682195)

Milne, A. J. (2007, January/February). Entering the interaction age: Implementing a future vision for campus learning spaces today. *EDUCAUSE Review, 42*(1), 12–31.

National Association of Manufacturers, The Manufacturing Institute for Workforce Success, & Deloitte Consulting LLP. (2005). *2005 Skills gap report: A survey of the American manufacturing workforce.* Washington, DC: National Association of Manufacturers.

Nielsen Media Research. (2006, December 19). *Nielsen study shows DVD players surpass VCRs.* Retrieved June 18, 2007, from the Nielsen Media Research Web site: www.nielsenmedia.com

Nora, A., Barlow, L., & Crisp, G. (2006). Examining the tangible and psychosocial benefits of financial aid: Student access, engagement, and degree attainment. *American Behavioral Scientist, 49,* 1636–1651.

O'Harrow, R. (2006). *No place to hide.* New York: Free Press.

Oblinger, D. G., & Oblinger, J. L. (Eds.). (2005). *Educating the net genera-tion* [E-book]. Retrieved from the EDUCAUSE Web site: www.educause.edu/educatingthenetgen

Roueche, J., & Jones, B. (2005). *The entrepreneurial community college.* Washington, DC: Community College Press.

Roueche, J., & Roueche, S. (1999). *High stakes, high performance: Making remedial education work.* Washington, DC: Community College Press.

Spann, M. G., Jr. (2000, February). *Remediation: A must for the 21s- century learning society.* Denver, CO: Center for Community College Policy (ECS Policy Paper No. CC-00-4). Retrieved February 15, 2007, from www.communitycollegepoli-cy.org/pdf/3347_Spann_remediation.pdf

Stanyon, J. (2004.). *Challenges of the future: The rebirth of small independent retail in America* [White paper]. Retrieved June 18, 2007, from www.retail-revival.com/home.htm

U.S. Census Bureau. (2004, March 18, 2004). *U.S. interim projections by age, sex, race, and Hispanic origin* [Data file]. Retrieved February 9, 2007, from www.census.gov/ipc/www/usinterimproj

Vaughan, G. B. (2005, October 28). (Over)selling the community college: What price access? *The Chronicle of Higher Education, 52*(10), p. B12.

Wallin, D. L. (2004). Valuing professional colleagues: Adjunct faculty in commu-nity and technical colleges. *Community College Journal of Research and Practice, 28*(4), 373–391. (ERIC # EJ682218)

Western Governors University. (2006, November 1). Western Governors University Teachers College receives NCATE accreditation [News brief]. Retrieved February 18, 2007, from www.wgu.edu/about_WGU/ncate_accreditation_11-1-06.asp

2

Guilford Technical and Community College: A Story of Patience, Persistence, Perception, and Change

Donald W. Cameron

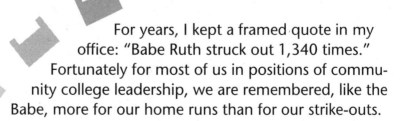

For years, I kept a framed quote in my office: "Babe Ruth struck out 1,340 times." Fortunately for most of us in positions of community college leadership, we are remembered, like the Babe, more for our home runs than for our strike-outs.

—*Donald W. Cameron, Guilford Technical and Community College (NC)*

Guilford Technical and Community College (GTCC) is located in the rural Piedmont region of North Carolina, east of the Blue Ridge Mountains. The college began as a technical school and has a long history of partnerships with area industries. In the past 25 years, President Donald Cameron has built critical relationships with the local public schools. His persistence and enthusiasm have won the community's support for Tech Prep initiatives and an early college high school, both model programs. These initiatives have increased the percentage of local high school graduates enrolling at Guilford, answered area concerns about building the changing local economy, and increased the number and success of students transferring to 4-year colleges.

Persistence and patience have been the core values of the GTCC leadership. Building significant relationships and earning the trust of college and community members took time, but the rewards for the college's commitment have been enormous for the students, the college, and the community.

E. K. FRETWELL, FORMER CHANCELLOR at the University of North Carolina at Charlotte, loves to say, "Universities often move at amazing speed—slower than you think." Presidents of community colleges, conversely, pride themselves on their colleges' abilities to respond rapidly to changing needs. Sometimes, though, change comes slowly—even in community colleges. Sometimes desired change comes only after much effort and several false, or less than successful, starts. Sometimes change comes only as a result of pressure by outside forces.

The relationship between a community college and the public schools in its service area is critical. If that relationship is positive and interactive, benefits accrue for the college, the public schools, and the community. This story is about the growth of such a relationship, one that began as weak—not negative, but weak. Over time, it grew into one of the strongest community college–public school relationships in North Carolina.

My story is one of slow, patient change. I would like to claim that I produced this change and that it would not have happened had I not been president, but that would be less than honest. Quite frankly, I do not know if it would or would not have occurred. I can say that it is a story of patient and persistent leadership that eventually produced results I never dreamed of when I began.

I am one of those community college presidents who served first as the chief academic officer before being selected as president. There are advantages and disadvantages to that situation. You have valuable history and knowledge to transition into your new role, but you can be hindered by established relationships and assumptions. Patterns develop that inhibit the possibilities of change; in many ways, meaningful change in the culture of the college may be more difficult to accomplish in this situation than if you had come from the outside.

When I became president of Guilford Technical and Community College (GTCC) in 1991, I had served 10 years as its executive vice president and chief instructional officer. This was my first presidency, and I was excited. I inherited a strong college—one well respected in the community, in the state, and, I dare say, in the nation. However, there were changes that I and my board of trustees wanted to make; for example, the college's long-standing, weak relationship with the public schools.

GTCC opened in 1958 as one of North Carolina's first industrial education centers, the forerunner of community colleges in this state. These centers were established to prepare citizens for jobs created by a state economy rapidly changing from one based primarily on agriculture to one based on manufacturing. For Guilford County, an urban county in the center of the state, manufacturing in 1958 largely meant furniture and textiles. Back then, Guilford County was home to many of the nation's best-known textile and furniture companies. High Point, the second largest city in the county, is still known as the "Furniture Capital of the World."

In the first 25 years of GTCC's history, the college developed a wide array of technical and vocational programs in manufacturing, business, engineering, and allied health. In 1983, a college-transfer program was added with considerable opposition at both the local and state levels. At that time, the board of trustees insisted that "technical" remain a part of the institution's name to demonstrate its continuing commitment to occupational training as the primary function in the college's mission.

As a new president, one major frustration (shared by previous presidents) was a weak relationship between the college and the local public schools. When I became president in 1991, Guilford County had three public school systems (city systems in High Point and Greensboro, and a county system). It was my view and that of my board that, for the most part, those three systems viewed their primary missions as preparing high school graduates for 4-year college work.

GTCC'S COMMUNITY IMAGE

In the late 1980s, the president and I frequently talked with the superintendents about Tech Prep. Only one of the three superintendents gave much attention to the Tech Prep movement, which had grown rapidly in North Carolina, as it had in other states, at that time. The superintendents were polite and supportive in their rhetoric, but real progress occurred only in isolated high schools. As chief academic officer, I frequently compared our enrollment statistics with other community colleges in North Carolina, and we were always well below the state average in the percentage of local high school graduates who enrolled the following year in our college.

I understood some of the reasons we had problems attracting a large percentage of graduating high school seniors. For one thing, Guilford County is home to two branches of the University of North Carolina and to four private, church-related colleges. Also, GTCC's strict adherence to its original mission of providing short-term (2 years or less) job-training programs, coupled with its relatively late addition of a college-transfer program, meant that a large number of local high school graduates never considered us as a postsecondary option. Moreover, like most community colleges, we often were seen as a second choice for students who could not enroll in a "real college." We knew, based on both anecdotal and first-hand knowledge, that most of the high school principals and high school guidance counselors did not promote GTCC actively. Thirty years after our creation, most of the high school leaders in our county still saw us in the traditionally negative light that was part of most community colleges' early years.

These facts bothered me when I was a vice president. First, they hurt my feelings. I knew that we were a high-quality institution that provided a wide range of high-quality programs. Indeed, I felt there was an elitist attitude behind the promotion of other colleges and little consideration of GTCC. It also bothered me that the failure of these principals and counselors to promote GTCC as a first option for their graduates hurt our growth and budget. North Carolina's community colleges operate on a full-time employee (FTE) based funding formula; the more a college grows, the more state funds it receives.

AREA SCHOOLS ASSISTANCE PROGRAM

Two years after my arrival as the vice president for instruction, we initiated the Area Schools Assistance Program (ASAP). We hired one guidance counselor from each of the county's high schools to work for GTCC during the summer. These counselors were charged with calling each June graduate of their respective high schools to talk about the student's postsecondary plans. As part of their training, they were given a review of GTCC programs and admissions policies.

Today, after 25 years, the ASAP program still benefits both the public schools and GTCC. The public school counselors, although being paid by GTCC, conduct a graduate survey as part of their regular job responsibilities. They are able to be a recruiter for GTCC as they talk with graduates who have not made definite postsecondary plans. When these students are identified, GTCC responds with mailings and phone calls, attempting to recruit and enroll these students in the fall semester.

As a result of ASAP, we have been able to recruit more students, and I am sure that it has contributed to our overall growth. More importantly, it has built strong and informed friendships with at least one counselor from each high school. Even after the summer work is over, these counselors return to their regular jobs more informed about GTCC and its programs. These counselors have become our ambassadors.

As I look back on ASAP, it is as an example of an initiative that actually turned out much as I imagined it would. One lesson I learned is that building partnerships is easier if all partners clearly benefit. For example, the high school counselors earned paid summer employment and had an established vehicle for gathering important, useful graduate information. In retrospect, I believe that effort paved the way for a transformational change in the relationship between GTCC and the Guilford County Schools.

TECH PREP PARTNERSHIPS

In 1993, just 2 years after I became president, legislative mandate merged the three school systems. This merger was extraordinarily controversial; most observers believed that had the question of merger been put to a public referendum, it would have been defeated. For the GTCC trustees and me, it presented another opportunity to forge stronger relations with a single board of education and a single superintendent.

One major, outside factor that made this a likely possibility was the country's changing economy. During the late 1980s, North Carolina's economy, especially Guilford County's, changed dramatically. Many of the local textile and furniture companies were acquired by national and international conglomerates. The North American Free Trade Agreement accelerated this change as many textile and furniture manufacturers moved their operations offshore. Almost weekly, area newspaper headlines carried stories of plant closings and increasing unemployment.

Local business leaders, chamber of commerce officials, and economic development groups began to voice concerns about their ability to recruit new industry to a county dominated by a relatively unskilled workforce. The themes raised locally echoed those of several national and state level reports. At approximately the same time, the governor of North Carolina appointed a taskforce on workforce preparedness that resulted in broad publicity about North Carolina's changing economy and the lack of both basic skills and technical skills in the workforce.

Local leaders' growing concerns about workforce preparedness began to focus on the newly merged school system. Feeling the pressure to respond, a newly appointed board of education began to talk with GTCC trustees and me about how to address these concerns. Indeed, it could be said that we were being asked to develop a plan that would not only address how the college could respond to the changing local economy but also how this new unified school system could be involved more effectively in the effort. The changes that we had been seeking for more than a decade were coming about—not primarily as a result of our efforts, but as a result of outside pressures.

This opportunity also presented some dangers and dilemmas. Most of the people asking GTCC to develop this plan neither worked for nor governed the public schools. They were business and industry leaders, chamber of commerce officials, and economic development professionals. I had to offer suggestions without inviting accusations that I was developing policy for the public schools. When I approached the new superintendent—a community college graduate—to discuss a Tech Prep partnership, he was enthusiastic. We developed a close working relationship that was supported by a wide variety of community leaders. The first joint decision was to hire an outside marketing group to analyze the state of the workforce in our community. The study, which involved more than 700 people in focus groups and telephone interviews, confirmed what we had been saying for some time—the college and the public schools needed to work more closely to prepare the county's present and future workforce. The Partnership for Guilford County Workforce Preparedness, a short-term and long-range plan, came out of the study. The study benefited from widespread publicity that heightened awareness of the gap in the county between employers' needs and employees' skills. Eventually, 10 workforce councils were organized around certain job classifications of business and industry.

The superintendent was enthusiastic from the beginning. He genuinely believed that a Tech Prep option focused on preparation for the 4-year college was needed in a public school system. However, it is also true that as a new superintendent, it was expedient politically for him to make Tech Prep work. If he did, he would gain the support of key business and industry leaders—essential friends as he lobbied county commissioners for increased funding.

What emerged, although relatively late in coming, was one of the most successful Tech Prep initiatives in the state and, perhaps, in the nation. Local businesses contributed more than $2 million to fund the Tech Prep initiative, including Tech Prep graduate scholarships, faculty return-to-industry experiences, and instructional equipment. Every public high school in the newly merged system implemented a comprehensive Tech Prep curriculum that included a career awareness curriculum in the elementary schools, a career exploration program in the middle schools, and a career preparation focus in the high schools.

The results have been tangible for GTCC. The percentage of Guilford County high school graduates enrolling at GTCC increased. In 2000, the first year that Tech Prep scholarships were available, 10 were awarded. In 2003, 85 were awarded, and in the fall of 2006, 191 were awarded. A by-product of that success has been extraordinary and favorable publicity for GTCC and the public school system. The Tech Prep initiative received the Magna Award for Outstanding Programs in Student Achievement from the *National School Board Journal,* and the Dale Parnell Award from AACC.

Regrettably, we have not tracked the success of these Tech Prep students adequately after leaving GTCC. Although we follow up on our graduates generally, we have not disaggregated the data. We know from graduate and employer surveys that a large percentage of our graduates have found jobs and that their employers are satisfied with their skills. We have committed ourselves to doing a better job of tracking the individual postgraduate success of our Tech Prep students.

MIDDLE COLLEGE

Almost 10 years after the birth of the partnership between Guilford County and GTCC, it continues to grow. When a new school superintendent was named several years ago, the school board explicitly sought someone who would continue to support the initiative. Although members of the school board and GTCC's board of trustees have come and gone, support for Tech Prep remains a top priority for both. I believe this success led to another major partnership, the development of North Carolina's first middle college high school.

In 1999, the Guilford County Public Schools selected a new superintendent. I was determined to ensure the continued success of our Tech Prep partnership, so I made arrangements to visit with him even before he arrived in North Carolina. I journeyed to Franklin County, Tennessee, armed with evidence about our initiative. We met, and, frankly, it was an easy sell. Then he turned the tables and took me to Nashville Technical Institute where he had helped develop a middle college. At the end of my visit, he asked me to support the development of a middle college on GTCC's campus.

I presented the concept at the next board meeting after my return to North Carolina. They were interested but had some concerns. One concern regarded potential behavioral problems on campus that might be caused by an infusion of 16-year-old students. They were concerned about issues of space for the middle college classes and their staff. However, they gave me permission to pursue the idea and come back to them again. I began to discuss the idea with senior staff and, eventually, with the entire faculty and staff. I repeatedly heard concerns similar to those raised by the board in that initial meeting. After the new superintendent arrived, he and I met frequently to discuss many issues; the idea of a middle college was always one of them. Although the middle college began in New York, almost 30 years before our discussion, none had been implemented in North Carolina.

By definition, a middle college is a small autonomous high school located on a college campus that serves students who are capable academically but who have become disengaged from their traditional high schools. Many middle college students have dropped out of school, and most of the remaining students are likely to do so. The essential idea of the middle college is to put these students into a new environment on a college campus where they can take high school classes along with college classes. The emphasis is on small classes, intensive counseling, a broad range of support services, and high expectations for each student. Public marketing focuses on the middle college as an educational alternative for the bright student who is not finding his or her needs met by the traditional high school. Obviously, that mission is in harmony with that of a community college.

Several months passed with many formal meetings and informal discussions, followed by the public school board's and GTCC's board decision to establish North Carolina's first middle college on our Jamestown Campus, to open fall 2000. Concerns among GTCC's faculty and staff remained but, for the most part, vanished as the first year moved along. Middle college classes were scheduled during the afternoon when many classrooms were vacant between the morning rush (when the campus operates at almost 100% occupancy) and the beginning of evening classes at 5:00 p.m. Office space for middle college faculty and staff was provided in two large rooms in the least desirable building on campus. The middle college staff did not mind; after all, most of them had no offices at all in their previous high school settings. Furthermore, although they had less-than-desirable office space, they taught in the best classrooms on campus. Recently, another facility became available on campus, and we remodeled it into office space for the middle college faculty and staff. The feared behavioral problems failed to materialize, and most of the middle college students blended right into the campus.

Dozens of logistical details had to be worked out: where to unload the school buses, how and when to feed the students, how to register them for college classes, and the like. All these issues and larger ones were solved, in large part, because the new superintendent and I worked closely together on the implementation. He had opposition from some of his staff and some high school principals, but together we moved the idea forward. One key to success was that he and I always spoke from the same script. Within GTCC, I consciously made the middle college one of my key initiatives. I introduced the middle college faculty and staff at the all-personnel meeting that opened the academic year. At various meetings throughout the year, I mentioned its successes. My plan was to make the middle college faculty feel like a part of the college community and to help GTCC's faculty and staff see the connections between our missions and work. I believe the plan was successful.

The superintendent helped win over his own critics, and some of mine, by making excellent choices for the founding principal and other positions on the middle college staff. Personnel from within the existing system were invited to apply for transfer to the new middle college. The superintendent said that the key criteria in making his personnel decisions were to select professionals with proven records and faculty and staff who had strong reputations for being student focused.

Another key decision was to appoint a long-time GTCC faculty member as the college liaison for the middle college. She has been instrumental in working out details such as space issues, registration procedures to enroll middle college students into curriculum courses, calendar alignment, and a host of other operational details. Because she was both a senior faculty member and a well-respected colleague, she was able to persuade critics of the middle college away from their negative positions. She worked individually with many faculty members who were skeptical about having high school–aged students enroll in their college-level classes. Because of their prior relationships with her, they were willing to give the idea a chance. Seven years later, the students' successes have been publicized throughout the county, state, and nation. GTCC now has three early/middle colleges (adding grades 9 and 10) on three of our campuses. As a result, we now have 14-year-old students on campus. Three private colleges in the county and one branch of the university also house a middle college now.

The results of the middle colleges have been phenomenal. The graduation rate for Guilford County's middle colleges has been 85% compared with a 63% rate for the county's traditional high schools. The GTCC middle colleges have been recognized with a host of awards for outstanding performance. Students and graduates have been featured in local and state newspaper stories, in *Newsweek,* and on the *CBS Evening News.* A graduate of the GTCC Middle College at Jamestown is ranked number one in his class at North Carolina State University; another graduate transferred 42 credits to the University of North Carolina at Chapel Hill. The student featured on the *CBS Evening News* graduated from GTCC's heavy equipment program only one semester after he received his high school diploma. These stories are even more remarkable considering that almost all of the students enrolled in the middle college were either high school dropouts at the time or had been identified as students likely to drop out.

There have been significant positive results for GTCC, which I consider by-products. The middle college has brought numerous first-time visitors to GTCC, including parents of potential students, high school faculty and administrators, visitors from across North Carolina and outside the state who are contemplating the start of a middle college, and numerous state officials. Currently, there are 29 middle colleges across North Carolina; most trace their roots to GTCC's first experiment. Without a doubt, the middle colleges have strengthened the college's overall relationship with the Guilford County Public Schools, including the existing Tech Prep program. Increasingly, the faculty of the middle college is participating in joint professional development opportunities with GTCC's faculty.

Moreover, the positive public relations generated for GTCC are incalculable. Innumerable parents of middle college students have given me their testimony that GTCC's middle college saved their children. Indeed, middle college graduates themselves have become public advocates for the program. One counselor, who was an original member of the staff, has told me that most of the program recruitment is conducted by students and parents who tell others about their experiences with the program.

Finally, the middle college has become a highly successful recruiting tool for GTCC, one that I never imagined when we established the ASAP program 25 years ago. Thus far, 86% of the GTCC Middle College graduates continue their education at GTCC.

CONCLUSION

This is a story of slow and profound change. The changes described here took 25 years, but GTCC now enjoys one of the most mutually beneficial relationships I know of between a public school system and a community college. Obviously, I cannot take all of the credit for the change, but I will take some because I did some things well.

One thing I learned was to see the issues from the perspective of the public schools rather than from the college. Many of these changes came about because there were distinct advantages that would come to the public schools if they engaged in the partnership. The success of both the Tech Prep initiative and the middle college is largely the result of a relationship of trust that I was able to establish with the superintendents. Given the busy schedule of a community college president, it is difficult to find time to build a close relationship with someone outside the organization. I made sure that I took the time to get to know the superintendents on a personal and a professional basis. The trip I made to Tennessee to meet the new superintendent before he moved to North Carolina was pivotal to our future work.

One lesson I learned early in life was reinforced by each of these projects: Teamwork is essential. I was a good high school and college baseball player, and I coached as part of my first teaching assignment. Programs like those described here do not happen because of one player; that would be impossible. The superintendent and I had to be team players for Tech Prep and the middle college, and we had to ensure that our staff members were team players as well. At times, we had to arbitrate differences between public school and college staff involved in the project; when the superintendent and I had differences, we talked about them privately, never publicly.

During the development stage of these programs, I often felt like the coach I used to be. Often I needed to inspire others, sometimes to believe in an idea they had doubts about, sometimes to move beyond their skepticism to give something a try, and sometimes to attempt something they felt would probably fail. The strongest leadership trait I brought to these tasks was an ability to relate the college's mission to others. For me, implementation of both the Tech Prep program and the middle college was clearly part of our college's mission. It is true that the middle college was more on the edge of our mission, but I knew it was important for the community. Sometimes we need to remind ourselves that an important aspect of the mission of a community college is to assist in solving community problems even if there is no obvious and direct benefit to the college in doing so.

At least one of my board members, who had some doubts about the middle college, has told me that he was won over by my own enthusiasm for the project. Many people have observed that the most important task for a community college president is to articulate the mission. In many respects, that is what I kept doing in this process: articulating the mission and explaining how these new directions fit into that mission. For years, I kept a framed quote in my office: "Babe Ruth struck out 1,340 times." Fortunately for most of us in positions of community college leadership, we are remembered, like Babe, more for our home runs than for our strikeouts. The story of GTCC's changing relationship with the public schools is about purpose, patience, persistence, and execution: essential factors for bringing about transformational change.

3

Chaffey College: Transforming Basic Skills for Successful Student Learning

Marie Kane

I believe any significant institutional change must be evidence based ... It is ultimately the students, their families, and society as a whole that benefit when the underprepared student of today becomes the transfer student of tomorrow.

—*Marie Kane, Chaffey College (CA)*

Founded in 1883, Chaffey College serves the residents of the Inland Empire in the west end of San Bernardino County, California. California's explosive population growth and large numbers of underprepared students complicated higher education services across the state, but the increasingly diverse and poor Inland Empire has faced the worst of it. Chaffey College administrators and faculty confronted the difficult issues facing the college and created the Basic Skills Transformation Project that improved student performance dramatically.

Careful research and assessment showed Chaffey College the direction it needed for change. The leadership team, headed by President Marie Kane, valued consistent communication of outcomes and disciplined decision making to encourage the transformation. With strong state support and a trusting, engaged faculty, the college created an Education Excellence Center that now boasts compelling evidence of student success.

At the heart of Chaffey College's success is the belief that underprepared students can overcome the problems and stigma of needing basic skills instruction and become tomorrow's transfer students. Courage to change radically and to believe continually in this new vision—expressed by the whole college—gave this transformation life.

Author's Note. Linda Howdyshell, vice president of instruction at Chaffey College, made significant contributions to this chapter and to the work of the Basic Skills Transformation project.

P ERHAPS THE MOST EXTRAORDINARY AND pervasive challenge facing community colleges today is the underpreparedness of entering students. Nationally, reports such as *America's Perfect Storm: Three Forces Changing Our Nation's Future* from the Educational Testing Service (Kirsch, Braun, Yamamoto, & Sum, 2007) present frightening possibilities for the future of the nation. The report suggests that divergent skill distributions, a changing economy, and demographic trends will have considerable impact on our future national prosperity. The first of these forces is

> the wide disparity in literacy and numeracy skills among our school-age and adult populations. High school graduation rates peaked at 77 percent in 1969, fell back to 70 percent in 1995, and have stayed in that range into the current decade. The graduation rate for disadvantaged minorities is thought to be closer to 50 percent. (p. 3)

The *Perfect Storm* report further suggested that literacy and numeracy skills are distributed unevenly across groups defined by race/ethnicity, country of birth, and socioeconomic status. In describing demographic trends, the report cites projections that our national population will become increasingly diverse, with immigration having a significant impact on the workforce and general population.

Our challenge is even greater in California, Chaffey College's home, where population diversity increases seem to contribute to the gap in achievement levels between population subgroups. A report published by California Tomorrow (2007), *California Community Colleges Struggle to Meet the Challenges of the State's Underprepared Workforce,* suggests the same three forces cited in *America's Perfect Storm:*

> But community colleges are also facing tremendous challenges that threaten to undermine their capacity to maintain, improve, and expand their innovative workforce preparation and basic skills programs. Among these challenges are the pressures of unprecedented enrollment demand for the accessible and affordable educational programs, the growth in underpreparedness among students entering their doors, and the challenges of developing and sustaining high cost instructional approaches and support services that are essential to meet the needs of students who are learning English, working several jobs, raising children and helping to support extended families. (p. 3)

In *Rules of the Game,* published by California State University, Sacramento, the authors cited low rates of degree completion or certificate attainment in California's community colleges as a danger to California's future economic status: "Access

41

without completion gives California's college students a false sense of opportunity and could jeopardize the state's competitive edge in the global economy" (Shulock & Moore, 2007, p. 4). As was stated in California Tomorrow's report, as the "on ramp to postsecondary education and workforce training for millions of Californians," community colleges are positioned uniquely to provide solutions to these challenges (California Tomorrow, 2007, p. 11).

THE CHAFFEY COLLEGE CONTEXT

In the late 1990s, Chaffey College board members, administrators, and key faculty members recognized the impending crisis in serving underprepared students. We were experiencing steady, strong growth and an increase in the diversity of our student body. Reflecting the population of the cities within its district, in the 1999–2000 academic year, the college served 25,046 students, including 32.6% identifying themselves as Latino, 36.2% identifying as White, 12.3% identifying as Black, 6.9% identifying as Asian/Pacific Islander, and smaller percentages identifying themselves as Filipino and Native American.

College leaders, including then-Vice President of Instruction Don Berz, a driving force behind the project, as well as leaders from faculty and administration, identified significant and systemic shortcomings in the delivery of basic skills instruction—that is, below college-level mathematics, reading, English, and ESL courses. Members of the governing board and I acknowledged the negative findings and supported necessary change. I became president at Chaffey College in the spring of 2001, and I immediately became a strong and consistent supporter for this work of improving basic skills instruction for students.

Disheartening Data

In 2001–2002, the project's baseline year, 71% of all first-time students were assessed at the precollegiate level in reading, English, or computational skills. At that time, the college basic skills program was a standalone organizational unit, separate from college-level mathematics, reading, and English. The basic skills program suffered from a lack of faculty leadership, limited budgets, and poor facilities, and it duplicated services.

Research from 1999 to 2000 indicated that the delivery and support of basic skills instruction were not serving students at what the college considered to be an acceptable success rate. Students were successful in precollegiate skill level courses only approximately 50% of the time. Only two thirds of those successful basic skills students subsequently enrolled in transfer or degree-applicable courses, and only 56% of that group were successful in those courses. In other words, only 18% of students starting in basic skills courses were successful later in transfer or degree-applicable courses. The data concerning students earning associate degrees or occupational certificates were more disheartening. Only 7% of associate degree earners and only 11% of certificate recipients had completed at least one basic skills course previously. Clearly, we were not achieving our goal of using the basic skills as a pipeline for future graduates and certificate recipients.

Partnership for Excellence

During that same time, the California Community College system made a mutual commitment with the State of California to create the Partnership for Excellence (PFE). This partnership had the goal of significantly expanding the contribution of the community colleges to California's social and economic success. PFE was structured in phases, with substantial financial investment by the state in exchange for credible commitment from the system of colleges to specific student and performance outcomes.

The PFE primary goals for improvement were in the areas of transfer, degrees and certificates, successful course completion, and basic skills improvement. Chaffey College's 1998 to 1999 appropriation from PFE was $1.1 million. Consistent with the budget act language, funds might be used in any manner, decided locally, designed to bring progress on the goals. Under our governance process, I formed a task force of administration and faculty members to identify goal areas, strategies, and estimated expenditures.

The opportunities provided by PFE could not have appeared at a more propitious time for Chaffey College. Its PFE Task Force, recognizing the current and impending crises in the delivery of basic skills instruction, conceived of the Basic Skills Transformation Project. Its motto became, "The underprepared student of today is the transfer student of tomorrow." The PFE Task Force presented an educational moral imperative to the college: take students from their entering skill level to a level that could earn them an associate degree or occupational certificate or prepare them for transfer.

The governing board and college community embraced the project, understanding that we must find ways to improve service to the growing number of underprepared students entering Chaffey College. Our administration and board made the commitment that no permanent employees would lose their positions, even if the current basic skills program and departments were changed radically. With widespread support, the college committed its PFE funds as an investment in and for the future toward that goal, and the Basic Skills Transformation Project was launched.

THE BASIC SKILLS TRANSFORMATION PROJECT: THE PROCESS

Our first step in the project was to engage an external review team of six recognized experts in instruction and basic skills in California community colleges. The review was treated as a focused "mini accreditation" to examine every aspect of the college basic skills program. The team did extensive research and spent 2½ days at various college sites observing program components and interviewing faculty and staff. In its report, the team recognized that the current program was a mixture of services and courses that were not well integrated throughout the college. Staff, faculty, and administrators were frustrated by trying to succeed while competing for resources in a fragmented environment. These findings, coming from a team of outside experts, articulated the perceptions of many at the college and thus were surprisingly well received. Some of the faculty and staff members who were then working within the basic skills department were feeling something like "second-class citizens"—unappreciated and undervalued. The outside review helped give them a voice.

The team's recommendations were intended to assist the college in developing a program in which math, English, and ESL courses were aligned; staff understood the available developmental education programs and services; skill assessment and placement was effective; and resources were allocated appropriately. The review team presented significant recommendations that would completely transform the college basic skills program. These recommendations would make wide-ranging changes in curriculum, organization, student assessment and placement, technology, support services, and facilities. In addition, the report recommended the creation of "student success centers," including a writing center, a math success center, a reading/ESL success center, and four multidisciplinary success centers.

The college adopted the team's recommendations, and a broadly based task force was given the task of implementing them. The basic skills courses were reorganized so that precollegiate English, mathematics, reading, and ESL became part of the instructional unit that offered the full sequence of those courses. The college agreed with the recommendations regarding assessment and placement and initiated a comprehensive, research-based study of placement and prerequisites. A computerized assessment system was added in the fall of 2001. Although the requirements to add a course prerequisite are quite rigorous for California's community colleges, as of the fall of 2007, almost 300 courses have validated and enforced prerequisites appropriately.

Student Success Centers

Perhaps the most challenging and exciting innovation resulting from the team's recommendations was the success centers. The mission of the success centers is to give students the resources they need to be successful in achieving their academic and life goals. The success centers are welcoming, easily accessed by students with a college ID, and open 70 hours per week. The centers serve all students, not just those with basic skills. We found that part of the "transformation" required changing remedial laboratories into resource centers for all students, thus removing the stigma associated with "needing to be fixed." Honors students, basic skills students, transfer students, and occupational studies students come to the centers for directed learning activities, workshops, study groups, tutoring, and laboratory resources, which vary from self-paced instruction to videos and software.

The centers are also a resource for faculty. When their students require additional instruction, instructors refer them to the centers. Faculty members also collaborate with a success center coordinator to develop workshops, create supplemental learning tools, or learn different instructional strategies. These multiple purposes require faculty leadership; therefore, each of the six success centers is staffed with a full-time faculty member. These instructional coordinators teach "just-in-time" workshops, hire and train tutors, manage intake, work with instructors to create supplemental instruction projects, and coordinate operations for more than 9,000 students each semester and for approximately 181,000 interventions of 15 minutes or more. In addition, each center employs instructional assistants, additional faculty, student tutors, and aides.

Educational Excellence Center

To accommodate the success centers, we needed appropriate and sufficient space at the main Rancho Cucamonga Campus and the three outreach centers. Only because the commitment to the Transformation Project was so pervasive within our college could this happen in an institution where space was at a premium. With the required approval from the state system office, Chaffey College committed several million dollars from its share of future PFE funds toward building a facility to house a multidisciplinary success center and a language laboratory.

During the building planning process for the Educational Excellence Center, another unexpected financial problem arose from sudden national cost inflation for construction projects. Cost estimates during planning indicated that the building could not be built as planned with the available financial resources. The college president and executive leadership team worked to modify the scope of the planned building so that existing capital bond funds could be added. After years of planning, approval processes, and construction, this building, the Educational Excellence Center, opened in the spring of 2007.

SIGNIFICANT OUTCOMES OF THE BASIC SKILLS TRANSFORMATION PROJECT

From the beginning, the college created and funded a comprehensive research evaluation component, and it continues to support this function as an integral component of the project. The statistical evidence of the success of the success centers is compelling. In 2005–2006, students accessing the resources of the success centers were 15% more likely to complete a course successfully than students enrolled in the same section who did not access a success center. Success centers had a statistically significant positive impact on all student subgroups, including those defined by gender, ethnicity, age, GPA, and prior college attendance. The greatest impact was on the success rates of first-time students.

We continually assessed the success of basic skills students and our delivery of instruction and support services to those students. The results 6 years later are encouraging, despite the decreases in the levels of preparedness of entering students. Although the proportion of students who place into college-level English has remained constant over the past 5 years, the proportion of students who are prepared for college-level reading has dropped dramatically, and the proportion of students ready for college-level mathematics has not improved.

Although the skill levels of entering students have decreased, the success rates for these Chaffey College students have increased. The basic skills course success rate increased from 57% in 1997–1998 to 64% in 2004–2005. The likelihood of former successful basic skills students enrolling in transfer- or degree-applicable courses increased even more dramatically, from 66% to 87% over this period. Perhaps most importantly, the percentage of Chaffey students who earn associate degrees or certificates has increased steadily since the beginning of the Basic Skills Transformation Project. In 2004–2005, more than 40% of certificate recipients and more than 30% of degree recipients had been basic skills students. Although we have not reached our goal of preparing every basic skills student to succeed in attaining a degree or certificate or in transferring, we are clearly on the correct path toward that goal.

The ongoing and increasing success of this multiyear, systemic transformation project has had a profound impact on Chaffey College. A stigma is no longer attached to being a basic skills student, because students of all skill levels participate in the success centers. The faculty and staff who work with basic skills students also work with honors students, occupational students, and students from across the college—clearly not "second-class citizens." Rather, the faculty and staff who work in the success centers are regarded as a valuable resource to other faculty. As a secondary effect, the college's reputation among its peer colleges in California and across the country has been enhanced. Faculty and staff frequently are asked to give presentations to other colleges or to host visiting teams from other colleges. State leaders often refer to the "Chaffey model" as exemplary in its ability to assist thousands of students each year.

LEADERSHIP CHALLENGES AND LESSONS LEARNED

Chaffey College's Basic Skills Transformation was based on a sustained commitment, including a strong financial commitment throughout the institution. During the 2002–2003 academic year, California faced a critical economic downturn, and colleges were required to make a 7% midyear budget cut. This budget cut was exceptionally difficult, and some colleges were forced to issue layoff notices. For Chaffey, the commitment to the Basic Skills Transformation Project did not waiver in the face of financial crisis. Although there were some necessary reductions in hours for part-time employees across the college, there was no substantive decrease in success centers. The executive team clearly articulated that the Basic Skills Transformation Project was core to the mission of the college and would not be abandoned.

The state of California ended its PFE compact with its community colleges in 2004–2005. We at Chaffey College, however, continue our commitment to basic skills programs in providing human resources, appropriate space, and operational dollars. The college is convinced that these investments result in improved retention and student success and that the resource commitment is well founded.

We believe any significant institutional change must be evidence based. From the beginning, a well-designed assessment was part of the plan. The regular dissemination of the outcomes provided evidence of the success center's effectiveness, identified practices requiring adjustment, and gave encouragement to the entire campus that the sustained financial commitment pays off in retention and success. Ultimately, it is the students, their families, and society as a whole that benefit when the underprepared student of today becomes the transfer student of tomorrow.

REFERENCES

California Tomorrow. (2007). *California community colleges struggle to meet the challenges of the State's underprepared workforce.* Oakland, CA: Author.

Kirsch, I., Braun H., Yamamoto, K., & Sum, A. (2007). *America's perfect storm: Three forces changing our nation's future.* Princeton, NJ: Educational Testing Service.

Shulock, N., & Moore, C. (2007). *Rules of the game: How state policy creates barriers to degree completion and impedes student success in California community colleges.* Sacramento, CA: California State University.

4

Iowa Central Community College: A Phenomenal Experience

Bob Paxton

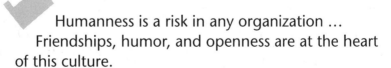

Humanness is a risk in any organization …
Friendships, humor, and openness are at the heart
of this culture.

—*Bob Paxton, Iowa Central Community College*

Iowa Central Community College recreated the belief among faculty, staff, and administrators that students come first. In rural north central Iowa, where the population and economy were both dwindling, investing in the future required focused decision making and the courage to change a culture of mistrust to a culture of common vision. Valuing humanness and leading with integrity, President Bob Paxton built relationships with individual members of the college community and initiated the momentum to transform the college from a struggling Midwestern institution to one of Iowa's leading training centers.

Crafting win–win community partnerships created resources that helped the college grow. Morale and enrollments increased, buildings were constructed, new programs began, and donations poured in, while tuition rates dropped. Most importantly, these developments ushered in countywide support for the college's future. Iowa Central Community College has moved from a college with a dwindling enrollment to a thriving hub of arts, culture, innovation, and excellence. Remembering that education is a human endeavor, Iowa Central Community College has cultivated relationships and opened doors it never could have imagined.

PICTURE THIS: YOUR FIRST DAY as a college freshman you are greeted by "Donuts with Doc." The next night is a hog roast, where you chat with other students and your instructors. Bingo, movie night, and many other lively events kick off the semester. You have more to look forward to throughout the year: athletic events, theater performances, art shows, an international festival, and a hilarious lip-sync contest in which students engage in friendly competition for scholarships while staff engage in "serious competition" for trophies and bragging rights. On top of all of this, you feel encouraged academically and know that this place cares about student life and learning. No wonder enrollment has increased again this semester.

The remarkable growth and success of Iowa Central Community College, in rural north central Iowa, did not happen by accident. The student-first vision extending into every corner of the institution has produced a collegial atmosphere of achievement that encompasses academics, vocational training, community partnerships, athletics, and the arts. Although many changes have occurred on the Iowa Central campus since 1994, 25 consecutive semesters of growth point to its greatest resource: people who believe in the college and its mission. This culture transformation resulted in success for our college and those it serves.

THE PAST

Three public junior colleges in north central Iowa merged to form Iowa Central Community College on July 1, 1966. Although the history of Iowa Central proper dates back only 40 years, the history of providing service to the community dates back more than 80 years. Fort Dodge Junior College had been in operation since 1921, Webster City Junior College was organized in 1926, and Eagle Grove Junior College originally was incorporated in 1928. In 1971, the Storm Lake Workforce Center opened.

It is well documented in the literature (Baker, Roueche, & Gillett-Karam, 1990; Collins, 2001; Gardner, 1990; Roueche, Baker, & Rose, 1989; Vaughan, 1992) that leadership philosophy directs an institution toward attaining its goals. Iowa Central Community College has evolved through different administrative leadership over its 40 years of operation. Over these years, key leaders and staff members have contributed to the success that Iowa Central reaps today. For its first 20 years, the college was led by an autocratic leadership that put the organization in a strong position for facilities and financial reserves. Although such a leadership style has its benefits, broader involvement is necessary for the longtime viability of an organization (Blanchard & Hershey, 1969). As the administration kept abreast of trends in education, the concept of the long-range plan took hold in education. In the 1980s, Iowa Central developed a broad and, looking back, unmanageable

51

10-year long-range plan that was difficult to understand, much less carry out. It contained no measurable outcomes, nor were outcomes considered during planning processes.

Iowa Central went through a period of laissez-faire leadership. Enrollment growth plateaued, then began to slide backward. An overall complacency set in within the organization. There were employees who wanted the college to succeed, but little enthusiasm registered among its leadership. In the spring of 1994, the Fort Dodge Center was suffering from many maladies—head count was approximately 2,100 students, and credit hours were down to 22,000. Only 80 students lived on campus in outdated high-rise dormitories located far from classrooms, the auditorium, and the gymnasium. Campus safety was a real concern. There were internal issues between staff and administration. Very few partnerships were in place, and financial reserves were depleted. The State Board of Education was considering taking over management responsibilities of the college. We were at a crossroads in our development. Recognizing this, the college board determined the need for a new direction. The board had the opportunity to hire a new college president and identified three important elements that had to be addressed by this new leader: the ability to bring staff together in a unified direction; the ability to increase enrollment; and the ability to develop stronger partnerships with area business, industry, and high schools.

I began my role as president in January 1995, which proved to be a great time to make critical changes to the college to enhance enrollment and programs for the upcoming fall semester. As a first-time president, I approached this post with enthusiasm and idealism. I quickly realized I was faced with some serious issues that had to be addressed immediately. Had I not been blessed with great community college mentors and leaders throughout the previous 13 years of my career, I am sure I would have failed miserably. Although several employees were anxious to make changes, a culture of mistrust and frustration existed within the organization. Some employees had been hurt by the organization, were burned out, did not see a need for dramatic change, and were resistant to any change. A tone had to be set at the first all-staff meeting in January. At that time, we voted to eliminate reserved parking for employees, the first step toward establishing a student-centered philosophy. As small of a modification as that might appear, it set change in motion within the organization.

Because we had to address so many priorities at once and set direction for the college, the board and I were autocratic in our approach to both. Because the college had severe financial problems, we knew we had to eliminate staff. Staffing was consuming well more than 80% of the budget. We offered an early retirement incentive, and more than 20 people accepted it. We had the highest tuition rate in the state and made a bold move by lowering tuition $10 per credit hour to enhance recruitment efforts.

During the first months, I spent time meeting with staff, students, and secondary school officials, and I made visits to industry and community leaders. During the year, each day was targeted to set the tone of where we were going as a college and communicating that loud and clear to our staff and region. I knew that staff development was essential to turn the corner and change the culture of the college. That first year, we began to invest significant funds into staff development. The reins of the organization were given over to the staff members as they began buying into this philosophy. As a result, my leadership style has changed drastically over the last 12 years. For example, to initiate the culture change necessary to bring about the needed increase in enrollment, we formulated institutional growth strategies , developed a manageable 3-year strategic plan with collegewide input, made staff development a priority, and introduced shared governance with participation and empowerment of people from all ranks of the staff.

Three of the most crucial areas we addressed that first year were fine arts, athletics, and industry training and partnerships. New staff and funds were pumped into music and theater to make those programs outstanding. The board decided to redirect athletic programs to recruit local student–athletes first. We brought in new coaches and put systems in place to hold students accountable for their behavior and commitment to the classroom. Significant effort and focus was placed on industry training. Industrial trainers were employed to do on-site training, and new technical programs were created to address the needs of industry.

From the low point of 1994 sprang changes that have turned Iowa Central into a model institution. Despite our location in the middle of a nine-county rural region suffering from acute population decline, we are one of the fastest-growing community colleges in the country. In 1990, the nine-county service area population was 144,805; the most current population estimate is 138,972 (2004). The number of high school seniors in the service area dropped from 2,062 in 1996, to 1,649 in 2006; yet, our enrollment increased from 2,515 in fall 1995, to 5,491 in fall 2006 (see Figure 4.1). We now have the highest market penetration rate in the state. Such a monumental achievement is possible only when the organization is viewed by the public as a students-first college.

THE PRESENT

Students First

Iowa Central's students-first philosophy has been the driving factor in its success. We are invested in our students and stakeholders and take great pride

Figure 4.1 Enrollment at Iowa Central Community College: 1996–2008

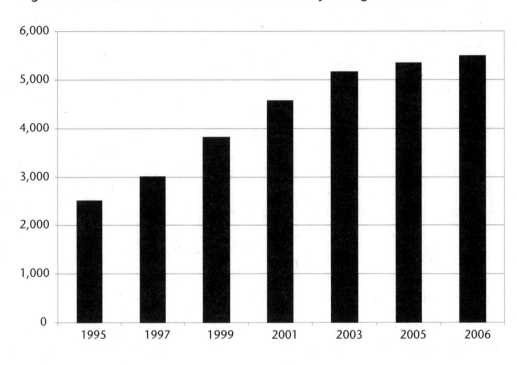

in presenting an attractive, fully functioning learning environment. We modeled our presentation of activities, academics, and student involvement after private 4-year colleges but at a greatly reduced cost to the student. Today's Iowa Central students operate within an environment where success is expected, while they receive help and encouragement from every possible source. The multipurpose Student Success Center offers students assistance in any academic pursuit and includes free tutoring. To meet students' academic needs, we have reinvented the college as an institution that sets high standards and demands accountability across the board. Student grades and attendance are monitored closely, and systems are in place to issue alerts to students, instructors, and advisors when student achievement slips below desired levels. Methods used to keep students, faculty, coaches, and advisors informed regarding a student's progress in course work include the following:

- The System for Tracking Achievement and Retention is used to alert students when the instructor has a concern about course progress or to applaud students who are doing well. Faculty members submit the information electronically in 2-week intervals. Students receive an e-mail of the report immediately, and a letter is mailed to the student.

- The Athletic Code of Conduct and a list of athletic requirements describe expectations for student athletes.
- The Electronic Gradebook Program gives students daily feedback regarding assignments and grades in their respective courses.
- Student athletes are required to provide their grade sheets to their coaches three times per semester, denoting the current grade in the course and including the faculty member's signature.

Student life embraces more than academics. To achieve a more collegial atmosphere on campus, and as an outgrowth of the 1994 campus security concerns, we embarked on an aggressive new campus living plan—student apartment buildings. Close to central campus with easy access to classrooms, activities, and the cafeteria, the new apartments and a strict code of conduct have eased security issues and provided a new approach to student housing. As the demand for on-campus housing increased, we constructed more state-of the-art, energy-efficient, three-story brick apartment buildings at the rate of one per year; now we have 12 fully occupied. Only 80 students lived on campus in 1994; 738 resided in the new apartment buildings by fall 2006. High-quality student apartments benefit the college—housing serves as a recruitment tool, because the apartments are often the deciding element in a student choosing Iowa Central. Further, apartments promote a collegial environment for the traditional student. Student housing changes the college culture and promotes better student retention. Recently, we established learning communities within the apartments in which students are grouped by their respective majors.

Student activities are an integral part of Iowa Central. In 1995, the board endorsed the plan to build credible, competitive athletic programs and a dynamic, exciting fine arts program focused on theater and vocal and instrumental music. Scholarship budgets were strengthened, and new staff members were recruited in these areas to bring a new vision. There were three primary reasons for these bold moves: to build enrollment from a strong local and regional base, to develop and create community pride and create excellence in the minds of the community, and to create a collegial culture with many activities on campus for students. The results have been phenomenal; growth in enrollment, as a by-product of this initiative, has been tremendous. We remained successful in recruiting students for these activities, and these students bring others with them to the college. Scholarships and activities enable us to attract some of the better athletes and fine arts students in the region who otherwise might have attended a private college or decided to drop activities altogether and attend a university.

Redefining these areas has developed broad community support. Excellent student theater productions draw sell-out crowds. Thousands of elementary and middle school students come to campus for matinees. The annual fall play, the spring musical, concerts throughout the year, and 18 athletic programs—many of which have succeeded at the regional and national level—have received excellent press, promoting community support. Fort Dodge community members, Floyd and Gloria Magnusson, said

> *We're so proud of Iowa Central Community College and the leadership of Dr. Paxton in the promotion of fine arts for our region. We take pleasure in being able to attend these wonderful productions and events. We feel that the staff at Iowa Central is amazing in how they can pull out the highest quality of music and talent from the students.*

The collegial atmosphere attracts students to campus and encourages them to be involved in a host of organizations and activities, positively affecting both recruitment and retention. For these reasons, as well as for its strong business ties, the community openly values Iowa Central. The local newspaper, *The Messenger*, recognized Iowa Central as one of the best assets of Webster County in a front-page article ("How Does Webster County Stack Up," 2007).

Educational Offerings

Students and stakeholders seek transfer courses, career programs, and vocational programs. The success of these programs relies on recruitment and retention of excellent faculty members who understand and believe in students, recruitment, a skilled workforce, and students prepared for upper-division college work. The faculty understands the need to set high expectations and provide the support and structure that students need to be successful. All sectors of enrollment have grown substantially, particularly career programs. Technical programs struggle in many colleges; the tendency is to place blame on outside factors such as equipment, high schools, and industry. However, the problem often lies with us as institutions and our unwillingness or inability to grow programs. We are always better off not offering programs than allowing them to struggle along with low enrollment. The foundation to any successful transfer or career program lies not in facilities, equipment, or need for employees in the field but directly with the enthusiasm, commitment, and focus of the instructors of the programs. We have eliminated few career programs; instead, we have focused on student recruitment and retention. In fact, over the past 10 years, we have modified several programs and added more than a dozen applied science programs, including transportation management, health and beauty management, culinary arts, biofuels technology, and electrical maintenance.

Faculty and staff have embraced the reality that enrollment is critical to the long-term viability of programs. All faculty members visit area high schools and call prospective students. There was some opposition in the beginning years; however, the results are overwhelming, and faculty and staff take pride in the results. Staff development, focused on building a cohesive staff, has been a critical component of creating this positive, collegial climate. One of the anchors to staff development is the National Institute for Staff and Organizational Development (NISOD) conference. Each year, 25 to 35 Iowa Central employees travel by bus, car, and plane to this international conference in Austin, Texas, where they learn, dine, dance, and celebrate teaching and learning excellence together. Nursing instructor, Jane Townsend, said of the event:

> *One of the unexpected benefits of attending the NISOD conference was getting to know, on a personal level, many of my fellow faculty and staff members. I feel like I came home with true friendships that will help foster a sense of community within Iowa Central. I also believe we have a great faculty, and I am proud to be a part of it.*

Off-campus academic offerings thrive, as well. We lead the state in providing college classes to high school students. Iowa Central Community College launched Project Earlybird (college credit offered to high school students) in the fall of 1995. In this project, Earlybird classes allow rural secondary schools to offer rigorous and expanded educational programs to their students. For the 2006–2007 academic year, 4,019 students were enrolled in Earlybird courses for 19,472 credit hours. The high schools pay tuition costs for their students. High school students (with school district approval) earn college credits toward an associate of arts degree, an associate of science degree, an associate in applied science degree, a diploma, or a certificate. These credits are accepted by most 4-year institutions, saving families in Iowa Central's region thousands of tuition dollars. These courses are instrumental in recruiting students to Iowa Central once they graduate from high school.

We are connected closely with area high schools and have partnered with two high schools to form charter schools: Southeast Webster-Grand School in 2004 and Storm Lake School in 2005. These two charter schools offered educational opportunities for 65 students during the 2006–2007 academic year. Southeast Webster-Grand Charter School allows high school students to take advanced courses that otherwise could not be offered in a small rural school district. Storm Lake Charter School allows minority students to attend an extra year of high school and

Iowa Central simultaneously, providing a critical structure for student success. The Storm Lake Charter School was designed to serve students for whom college would be an enormous economic challenge or for whom poor English language skills would have compromised their academic and vocational opportunities. The charter school purchased a school bus to transport students 60 miles to the Fort Dodge campus. With the large influx of "New Iowans" to Storm Lake, a local workforce grows and addresses Iowa's increased diversity—an indirect benefit to the Fort Dodge Center, creating more diversity on campus and across the state.

More unique educational offerings are under way. Area high schools and Iowa Central are creating a rural model that fosters the implementation and growth of Project Lead the Way—a preengineering program. This model ignites young people's interest, provides a head start in manufacturing and engineering careers, and creates a seamless transition for students to move from the secondary level into higher education.

Recruitment

When I first came to Iowa Central, I believed we could build this college into something special in spite of its being located in a region that was experiencing a population decline. I also knew it would take a mind shift by the staff to get it accomplished. We have worked hard to increase enrollment and credit hours by 250% since fall 2004. The increase to almost 5,500 students, taking almost 55,000 credit hours, is remarkable in a region hit hard by job losses and out-migration.

This growth has been accomplished through a multilayered approach. First, all aspects of the college became involved in an image-building transformation that catered specifically to customers, whether customers were current students, students in regional high schools, community partners, or partners in business and industry. In addition, Iowa Central adopted a proactive position, courting students, courting partnerships, and anticipating community and regional needs. As president, I took and still take a very active role in recruiting, developing and fostering partnerships, and forecasting future needs of the college. It is essential to model behaviors crucial to college success. Another step was to make the college comfortable and affordable through wide-ranging scholarship opportunities at institutional and department levels, inviting and encouraging students to take part in the Iowa Central experience. Gerry Miller, involved in Student Ambassadors and other activities, enjoys being a student: "Iowa Central has been a true stepping stone for students who want a positive start in college. It has allowed me the chance to get a firm grip on college life before venturing off to a 4-year university."

Twelve years ago, the concept of the entire college focusing on enrollment management was established, and I observed:

I believe that in order to have excellence in the management of enrollment a college must have each and every member of the institution pulling together to maximize the opportunities for increased enrollment. It cannot be the sole responsibility of the admissions staff. All faculty and personnel must be involved in this process.

From that point, collegewide involvement in recruitment and student services has played a critical role in the process that fostered this amazing rebirth. It begins with an open-door policy that welcomes visitors to the campus at any time. Staff members take pride and ownership in an environment that is available to current and prospective students.

The entire college is involved in the recruitment process. Admissions staff members arrange campus visits at prospective students' and parents' convenience. Students take tours with departmental representatives and meet faculty and program coordinators. Student ambassadors give students peer connections to the college. On organized Junior and Senior Visit Days, students and their parents tour the campus, visit with department heads and instructors, eat lunch in the cafeteria, and chat with current students. Three-week periods are blocked off each fall and spring for all college personnel to make personal phone calls to thousands of prospective students. Student Services representatives visit 85% of all Iowa high schools, routinely call students, and follow up on their requests for information and visits.

Increased enrollments and changes in the student demographics led to a change in the perception of quality of the college. An entering new student opinion survey is conducted during the sixth week of freshman orientation classes every fall semester to gather information. Results of this survey are analyzed and used to target areas that need improvement. As Figure 4.2 shows, progress is sometimes slow, but consistent effort will bring about desired change.

Quality breeds quantity, and students rise to the level of expectation. Consequently, Iowa Central has experienced growth in numbers, increased support from area high schools, and increased participation by all constituents. When high-quality students experience high-quality transfer experiences, it is a win–win experience for Iowa Central. When high-quality graduates from industrial technology programs, health sciences programs, and career option programs obtain employment to enhance the economy of Iowa, it is a win–win experience for Iowa Central and the community.

Figure 4.2 Entering Students' Opinions of Iowa Central Community College: 2004–2006

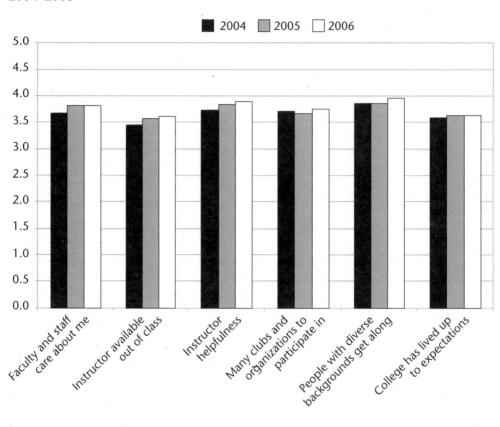

Note. 1=Strongly Disagree, 2=Disagree, 3=Neutral, 4=Agree, 5=Strongly Agree

Partnerships

"First it is necessary to stand on your own two feet. But the minute a man finds himself in that position, the next thing he should do is reach out his arms" (Hunter, 2003). Under Iowa Central's current leadership with partnerships with business and industry and private citizens, an entrepreneurial spirit has proven to be a critical component to the success of the college. Cultivating working relationships with the communities we serve and with business and industry within these communities has made us a leader in regional economic development. The college's flexibility and willingness to respond quickly to the needs of area employers has made it the hub of regional workforce training.

Initially, it was critical that we established partnerships beneficial to the college and the partnering entity. It was important to be successful in these early partnerships and to establish a positive record. We had to establish a close link with industries.

Today, many businesses and industries believe we are crucial to their success. One of our industry leaders, addressing the local Chamber of Commerce, stated, "C&S Products and many other industries in this area would not be viable today without Iowa Central, and many new companies have even decided to locate here because of Iowa Central."

One of our first steps was to transition some traditional faculty positions into industrial trainer positions. These trainers were full-time college employees who taught part time in the technical programs and then provided industry training within industries on a part-time basis. This step enabled us to create a connection between industries and Iowa Central's technical programs—to develop a trust in the quality from technical programs. It also led to our offering significantly more on-site industry training. The relationship has proved invaluable as the organization has moved forward the last 12 years.

From this beginning, we cultivated some traditional partnerships, including excellent relationships with the Regional Medical Center and the YMCA. A partnership with Trinity Regional Medical Center has produced even more educational opportunities for hospital employees, programs for the community, and health care providers. This partnership has created an interesting dynamic; when the region needs to move forward with innovative solutions, it is not unusual to witness these two forces leading the way. As in most communities, the YMCA was seeking program revitalization. Within a week of discussing possibilities, Iowa Central created a partnership with the YMCA, and 6 months later, the college assumed leadership. The result has been hundreds of new members, a new on-campus location, and a communitywide recreational system.

We have established an important partnership with *The Messenger,* the regional newspaper. We first began work with the newspaper with an annual fine arts program, "This Is Entertainment," a production held in the college auditorium before 1,200 people. The proceeds from this event went to area high schools for their fine arts programs. From the beginning, the college established a variety of events, including home and garden, sports, and agriculture shows. The regional newspaper handles the advertising and coordinates booths for these events. The college established six tuition scholarships with the *Messenger* in trade for college advertising. The newspaper awards these six full-tuition scholarships to eligible high school graduates each academic year.

We have established some unique partnerships, as well. For example, most cosmetology programs in Iowa are operated by private, for-profit colleges. Rather than creating our own cosmetology program, we established a partnership with LaJames International College, which has several sites throughout Iowa and other states. To provide an associate of applied science degree in health and beauty management, Iowa Central works side-by-side in recruiting students for cosmetology and providing the essential business and communications courses students need for completing a cosmetology program. A local businessperson purchased the Willow Ridge Golf Course and its on-site restaurant. The college manages the golf course and has established turf management, culinary arts, and hospitality management programs. This partnership provides an outstanding laboratory for all three programs; the accounting program manages the financial aspects of the club, giving students real-life accounting experience. We have created partnerships with trucking companies using biofuels. The college has become the state quality-testing center for biodiesel. The state's Department of Homeland Security has partnered with the college to provide statewide training for first-responders in security initiatives.

To make these partnerships work, it was critical to seek alternative funding aggressively. A grant writer had limited success, and I was not entirely happy with our overall efforts to develop alternative funding. I turned to a former state senator, who lived in the area, knowing that he still had strong political ties in the state and in Washington, DC. I actively sought him out and employed him to improve government relations at local, state, and federal levels. That accomplished, we actively recruited a former bank president who had great ties in the community and employed her to oversee the college's foundation.

In 2005, the foundation embarked on its first capital campaign in 40 years to raise money from the private sector. The best private partnerships often begin with the college's alumni. One partnership has been developed with an Iowa Central alumnus, Don Decker, and his family. In August 2006, the Decker family's $1 million commitment to the college was the first step toward taking the transportation and logistics programs to the next level. In March 2007, the Crimmins family, which includes many alumni, donated a 94,300-square-foot building, located on 25 acres of land and worth $3 million, to the college. This building will be used for equestrian events, the home and garden show, and other events cohosted with the regional newspaper. These partnerships have proved invaluable in creating tremendous linkages with the region.

With state funding cutbacks and budgets strained with steadily increasing enrollment, Iowa Central has realized the value of private entrepreneurial partnerships to finding alternative revenue streams. In the past 3 years, we have acquired an impressive $12 million in direct appropriations, grants, and gifts from members of the community. We have been successful in securing direct appropriations to establish new programs, most recently resulting in a dental hygiene laboratory, homeland security programs, and a biodiesel transportation efficiency study with a local trucking firm, as mentioned earlier.

Leadership

Iowa Central has experienced a significant change in "campus think" over the last 12 years. Faculty and staff members used to work in silos, without much thought or information about their colleagues' job responsibilities. An admission representative's job was to get students enrolled in classes. Faculty members taught the course material in the classroom. Coaches coached. Financial aid monitored money, and the business office collected money. There was a clear pattern of "to each his own" throughout the college. This old notion began to disappear as we embraced the philosophy that recruitment and retention of students is everyone's number one priority—a new concept for many. However, this concept saved the college and helped us increase enrollments and raise employee morale. We worked to bring cohesiveness to the organization. It was obvious we had to downsize administrative staff and remove bureaucratic functions within the organization.

I required the vice president of student development and vice president of instruction to work closely together and to encourage the student development staff to work more closely with faculty. Continuous Process Improvement (CPI) practices—a method whereby the decision-making routine of the institution is distributed to the persons most closely involved with the process—were implemented, and staff members were trained to work in cross-functional teams. CPI teams are empowered to address specific challenges by developing new or improving existing processes and implementing these changes into college procedures. For example, one of the first successful CPI endeavors involved the signage team, which provided aesthetically pleasing and consistent internal and external signage at the Fort Dodge Center.

The college has many systems and processes that change over time as personnel come and go. An instructional systems and process improvement team was created to monitor and ensure consistent application of processes dealing with grading, awarding advanced standing credit and degrees, test taking, grade requests, number of incomplete grades issued each term, and a myriad of other issues related to instruction—for example, Internet-guided self-study courses, transcripts, grade changes, and student withdrawals for nonpayment. The team collects data regarding course offerings, athletic code of conduct enforcements, online course registration drops, and the like, and presents this information to the board of trustees once each year. Such teams have made multiple processes more efficient and helped improve morale.

Improved morale is validated by responses to our internal environment survey, a survey distributed to all employees every 2 years. Figure 4.3 shows responses over time in five categories of this survey: administrative practices, climate, individual and team practices, performance goals and feedback, and training and education. The figure shows an increase in "strongly agree" responses, reflecting increasingly positive perspectives on the overall college environment.

Iowa Central staff members take pride in promoting a positive, unified, all-inclusive college experience for our students. These survey results clearly indicate that the majority of employees agree or strongly agree that Iowa Central exhibits a positive internal environment. Culture is created by people who bring perceptions, work ethic, and skill sets into an organization; our culture is unique. We adopted the belief that the college is only as strong as its weakest link and successfully presented a collegewide blueprint for the pursuit of service excellence. Employees understand that we can be the best only if we have the best people on the team. Our organization has become lean and efficient. The introduction of shared governance with participation and empowerment of people from all ranks of the staff created an initial culture shock. However, today we have achieved a unified coalition of faculty, staff, and administrators who work together to provide excellence in teaching and learning for students and other stakeholders.

The journey of Iowa Central was validated June 2007, when area voters overwhelmingly approved a bond issue to enhance the future of the college. The $18 million bond issue will provide a biosciences building, a learning resource center, infrastructure improvements, and more. The community's support proves that it believes in Iowa Central and the future of the rural region it serves.

CONCLUSION

Humanness is a risk in any organization. Some organizational theorists maintain that deep friendships can be attributed in the long run to organization humanity. Friendships, humor, and openness are at the heart of this culture. Everyone here understands that our success lies in working hard, having fun, and focusing on the college together.

We never rest on the status quo. Staff members are willing to take risks, be flexible, and change to meet needs and find niches. We take an entrepreneurial approach to meeting student and community needs. The focus is always on the student. Although the heart of Iowa Central is its faculty and staff, its soul is in its students. To maintain this focus, we must take risks, aggressively seek alternative funding, create unique partnerships, and believe that the sum of the college whole is always bigger than any of its parts.

REFERENCES

Baker, G., Roueche, J., & Gillett-Karam, R. (1990). *Teaching as leading: Profiles of excellence in the open-door college.* Washington, DC: Community College Press.

Figure 4.3 Employees' Ratings of the Iowa Central Community College Environment: 1999–2007

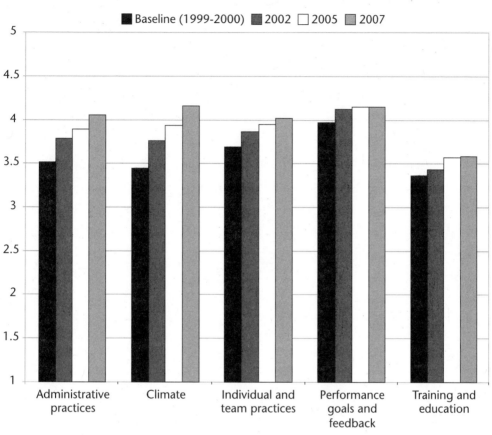

Note. 1=Strongly Disagree; 2=Disagree; 3=Neutral; 4=Agree; 5=Strongly Agree

Blanchard, P., & Hershey, K. (1969). *Management of organizational behavior: Utilizing human resources.* Englewood Cliffs, NJ: Prentice Hall.

Collins, J. (2001). *Good to great.* New York: HarperCollins.

Gardner, J. (1990). *On leadership.* New York: The Free Press.

"How Does Webster County Stack Up?" (2007, May 2). *The Messenger,* pp. 1A, 3A.

Hunter, K. (2003, November). "Thought for today." *O, the Oprah Magazine.* Retrieved April 4, 2007, from www.oprah.com/spiritself/insp/tft/2003/ss_insp_tft_20031110.jhtml

Roueche, J. E., Baker, G. A III, & Rose, R. R. (1989). *Shared vision: Transformational leadership in American community colleges.* Washington, DC: Community College Press. (ERIC # ED307013)

Vaughan, G. (Ed.). (1992). *Dilemmas of leadership: Decision making and ethics in the community college.* San Francisco: Jossey-Bass.

5

Transforming Morton College

Brent Knight

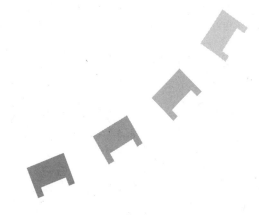

A sound management team that continually demonstrates commitment with high expectations of themselves and all in the organization is critical to any transformation.

—*Brent Knight, Morton College (IL)*

Morton College faced a monumental task: to completely transform the college from its former dilapidated self to a new, vibrant pillar of community pride. Located in a suburb of Chicago, this community's college would need to look and feel as if it was proud to be a part of the once eastern European and now Latino neighborhoods where it resides. President Brent Knight was hired to accomplish this task. He discusses lessons learned from years of experience and the importance of building a strong leadership team and community advisory committee to assist a dramatic transformation.

For people to believe a significant amount of change was occurring, they needed to see it. Knight and his teams worked diligently to give the campus a facelift. Creative architectural and interior design elements adorn the campus with a unique blend of art, pop culture, and history, celebrating the past and present of Cicero, Illinois, and its proud residents. Their momentum propelled faculty and staff to buy into the structural changes, generating programmatic and functional changes as well.

ARLY IN MY GRADUATE STUDIES, I learned that leadership is paramount for a community college president. Although administration is important and needs to be done, leadership is the most crucial endeavor. I also learned that, for the most part, change in education is incremental, and true innovation is not a regular occurrence. Too many educators are content with the status quo and spend more time thinking about their retirement than risking new endeavors. All organizations, and those who lead them, must seek continuous improvement, regardless of whether those leaders are new presidents or presidents in the last stages of their careers.

It is my belief that all organizations have inherent strengths that, if understood, can and should be built on; yet, I think that there is a place for a Maslow-type hierarchy. First, we seek to establish basic organizational needs and operating necessities. Then, we move up the pyramid toward an organization that truly, and perhaps uniquely, seeks perfection. More status is usually accorded to organizations and people that function at the top of the pyramid, but moving an organization up the pyramid at any level is worthwhile. Sometimes it is easier to be a president at the top of the pyramid or hierarchy than to struggle for survival at the bottom.

Organizations are also like sports teams—different specialties are required. A leadership team should seek and retain people with different strengths, and it should reflect the community. The development of future educational leaders is part of a president's job, and spending resources to help members of the team "be all that they can be" is a good decision. A leadership team must consist of leaders capable of functioning as a team, yet individual achievement is important. Stifling individual achievement and creativity reduces the chances that organizations can become better. Creativity, so important to growth, is too bound up by committees, and individual energy is not supported. If the organization or the team applauds the fine work of a team member rather than applauding itself, it encourages thinking creatively.

MARKETING AND ENTREPRENEURSHIP

I am a strong advocate of community colleges' marketing themselves and helping entrepreneurs. Historically, marketing has not been a significant part of the fabric of higher education (although higher education has become far more adept at promoting itself over the last 30 years), and entrepreneurship is more accepted as a valid concept for higher education in the 21st century than it was for most of the 20th; marketing and entrepreneurship practices were thought to be too businesslike and inappropriate then.

Marketing and entrepreneurship are companions of creativity, determination, freedom of expression, and energy. If a leader wants to create and develop a marketing-oriented organization, a team and a climate must be assembled, led, and supported. Leadership in such an organization is accomplished best by conceptual leadership, rather than by specific direction. Members of the organization need to know that failure, in the valid pursuit of an organizational objective, will not have negative consequences, except in the most extreme and unusual circumstances.

Community college presidents cannot achieve much without the full support of their boards. Usually, only boards have the authority to hire, start programs, and approve expenditures. Much has been written about the art of working with a board, being a leader, and pursuing collaborative styles that work in different circumstances. The key ingredient in winning the support of a board is earning its respect. Usually a president can sense the level of board support at any given moment—assessing debits and credits or points that might be in the bank in board support. If a president moves faster than a board might allow or exceeds its tolerance, that president will not exist long with the negative balance that pace creates.

Learning outcomes are similar to a corporate bottom line. Just how well did the organization do this year versus last in learning outcomes? The public will require higher education to offer improved evidence of learning outcomes in the short and long term. Community colleges will be under more pressure than other segments of higher education, primarily the result of significant differences between the average community college student and the average residential university student. Usually, the residential university student is the prescribed target for higher education and is familiar with the established norms. Can community colleges change organizationally to meet changing expectations, especially when university measures are the norm? The answer to this question is unequivocally "yes," unequivocally "necessary"—a tall order. But the challenges of tall orders can be met, beginning with an understanding of what needs to change. Once the *what* has been identified, the *how* must become a viable strategy.

THE CHARGE

All presidents have a starting point and first day on the job. The initial direction or charge by the hiring authority is critical if considerable change is a primary goal for an organization and its new president. Usually, a board of trustees, as the hiring authority, communicates directly to a new president a sense of what might be possible, what is necessary, what is expected, and what parameters are supported for speed or rate of change. This is not to be confused with what is said in a published job advertisement or a written employment contract; those documents may or may not be helpful in establishing true desires and expectations. A clearly stated charge at the point of employment and a consensus of what is to be done or what problem(s) should be solved will offer clarity and a sense of direction to a new president.

Regardless of expectations, a new president should attempt to understand the organization and the setting before embarking on a change process. Sometimes, in a crisis, allowing time for understanding may not be possible, and a leader may need to manage immediately. Nevertheless, decision making without understanding increases risk.

STAKEHOLDERS AND CONSTITUENTS

A new president faces multiple expectations. In addition to a board of trustees, other stakeholders may limit a president in terms of the rate of possible change. Aside from a board, the faculty is usually the primary stakeholder; employee groups, such as staff/classified members and administrators, are vital in any transformation, as well. A local newspaper might have expectations about what should be done and how fast change might occur. Sometimes constituencies may say that they would like to see change occur, when in fact their primary interest is to maintain the organization in a steady state. This bait and switch condition may cause a leader considerable difficulty.

If it appears that key stakeholders are not in favor of a change, then a president must work to bring them to a table of agreement about common, shared goals. A president may be handicapped or fail if the rate and extent of change are not supported by key stakeholders. If these people are not aware of the major issues facing an organization, then the president must provide rationale and leadership for change. Fairly or unfairly, a new president owns whatever troubles may exist in an organization after the first year.

Presidents are appointed formally and contractually, but they must earn the respect of key constituents to achieve maximum results. If a board and key constituents perceive a president as dedicated, working for the greater good, determined, fair, forthcoming, competent, and not self-serving, then support usually follows. Modesty and understatement usually are well received. If a president is not respected, change is not likely and may be impossible, and he or she may be stonewalled from taking action. Earning respect is a critical challenge and goal.

Achieving face time with key constituents is also critical. Seize key moments or circumstances to make points about personal values or personal perspectives. Be genuine, reveal some vulnerability, or convey an honest sense of yourself. These are all good ways to gain confidence and build trust within an organization. Appropriate stories about past experiences, successes, failures, family, parents, or the life and times in your youth all contribute subtle influences on how you are perceived. I watched one successful president invite small groups of faculty members for breakfast day after day until he worked through most of the faculty. A new president needs to exhibit some behaviors that enhance the transparency of his or her character.

BASELINE DATA

Regardless of the hiring authority, addressing baseline data, public perception, the image of the college, and internal climate should occur early in the transformation process; otherwise, the numbers may be contaminated over time or be too difficult to document. Instruments used to create these baseline data, which are assembled and addressed early on in the process, may be used to document change as the process develops.

When I was hired at Morton College in 2003, I was given clear direction with certainty and clarity. I was directed to "fix the college." Fixing the college meant that across-the-board changes were expected and that the college should be better managed, thus improving its image in the community. Changes in the operation were expected in the near term and would occur simultaneously with improvement in the college's image. Fixing also meant that there would be a marked improvement in pride in the college by the faculty, staff, students, and community.

I had been the president of an adjacent college some years before, and I was familiar with Morton and the geographic area. My perceptions were reinforced by discussions and early observations in my new role. The college had languished for some years, struggling internally and externally. I found that the primary problems were negative expectations and an acceptance of the idea that the college could never become better. Clearly, as a new president, I was careful not to criticize the organization or its employees, avoiding the likelihood that I would reinforce their perceptions and have them resent me early on.

Anticipating that considerable transformation would be forthcoming, the board supported a recommendation to appoint a blue ribbon committee of members of the community to study the college, how the community had changed, and what changes were needed. A blue ribbon committee can be useful in helping today's community to understand the college's mission. A series of community forums was held, data were assembled and discussed, and consultants were retained where expert opinions were warranted. Many did not know why the college was founded or its role in the community.

The most significant issue this committee addressed was major change in the community's demographics, which were originally eastern European and were now Latino. The adult and continuing education portion of the mission had been diminished over time as most of the college district's residents were now Latino.

Adult and continuing education opportunities were critical to serving the local community—as important as any other function of the college and an important reminder about the mission of the college. An important internal issue this committee addressed was the collective sense about how the college was being managed. Was there an expectation of a day's work for a day's pay for all? Did all jobs constitute a day's work? Were all employees assigned tasks that needed to be accomplished?

I prefer to assess employee effectiveness and efficiency as early as possible, implement whatever changes are needed, and proceed to build the organization. A sound management team that continually demonstrates commitment with high expectations of themselves and everyone is critical to any transformation. An organization cannot be and is not transformed if some employees are obviously not contributing their fair share. A leader cannot allow obvious examples of incompetence or lack of production to linger. "Putting the right people on the bus" and removing others is vital to transformation and best accomplished early in the transformation. An organizational bus needs to include a workforce that reflects the diversity of the community, because the residents are the true shareholders of any community college.

EFFECTIVE AND EFFICIENT ORGANIZATION

Early in my leadership education, I came to believe that any organization can and should be effective and efficient. All too often, public entities are not as effective and efficient as they should be, and this may make them difficult to sustain. Everyone in an organization needs to contribute, work well with others, understand roles, and make positive contributions. If I have low expectations for some and high expectations for others and make exceptions that condone less-than-optimum performance, the price is the idea that public employment provides a place for those who cannot perform adequately in private industry. Influence is better than control. Flat organizations require people to contribute and have a stake in outcomes. Hierarchical organizations breed feelings of being less or being diminished, and breed senses of inflated importance. Excessive hierarchy and its related protocols do not help people work together well.

Retailers might rearrange product adjacencies, improve in-store signage, run product sales, improve customer service, or change fixtures, but if a sufficient number of shoppers are not in the store, those management efforts may not matter. Likewise, for a college or university, improved instruction and learning conditions may be of little consequence unless students enroll in significant numbers to fund change and take advantage of the improvement. Similarly, if enrollment is in decline, then improvement in instruction may not be possible for fiscal or practical reasons.

MARKETING

Leading and change become especially difficult during retrenchment. A strong marketing program, as well as recruiting and retention, can alleviate a soft or declining enrollment condition. A strong marketing program needs to have breadth and depth, but a good place to start is understanding and making a plan to improve the image of the college in the community. If I could choose just one outcome for a college, it would be that the community and the college take pride in the college's work and its presence in the city.

Publicity

If a college has been the continued recipient of negative publicity, it is imperative to eliminate or reduce negative media coverage. Winning over the media is a challenging assignment. Members of the media become conditioned to attend board meetings, elicit comments from those who would make controversial statements, submit requests under the Freedom of Information Act, and write critical articles about a college when such stories are available and easily obtained. Negative press can become the media's steady diet, and the members of the public can follow negative press week after week, as if reading a novel.

When I was hired, Morton College had received less-than-desirable press coverage for some months, if not years. But I knew that if a president works on the root cause of the negative press problem with discipline, patience, and hard work, negative press can be reduced or eliminated over time. Winning over the media, explaining to those who offer and write negative headlines how they might be more constructive and how much damage that negative press does to a college, and offering better ideas are all part of important viable efforts to reduce habitual negative press. Some people believe that negative press is better than no coverage at all. Some people enjoy seeing their name in print, regardless of the coverage. They are reluctant to give up their fame, and the media are reluctant to give up someone who provides quotable statements.

You can create more positive publicity by explaining how the publicity game is played, showing the damage that it causes an organization, and providing suggestions to good citizens on how they might minimize continuing negative publicity. Overcoming damaging publicity demands hard work, patience, and persistence by the president and board chair.

College Image

Early in a transformation, there should be a review of all college symbols, logos, tag lines, colors, college seal, signage, stationery, publications, Web site, and the like. If fundamental change is to occur, symbols need to be ready to signal this change (e.g., good publications, a contemporary Web site)—all improved college communication tools that are parts of an improved college image. Educating college personnel on the proper and consistent use of media tools is critical. Communication is expensive; any information directed to the public should be as effective as possible. Sometimes a president may not be skilled in marketing and communication, so identifying someone internally who is and who has good judgment is worthwhile. I am always reluctant to delegate such matters to internal committees; sometimes the wrong committee can make recommendations that make things more difficult or worse (e.g., art does not lend itself to committee work, but rather to a good artist or designer).

How the college looks is important. An honest assessment of curb appeal, grounds, walkways, parking areas, horticulture, building exteriors, signage, and cleanliness is essential to creating an improved image. Some colleges and universities simply mow lawns and plow snow, and see that as the extent of their obligation. Dead plants or trees may not be removed in a timely manner because that is not part of mowing lawns or plowing snow. Trees are never trimmed, and shrubs become overgrown. Maintaining routine care of those important first impressions is required in improving the college image.

At Morton College, we needed a dramatic change in curb appeal. The parking lot is immediately adjacent to the street, and the shrubs designed to prevent a line of sight from the street into the parking lot were taller than the rooftops of the cars. A landscape architect was retained to improve curb appeal. A berm with plantings was created on the corner as a focal point, and the college logo was created in colored flowers. Irrigation was installed along the entire frontage; seasonal plants (e.g., tulips and mums) were planted in a serpentine shape. College landscaping personnel were trained, encouraged, and applauded for their efforts. Instilling a sense of college pride in those taking care of buildings and grounds is important and well worth the effort.

The college sought permission to hang street flags on municipal fixtures along streets adjacent to the college, as well as on all light poles in the college parking lot. Lighting was improved in the parking lot and along pedestrian walkways. New bilingual backlit signage was installed along key thoroughfares. A photographer was retained to secure professional photographs of the exciting new horticulture for use in publications and on the Morton College Web site. The media was encouraged to visit the college and photograph the grounds when plants were at their peak. All colleges need a literal front door that is obvious to a person visiting a college for the first time; otherwise, visitors can wander about shaking doors and asking for directions to college services. An architect can design an improvement that easily communicates the location of a front door. Morton College's front door was made more prominent with better signage and lighting.

The interior spaces of a college express the values of a college and offer the public a sense of what the college thinks of itself. If hardware is not in good repair, surfaces are dirty and worn, paint and carpet are not attractive, colors are tired and dated, and trash is obvious, the public goes away with an unfavorable opinion. Some of these changes and responses cost very little money to improve, and others may require some budgeting for the future.

Morton College had problems in all interior space categories; it had experienced scant improvement since it was built in the mid-1970s. In fact, the *Chicago Tribune* reported, in 2003, that the college was stuck in the 1970s. Over time, colleges can become cluttered. It is easier to add furniture and equipment than to remove; it can become no one's job to remove something that is broken, a fixture that is no longer used, or pieces of woodwork that are torn away. A stain on a carpet from a spilled large beverage might be a considerable eyesore that could last for 10 years unless a college has the discipline to do something about it. Libraries can become cluttered with fixtures and furniture that does not match or other items are no longer relevant to the library (e.g., technology has rendered them obsolete). Graffiti not immediately removed can spread throughout the campus. All of these eyesores can add to an already unattractive college. Word of mouth in the community advertises that the college is obsolete and is an undesirable destination, regardless of the acceptable quality of instruction.

Early in my presidency, we retained an architect to make a complete assessment of all buildings, grounds, and infrastructure. The architect provided a prioritized list of capital issues that needed improvement. Simultaneously, the faculty and staff provided input on capital matters most in need of attention from an instructional point of view. A fiscal consultant was retained to provide a plan for capital finance. This plan included fund equity and bonding authority, as well as federal, state, and foundation grants. All of these plans were presented to the board and key stakeholders.

A complete remodeling of the library and adjacent spaces was first on the structural transformation list. The library was simply unattractive and technologically obsolete. As soon as classes adjourned in May, the library was relocated on a temporary basis while the entire library facility was gutted and remodeled. The library reopened in January for the spring term. Student use of the library and personal computers in the library more than doubled. The new space became inviting;

form and function had been improved. Students discovered these college assets and used them.

A similar plan was made to improve all science laboratories the following year. A nationally renowned architectural firm, specializing in science laboratories, was retained as a consultant to the college architect. As a result, all science laboratories were gutted in mid-May, completely rebuilt, and ready for class in late August. In addition, all nursing instructional spaces were remodeled and equipped with modern, high-tech tools and equipment. ESL areas received major remodeling.

Promoting History and Roots

All remodeling improved the image of the college, a vital component to the strategic plan. The college, located in Cicero, Illinois, resides in a community that has had a less-than-favorable public image. However, Cicero and the surrounding communities have a notable past. The great Western Electric Hawthorne Works, which at one time employed more than 40,000 people and made the telephones for a nation, was located in Cicero; the world's largest aluminum rolling mill that made skin for World War II aircraft, and the factory that made the locomotives when the nation changed from coal to diesel, were located nearby. The community was known for its horse racing venues, the "Bohemian Wall Street" (because of its savings rate), and its magnificent places of worship.

The history of the community was studied, chronicled, and displayed at the college—the Hawthorne Works Museum will serve as an educational tool for the community and the college. Many large, colorful graphics were created and applied to hallway walls. Collectively, the museum, the historic graphics, and the remodeling made a striking physical difference in the college, but the most dramatic difference is in the pride within the college and the college community.

CONCLUSION

Almost all would agree that the college has changed considerably in 4 years, making a marked difference in the overall perceptions of residents who enter or drive past the campus. The history graphics have made the college unique and have been a considerable source of pride for the college and the community. The fiscal health of the college is sound. The nonteaching workforce is more inclusive of Latinos, who comprise the majority of residents and students. Higher expectations are held out for the workforce overall, and relationships with organized labor are collaborative and productive.

Relationships with local high schools have improved, contributing in part to record-level enrollments. The board of trustees is effective, and relationships with local media have improved dramatically. The new library has won three national design awards, including a prestigious award from the American Library Association. The college has won numerous awards for publications and publicity efforts and has improved the level of funding from private sources and state and federal grants vastly. Most importantly, the college is well positioned to continue improving all aspects of the college's operations.

REFERENCES

McSherry Breslin, M. (2003, September 5). Knight rides in to run Morton. *Chicago Tribune Online Edition.*

6

Richland College: Whole People, Whole Organization, Whole Lot of Fun

Stephen K. Mittelstet

Don't just do something; sit there!

—*Stephen K. Mittelstet, Richland College (TX)*

At Richland College, confronting difficult issues with honesty and integrity has become a way of life. With more than 20,000 students, this Dallas-based college serves a diverse student body whose members speak 79 first languages. Focusing on excellence involves constant evaluation, prioritization, and the ability to remember to be authentic in every interaction.

Student learning is the essence of life at Richland, and employees take great pride in celebrating their work. Thunderduck pride surrounds its learning college philosophy. President Steve Mittelstet discusses the journey the college undertook to become a rewarding and joyful place "to learn, to teach, and to build a sustainable local and world community."

In the late 1990s, Richland College started living by the seven Baldrige performance excellence categories. Fearless and continual communication allows Richland teams to use disciplined decision making, to strategically plan for the future, and to honestly evaluate their effectiveness: the qualities that keep Richland's boat afloat. Mittelstet compares this journey to rowing a boat, gently down the stream.

Author's Note. I am grateful for the expert aid that Richland's graduate assistant, Jenny Matthews, provided me in researching my various speeches, listening to my organizational plan, providing me with a beginning draft, and helping me with technical support in producing this chapter.

I BEGAN MY DOCTORAL DISSERTATION with a quotation from the 16th-century French essayist, Michel de Montaigne: "Bees steal from this flower and that and create therefrom a honey that is all their own" (Mittelstet, 1973). Throughout my tenure as president of Richland College, in the Dallas County Community College District (DCCCD), my Richland colleagues and I have been very busy bees.

Richland College—enrolling some 16,000 college-credit students (mostly college transfer) and approximately 6,000 noncredit workforce-training students each semester as reported in 2007—was conceived to open as a starter college in 1972. It was anticipated that Richland's enrollment would peak within a decade, during which time the remaining two DCCCD master-planned colleges would come online, and it would be determined whether contiguous Collin County, immediately to the north, would organize its own community college district. All this future growth was expected to shrink Richland College's geographic service area to approximately one fifth its original size. However, with seven community colleges and one branch of The University of Texas now located in the original area served earlier by Richland alone, Richland's enrollment did not peak or shrink commensurate with its reduced immediate service area; rather, it has continued experiencing robust growth.

Richland College continues to enroll more students than any institution of higher learning in Dallas County, with a 24% enrollment increase from 2001 to 2007. More importantly, Richland has a richly diverse mix of students. They represent 132 countries, speak 79 first languages, are 62% ethnic minority, and average 28 years of age. Despite this potentially challenging cultural milieu, Richland's student learning outcomes, student engagement, and student satisfaction data continue to set the pace in most aspects, compared with like-data of peer institutions nationwide.

Throughout its history, Richland College and its students, faculty, and administrative leaders received recognition and awards. In 2005, however, Richland achieved high marks in overall performance excellence, after a reaffirmation of accreditation visit from the Southern Association of Colleges and Schools, with no recommendations and numerous commendations. In 2005, the governor's office honored Richland College with the Texas Award for Performance Excellence. Richland is the first accredited institution of higher education in Texas to receive the state's highest quality performance award. Later that year, the White House and the U.S. Department Commerce, describing Richland as "world class," named Richland College the first community college recipient (and only the third higher education recipient) of the Malcolm Baldrige National Quality Award.

BUILDING TO THE BALDRIGE

Richland's earlier successes, like those of many institutions, were sporadic and not linked directly to our mission and vision statements (which were too wordy for any of us to remember, much less act on consistently). Our "pockets of excellence" frequently operated from organizational silos—sometimes "suboptimizing" one another and the organization as a whole. Instead of an ongoing, robust, agile, organic process, our "strategic plan" was a once-a-year activity, frequently isolated from other key processes such as budgeting. Our metrics to demonstrate achievement were neither defined clearly nor tracked systematically with clear measures, targets, and action plans. There is little wonder that we found it difficult to articulate our successes, which our increasingly demanding stakeholders judged to be more anecdotal than data supported. Watching our state funding for instruction plummet from nearly 70% to approximately 30% over just three legislative sessions, we realized our organizational behavior needed to become more focused, leaner, more productive, and more entrepreneurial. We had to not only examine costs but also diversify revenue sources.

Somewhere in the increasingly turbulent environment of the 1990s, Richland's joyful bees bumbled into the seven-category Baldrige performance excellence framework and began experimenting with it as the basis for our systematic continuous improvement, which continues to this day. I have come to view our Baldrige learning discipline as similar to rowing a boat. In truth, I shamelessly stole this metaphorical concept from good friend and colleague, Richland philosophy professor Luke Barber (Barber & Weinstein, 2006), whose co-authored human success book, *Gently Down the Stream*, organizes its lessons in success within the framework of the four strains of the children's round, "Row, Row, Row Your Boat." In fact, most of my best teachers in successful organizational behavior over the years have been Richland faculty. Observing faculty members like Luke engage their students through an ever-tailoring balance of support and challenge, I have gained insight into developing, leading, empowering, and engaging Richland's employees. Aside from my own growth, these lessons have benefited employee development and student success, and eventually transformed the way we educate our community.

Performance Excellence Principle #1: Row, Row, Row Your Boat

In likening Richland's Baldrige performance excellence discipline to the persistent learning required to excel in boat rowing, I have found that the demanding Baldrige discipline paradoxically has freed Richland to have creative, breakthrough innovations and to continuously nurture our whole, authentic selves. Baldrige discipline has created a college culture where it is safe to take risks and where people have fun in the process.

Figure 6.1 Richland College Performance Excellence Model

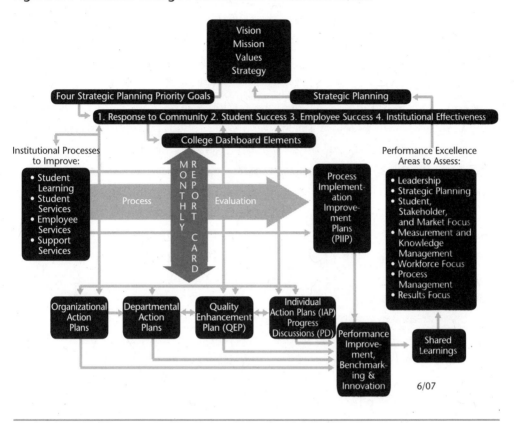

Richland's Baldrige-inspired boat-rowing discipline is depicted in a hot-linked graphic Intranet model that all Richlanders can locate easily and regularly to be reminded that our individual and small-group activities influence the whole (see Figure 6.1). In keeping with our tradition of lifting good ideas from others, we stole the basic elements of this model from an earlier Baldrige Award recipient, St. Luke's Hospital, of Kansas City, Missouri, and made our own honey with it. This model addresses everything our organization does—systems, processes, programs, activities (following an ongoing cycle of approach-deploy-learn-integrate). All these elements align with our organization's core business: student learning. Outcomes are measured for student learning, program success, and all other stakeholder segments. In addition, our trend-line improvements over time show marked progress toward ever-higher student and program achievement targets.

The first phase of our performance excellence model is strategic planning. Richland's planning–budgeting team meets in an annual 3-day retreat each August to update our strategic and operational plans. Plans are made based on the past year's performance and a wide variety of environmental input, which includes insights from our bimonthly Environmental Scanning Council and collegewide conversations such as the one that garnered organizational improvement insights from the more than 200 Richlanders who studied Friedman's (2006) *The World Is Flat* together.

Richland's strategic planning emanates directly from our vision, mission, values, and strategy. The strategic plan and its components must be stated clearly for collegewide deployment at all organizational levels, institutional learning, and integrating findings into the next (ideally improved) planning cycle. Over the years, we have simplified our mission and vision statements so that we, our students, and other stakeholders can remember and act on them. Our simply worded mission is "teaching, learning, community building," which is easily remembered as TLC. Our vision is that Richland be the best place we can be "to learn, to teach, and to build a sustainable local and world community." Similarly, we have narrowed our strategic planning priority goal areas to the following: response to community, student success, employee success, and institutional effectiveness. For these four priorities, we have a total of 16 key-performance indicators (KPIs), with 106 related measures that make up our scoring metrics.

To deploy and act on these priority and KPI areas throughout our organization, we have action plans at all these linked levels. Because we are accredited by the Southern Association of Colleges and Schools, which requires an ongoing quality enhancement plan, we help people understand how and where initiatives fit together in our model. Our goal is to have our efforts and decisions coordinate with the demands of multiple stakeholders rather than have numerous unrelated initiatives meeting the needs of these various entities. This approach keeps us focused on our vision and responsive to stakeholder expectations. Smooth-running processes and systems are essential to performance excellence. If these chronically break down, malfunction, or otherwise fail to deliver, even our top-performing employees will fail through no fault of their own. They will become discouraged and fearful of being unfairly punished, and they will start going through the motions to play it safe. Each day, they will check their passion, souls, and spirit at home as they head for work, leaving Richland with a soulless organization that obviously would not be good for anyone, including our students.

Richlanders have identified four major process areas—student learning, student services, employee services, support services—and nearly 60 subprocesses that have been implemented, reviewed, or improved in a systematic, eight-step discipline we call the PIIP (process improvement/implementation protocol). All these key organizational processes are archived on our Intranet. This is an example of how we share our learning across the campus so that we do not reinvent the wheel, start from scratch, or engage in redundant work. Each area in the performance excellence model occurs across all seven Baldrige categories and takes place in an interconnected fashion across these categories: leadership; strategic planning; student, stakeholder, and market focus; measurement and knowledge management; faculty and staff (workforce) focus; process management; and results focus. As our expert faculty do with our students, we use informal and formal formative and summative feedback (or leading and trailing indicators) to understand our progress. This feedback allows us to make "midstream" or in-process adjustments to get back on track, rather than waiting until the end of a semester or academic year.

Our formalized in-process, formative organizational feedback tool is what we call our monthly Thunion (Thunder Onion) Report Card. (Read more about this "thunder" business later in the chapter.) The Thunion provides monthly scores for the college as a whole and for each of our four strategic priority goal areas, each with different weights. The Thunion weights each KPI and produces a score based on the 106 metrics (mentioned earlier) and derived from data extracted from our database system, with these scores appearing in more detail in second and third layers (much like peeling back an onion). At a glance, this report card informs us on how we are doing, according to our institutional vital signs: green light indicates healthy, yellow indicates needing some explanation or conversation, and red light indicates there might be cause for concern or alarm.

The layers are specific enough that they can trigger monthly corrective action and deeper understanding at appropriate organizational levels, causing scores and, more importantly, performance that underlie the scores to improve by the next monthly updated report review. After each executive KPI review session, the monthly Thunion is made available to all Richlanders on the Intranet; we can all see its three layers electronically as a context for our own individual and departmental activity. Everyone has archival access to all previous reports for the purposes of comparison and research.

Because most of the data behind these metrics are extracted from our database, compiling the monthly report card is not as labor-intensive as one might think. The bulk of our organizational energies on reviewing these monthly reports is devoted to those few areas needing attention (yellow and red lights) in between reports and on launching, sustaining, revising, and, when appropriate, eliminating mission-related innovations as unanticipated opportunities arise. Again, focusing our joint organizational efforts on those few red or yellow lights allows us to pay attention and focus energy only on areas needing support.

Our summative end-of-year report includes multiyear trend data, as well as peer institution and best-in-class comparisons. We use this summative organizational report to inform internal and external stakeholders of our ongoing, results-oriented trends. We compare results against ourselves over time, segmenting by target populations for closing certain student demographic and other performance gaps. We also contrast results with local benchmark peer institutions and national "best in class."

Recently, I have come to view Baldrige as the wise Socratic teacher, firmly grounded in the belief that the answers lie within the student—asking rigorous questions over and over in a nonprescriptive way, helping the student find her or his own answers in life's journey to becoming the unique, authentic whole person he or she can become. Similarly, I believe the Baldrige framework can help each of our organizations become whole, high-performing institutions through the rigorous, nonprescriptive questions contained in the seven Baldrige categories. Of course, if all an institution does is row, employees will soon get bored, distracted from their mission, and exhausted. So, Richland has found that to relieve the exhaustion and transform the tedium, sometimes we simply need to say, "Don't just do something; sit there!"

Performance Excellence Principle #2: Gently Down the Stream

Richlanders have learned either to stop the rowing from time to time or, more likely, to get into such a systematic zone with the rowing that we can—in a very mission and vision-related fashion—virtually go "gently down the stream," even though that stream might be viewed by many as today's raging, turbulent rapids of change. We have found that it is easier for our high performers to go gently down the stream when our college maintains a culture that encourages and supports this gentler approach.

At the entrance to Thunderduck Hall—our front-door, one-stop matriculation building—all who enter are greeted by a large bronze plaque that describes Thunderduck culture, including the following excerpt:

> Stemming from Richland's campus agrarian roots and the ducks on our lakes long before we arrived, our mascot—R. Mobius Thunderduck (or "Moby Duck")—symbolizes the linkages, in Mobius-strip fashion, between one's inner life of contemplation and mindful reflection and one's outer life of service to others in creating sustainable local and world community for all.

Setting high standards and expectations for our interactions with one another, this organizational culture for students and employees is grounded in Richland's 10 behavioral values, developed and refined by and for employees and students for over two decades. Because we believe it is the whole person who best learns, teaches, serves, and leads, we (faculty, staff, and students) develop, renew, and affirm the following organizational "ThunderValues" for our learning and work together, both in the classroom and in our interactions with each other: integrity; mutual trust; wholeness; fairness; considerate, meaningful communications; mindfulness; cooperation; diversity; responsible risk taking; and joy.

It is not unusual for organizations to have formal values statements. It is more challenging for all within the organization to remember and act according to these values. Unlike our vision, mission, and strategic priority goals, however, we do not pretend Thunderducks can remember all 10 of these values. There are just too many, but we cannot seem to give any of them up for the sake of brevity.

We have developed numerous methods to reinforce the values in our hiring, screening, 3-year-long new-employee orientations, annual all-college convocation, and weekly staff newsletter. We try to assess how well these values are deployed throughout the organization, using an all-employee values survey, asking how well individuals, supervisors, Richland's Executive ThunderTeam, and the college as a whole model these values daily. Each of our employees turns on her or his computer each day and is greeted by a pop-up screen invitation to live our values at work. Featuring one ThunderValue each week is an illustration of that value at work on the campus, helping us all remember to go gently and innovatively in whatever mayhem might await us that day while maintaining our vision as our compass.

Individuals are not the only ones who reflect on the featured value for that week; our various employee and council meetings begin with conversations that illustrate the value in action in various parts of our campus as an appreciative inquiry context for their action-oriented agendas. Minutes of these meetings are circulated to the entire college and reflect these conversations. In a cascading effect, they spawn similar informal conversations among employees and students, many of which are featured as "ThunderValues in Action" reports in our weekly staff newsletter, *ThunderBridge,* for us all to enjoy.

Performance Excellence Principle #3: Merrily, Merrily, Merrily, Merrily

Culturally, an organization must be intentional in helping employees and students enjoy teaching, learning, serving, and building community—even in turbulent waters. Joy permeates Richland's learning and work—in and out of the classrooms, with employee recognition parades, spontaneous collegewide and local "laugh breaks," celebratory annual convocations, and just fooling around in the tradition of the classic Wise Fool.

Performance Excellence Principle #4: Life Is But a Dream

When Richlanders deploy the first three principles of performance excellence well, our organizational life is but a dream. When we do not, our organizational life is closer to the other end of the dream–nightmare spectrum. The dream plays itself out through organizational wholeness. This wholeness encourages whole, authentic faculty and staff to bring their whole selves to work every day. However, whole, authentic employees must have a nurturing environment at work, as many have been broken through years of bureaucratic dysfunction in a wide variety of institutions. Hence, the importance of professional development at Richland College is addressed through the expectations of our Thunderwater Organizational Learning Institute.

More than 200 Richlanders in the past decade have participated in a yearlong retreat series known as "teacher/leader formation circles of trust," based on the work of community activist and educator Parker Palmer. Their learning ripples through our organization and with our students in innumerable and varied, positive ways. *To Teach With Soft Eyes,* published by the League for Innovation in the Community College and edited by Richland professor Rica Garcia (2000), includes 23 essays written by Richland faculty, support staff, and administrators on the impact of this personal formation learning on various aspects of their work with students at Richland College and in the communities we serve. Richland professor Sue Jones serves as codirector and founder of the Center for Formation in Higher Education (CHFE), originally launched by the Fetzer Institute and the League for Innovation in the Community College. CHFE continues to train and support dozens of formation facilitators to offer ongoing formation learning experiences at colleges and universities throughout North America.

Our professional development for whole-person authenticity includes a 6-year intercultural competence international pilot series for all Richland employees, developed in conjunction with the Summer Institute for Intercultural Communications, the first series of which concluded with a longitudinal research study as part of a doctoral dissertation to determine whether the intercultural competence of an entire organization can be systematically improved over time. The study indicated that this systematic form of professional development can assist not only individuals but also entire organizations to improve intercultural competence. Richland concluded that this ongoing attention to intercultural communications improvement provides an excellent return on investment in student learning and employee success.

Our organizational value of honoring silence by cultivating space, time, and skills to hear and honor our inner lives (our souls) has helped us mold a learning work environment. Quiet reflection rooms, park benches, meditation gardens, fountains, waterfalls, a lakeside Peace Pole Trail, protected wildlife habitat, and the outdoor TLC Labyrinth are convenient places to get away, be silent, reflect, and express gratitude throughout our busy workdays. We are reminded to take time for this reflection quarter-hourly by the resonant peal of our carillon bells across the campus.

Many of the faculty, staff, and students who walk the TLC Labyrinth are those who have participated in the teacher–leader–service provider formation groups mentioned earlier. In these sessions, participants learn to interact in mindful, considerate, affirming ways with their colleagues, turning to wonder before judgment. We view whole-person formation as a lifelong journey. It is about who we are, what we value, and how we relate to one another and our students with our authentic selves. It is about using our gifts to help meet our community's educational needs and help our students and colleagues learn and live better with one another at Richland College and in their communities.

One of Richland's most enduring community-building professional development programs over the past two decades has been the Uncommittee Reading Circle. Each year more than 100 volunteers sign up to read monthly selections of works of fiction, alternating with works of nonfiction, from a wide variety of fields and authors worldwide. The purpose of the Uncommittee Reading Circle is not one of critical analysis but one of humanities-type synthesis, responding to such questions as "As a result of this reading, what was evoked from my life and what implications might those evocations have for my work with Richland students and colleagues?" These conversations, held informally and frequently in participants' homes without a formal facilitator, have served as indirect catalysts for several of the innovative programs described in this chapter, for strengthening Richland's community of trust, and for reinforcing Richland's ThunderValues.

More than 50% of Richland's classes are taught by adjunct faculty. Richlanders have worked diligently to include adjunct faculty in all aspects of Richland College life, especially in professional development. Adjunct faculty who complete a variety of professional development series related to their teaching and to Richland College culture receive a special certificate. These adjuncts are afforded certain privileges such as priority class scheduling and "bumping rights" over adjuncts who have not acquired the certificates when their own class sections do not "make."

VISION-INSPIRED DREAM: HELPING ROBUST RICHLAND DEFY PREDICTION

Had Richland College been a data-driven institution, it might have reacted to the accurate predictions of a shrinking service area in its starter college years and peaked in enrollment commensurately. But Richland chose to be a data-informed institution, choosing instead to anticipate the inevitable while steering a different mission- and vision-related course. The following are recent examples of how Richland has continued to increase student market penetration within its smaller service area and increase its service area through the advent of technology not available in 1972. All of these initiatives emanate from Richland's vision that it excel in building sustainable local and world community (economic, societal, environmental) through teaching and learning.

Aging Community (Societal, Local)

Richland's original predominant community demographics were young and Anglo. As this demographic has aged and diminished considerably over time, Richland has become more responsive to lifelong learning needs through its college credit program and its noncredit workforce retraining and life enhancement programs. Richland's dynamic Emeritus Program offers up to 6 college credit hours per semester tuition-free to anyone aged 60 years and over. The program keeps longer-living retirees engaged in their ongoing learning, new career training, and volunteer opportunities to serve the college and its younger students. One of these volunteer opportunities is the lively Conversation Partners, which pairs emeritus students with Richland's large population of ESL students learning English—an innovative cross-cultural, cross-generational learning program. Keeping older students in touch with families and friends through technology, including their international conversation partners who later return to their home countries, is another increasingly popular emeritus program.

Ethnically Diverse Community (Societal, Local)

As Richland's immediate service area demographics have become more ethnically diverse, especially with Latino, Asian, and Middle Eastern residents, we have added multiple ESL language-immersion programs, with several fast-track credit and noncredit options. We also offer more than a dozen other languages in our college credit program, expanding the traditional Spanish, French, and German offered early in our history. Our varied cultural studies curriculum includes courses such as Understanding Islam. Our workforce training now includes the nation's largest Command Spanish franchise, which tailors classes to specific industries and professions, such as police, emergency workers, food and hospitality workers, health professions, and an award-winning program offered to the military in Desert Storm to help U.S. forces communicate better with Spanish-speaking soldiers.

Richland also offers a variety of academic enrichment programs that give coherence and a more focused emphasis on the need to build sustainable community to the basic core curriculum required of all college transfer degrees. These emphasis programs include global studies, peace studies, mind-spirit-body health studies, honors studies, and three ethnic studies options (African-American/Black, Mexican-American/Latino, and Asian/Middle Eastern-American). These ethnic studies programs give every student a variety of opportunities to learn about common U.S. multicultural heritage, regardless of their own ethnicity.

Students may complete their entire core curriculum in any one of these emphasis areas and transfer to universities to continue a major in that area. Alternatively, they may take any of these special class sections as a way to study a particular subject area through a different lens than had they taken a more general section of the same course. Cocurricular outreach and student success programs such as Los Patos Listos (Smart Ducks at the Ready), African-American Connection, and Men of Color include mentoring volunteers from among Richland's employees to help case manage students socioeconomically at-risk and minimize student enrollment and performance gaps by ethnicity—with impressive results.

Workforce Needs (Economic, Environmental, Local)

Richland's Workforce and Resource Development offices work closely with local chambers of commerce and industry groups to fashion industry-specific and organization-specific training. These offices leverage government funds through various partnerships to help area industries offer the training to their employees. Working with groups such as the Garland Chamber of Commerce and the Hispanic Contractors Association, Richland helped establish the North Texas Manufacturers Association to gain critical mass for common training needs throughout the region. In addition, in cooperation with these chambers and the City of Garland, Richland's new Garland Campus will open in 2008 with a Leadership in Energy and Environmental Design (LEED) gold-certified Workforce Training Center in downtown Garland, not only offering the needed training but also offering it in a setting that demonstrates the critical role of designing sustainable community buildings. Garland Independent School District and Richland officials are brainstorming future facilities that will link P–16 career development and dual credit on this campus with local business partners.

Science, Technology, Engineering, Mathematics Deficit (Economic, Environmental)

Addressing local and national needs to increase P–16 seamless learning in science, technology, engineering, mathematics (STEM) fields, Richland College partnered with the Metroplex Technology Business Council, Richardson and Dallas Independent School Districts, and three area universities in attracting two of Texas's first four STEM high school academies to its service area. The partnership received several National Science Foundation engineering and computer science student recruiting grants. It also revised the freshman–sophomore engineering school curriculum into one common sequence at Richland and the three universities for seamless transfer. Another result was the start of the business–community college urban tree farm at Richland, from which thousands of native trees are transplanted into public places in the Metroplex to regreen the area and teach principles of sustainable community building.

For high school students ready to take college courses at the beginning of the high school junior year, Richland expanded its large dual credit program with area public, private, and home schools by opening the first community college charter high school in Texas. The Richland Collegiate High School for Mathematics, Science, and Engineering (RCHS) mainstreams 400 high school juniors and seniors through regular Richland College classes in a dual-credit approach, so that its students may graduate from high school and receive their associate degree simultaneously. Although RCHS offers no separate high school-level classes, it addresses lack of college-readiness through the developmental studies program and individual case management. Its first graduate—a 16-year old—earned his high school diploma and associate degree after just 1 year at RCHS/Richland and received a full-ride scholarship as a junior to The University of Texas at Dallas Engineering School. RCHS was rated "exemplary" by the Texas Education Agency at the conclusion of its first year of operation.

The increased science enrollment from these initiatives has resulted in the design of the area's first LEED-Platinum designed Science Building at Richland College–RCHS. The construction design is intended to teach science to students, businesses, and the rest of the community as a vital component of learning to build sustainable communities. The green building helps Richland meet its climate neutrality sustainable community commitment as a Presidents Climate Commitment signatory institution.

The Information Age and the World Community

Richland College served as an important community college resource in the development of College Learning for a Global Century, a 4-year curriculum launched by the Association of American Colleges and Universities in 2006. The curriculum was a result of extensive national conversations with business, government, and education leaders for helping U.S. students be positive, productive citizens. In addition, Richland was selected by AACC as a mentor college for service learning, the pervasive use of which contributed to Richland's being one of the first recipients of the new Carnegie Community Engagement classification for higher education. Service learning is also a strong component in the Richland–RCHS campus experience. Students produce a learning product demonstrating they have acquired the seven intellectual competencies of Richland's core curriculum and can apply them to concepts of building sustainable communities.

The exponential increase in the use of the Internet in distance learning has been a major catalyst for Richland's increased international learning program, leading to the establishment of such partnerships as the joint distance learning associate degree between Richland College and Saratov State University, Russia's second-largest university. Students from each location enroll in courses, learning from one another via the Internet, coupled with featured class sessions via live Webcasting. Such technology has assisted Richland in helping develop new community colleges in such places as the Mekong Delta in Vietnam and in the island nation of Mauritius, off the coast of India.

A key part of these programs is Richland faculty teaching faculty—in the partner countries—successful teaching practices in such subjects as ESOL and computer networking. Such initiatives have served to expand Richland's student recruitment service area globally. Richland's broadcast journalism KDUX Webcast radio station is not only teaching its students the principles of broadcast journalism but also serving international students at Richland's Dallas campus with opportunities and venues for communicating with family, friends, and potential students in their home communities around the world. Many people tune in around the globe to Richland's live video Webcasts to watch their students in Richland student success ceremonies such as semesterly Peace Pole plantings, international festivals, and graduation.

COMMUNITY COLLEGE LEARNING PARTNERS IN VISION ALIGNMENT

In conjunction with the teaching–learning components of Richland's mission and vision alignment, Richland College was selected to participate in the Lumina Foundation-supported Learning College Consortium (LCC), sponsored by the League for Innovation in the Community College. As an extension of Richland's LCC consortium achievements in improving its ability to increase student learning outcomes and documentation of these outcomes, Richland is leading a consortium of 16 community colleges selected from Continuous Quality Improvement Network institutions to create an "innovations distribution lab," to be launched by the first-ever Johnson Foundation–sponsored community college Wingspread Conference. The purpose of the lab is to help us all focus on the specific student learning outcomes that demonstrate whole-person competence in building sustainable local and world community. Richland has called on peer institutions to assist in this aspect of achieving our vision, and we are joined in this national initiative by award-winning innovative design business partner, IDEO.

RICHLAND COLLEGE IN 50 WORDS OR SO

After a lengthy interview with a *New York Times* columnist preparing a feature on the impact of our nation's exceptional community colleges, I was asked to describe Richland College in 50 or so words. I offered the following:

> *Richland College is a bumble of Montaigne's busy bees—stealing from this flower and that—striving to be authentic, whole-person Thunderducks rowing gently and merrily (as we make our own honey) with Malcolm Baldrige and Parker Palmer to our organizational wholeness dream of teaching, learning, and building sustainable local and world community.*

Apparently nonplussed by the multiple mixed metaphor, she printed several flattering things about Richland College, but not that description. I stand by this message; it works for us.

REFERENCES

Barber, L., & Weinstein, M. (2006). *Gently down the stream: Four unforgettable keys to success.* New York: Penguin Group.

Friedman, T. (2006). *The world is flat.* New York: Ferrar, Straus, and Giroux.

Garcia, R. (Ed.). (2000). *To teach with soft eyes: Reflections on a teacher/leader formation experience.* Mission Viejo, CA: League for Innovation in the Community College.

Mittelstet, S. (1973). *Humanities education in selected Texas junior colleges.* Unpublished doctoral dissertation, The University of Texas at Austin.

7

El Paso Community College: Climbing Ladders to Success

Richard M. Rhodes

The "Ladders to Success" framework that exists at El Paso Community College is possible because of the dedicated, committed, and entrepreneurial faculty and staff who have a passion to pursue the shared vision of student success.

—*Richard G. Rhodes, El Paso Community College (TX)*

In the far southwest corner of Texas, with Mexico and the Rio Grande to the south and the Guadalupe Mountains to the north, El Paso Community College (EPCC) serves a unique population that is isolated by geography but is multinational in vision. A mural by artist Amado M. Peña, Jr., depicts a multilevel pueblo with ladders to each level, symbolizing the learning journey. EPCC's creative leadership and passionate staff and faculty, led by President Richard Rhodes, nurtured the college to grow with the community's needs, much like a pueblo grows from the earth on which it was built.

Embracing and implementing learning college values, EPCC annually measures and evaluates student progress to improve the learning climate. The college has built successful early college high schools, a new community library, a leadership academy, significant community service projects, and a college readiness consortium that unites the public school districts, EPCC, and the University of Texas at El Paso in a partnership to bridge the gaps students face as they climb the rungs of education.

EL PASO COMMUNITY COLLEGE (EPCC) has adopted a new metaphor to describe our role in the educational continuum of students, faculty, and staff: "Ladders to Success" or "Escaleras al Progresso." This metaphor is the result of our special relationship with a special artist, Amado M. Peña, Jr. Our new journey in pursuit of entrepreneurialism, creativity, and excellence began in 2002, by virtue of a chance meeting with Amado at the National Institute for Staff and Organizational Development Conference in Austin, Texas. I have always been an avid fan of Amado's artwork. During this chance meeting, I asked Amado if he had ever painted a mural. His response was "no," so I emboldened myself to ask if he would consider creating his first mural for EPCC. After some thought and constant encouragement (harassment) by Shirley Gilbert, the "extra very special assistant to the president," Amado began to play with the idea by drawing a concept on a paper tablecloth. By the end of the conference, we had not only begun the agreement for a mural at EPCC but also begun something much more important—a relationship in which we had a friend for life.

I remember one special conversation we had at the beginning of the mural's concept and design. I was trying to describe my vision of what the mural should look like. About halfway through my discourse, Amado stopped me and said, "Richard, never tell an artist what to paint; just tell me the message you would like to relay." I said, "I would like to describe learning through the visual of a pueblo with multiple levels. To get to each level, the learner must climb a ladder. The ladder is the metaphor for the learning journey." With that brief description, Amado created the magnificent mural, "Ladders to Success." They say, "A picture is worth a thousand words." We say, "A mural that captures a vision is priceless."

I have a compelling desire to create acronyms to convey a message. One day I was writing a speech for a high school senior banquet on leadership and the community college when "acronymitis" took control of my thoughts. The result became a leadership mission statement for EPCC:

- Lead with passion
- Access
- Develop the team
- Develop the community
- Evaluate
- Respect the legacy and culture and resolve to make a difference
- Strategic partnerships

LEADING WITH PASSION

During fall 2002, we passed out hundreds of copies of O'Banion's *A Learning College for the 21st Century* (1977). We asked faculty, staff, and students to read it, share it with others, discuss the conceptual framework, and participate in future collegewide dialogues on its applicability to EPCC. We then scheduled a series of campus meetings to review and discuss the concept and philosophy to determine whether there was consensus that this was a direction worth embracing as a college family. We received strong concurrence for incorporating this philosophy into the culture of the college but not as a new program.

Through the dialogue, some of our faculty and staff decided there was an immediate application to develop a set of institutional core values. Although EPCC was created in 1969, and we had a shared vision statement and mission statement, we did not have a set of shared core values to use as the basis for developing decisions, policies, and procedures. After a yearlong dialogue on core values and their definitions, the college family was ready to adopt a shared set of core values:

- Communication. We value and encourage the open, interactive exchange of thoughts and ideas.
- Competence. We value excellence as our standard in teaching and learning.
- Integrity. We value honesty, ethical behavior, and professionalism in meeting our mission.
- Personal growth. We value the journey of faculty, staff, and students in becoming more conscious, productive, and contributing members of the community.
- Respect. We honor and value each other in our diversity.
- Student success. We value a learning environment that enables students to succeed.
- Trust. We value relationships based on honesty, reliability, and compassion.

On the adoption of these core values, our college family suggested that, as a learning college, we ask ourselves not only (1) does this action improve and expand learning? and (2) how will we know this action improves and expands learning? but also (3) does this action reflect our core values? Through this year of reading, discussion, reflection, and articulation of thoughts and ideas, I began to see a new passion and a focus on student success emerge. In *The Heart of a Leader*, Blanchard (1999) stresses the importance of this process, or rung on the ladder, that we just climbed. He stated,

Take time to identify core values. Identifying the core values that define your organization is one of the most important functions of leadership. The success or failure of this process can literally make or break an organization .... Draw in your people—everyone should have ownership in the process. Remember that rules can be imposed but values cannot. (p. 175)

The process of embracing the learning college philosophy and immediately putting it into practice in a meaningful and concrete fashion may have been the most pivotal and uniting step on the ladder to success.

PROVIDING ACCESS

EPCC serves the residents of El Paso County, a population of approximately 750,000. Of this population, 78.2% are of Latino origin, 26.6% of the children are living below the poverty level, and the median household income is $30,968, well below the Texas state average of $42,139 and the United States average of $46,242. Census data also reveal that 32.4% of the county's population ages 25 and older has not completed high school, compared with 21.3% for Texas and 15.9% for the United States.

Of the student population at EPCC, 85% of the students are Latino origin, 63% are female, and more than 70% are first-generation college students. More than 75% of our students are on financial aid; EPCC is the largest Pell-granting institution in Texas. According to the Pell Institute for the Study of Opportunity in Higher Education,

In recent years, college attendance for first-generation students has had a high profile in Texas. First-generation students—students whose parents did not attend college—have increasingly been the target of efforts to increase college-going and completion rates in the state. Such efforts demonstrate a growing recognition by State policymakers and educators that expanding postsecondary opportunity to students who have previously lacked college access—namely the state's large and increasing low-income, minority and first-generation populations—is critical to the future social and economic well-being of Texas. (2006, p. 5)

When you look at the demographics of El Paso, EPCC's student demographics, and the changing face of the state of Texas, you begin to understand the vision and charge of *Closing the Gaps 2015: The Texas Higher Education Plan*, produced by the Texas Higher Education Coordinating Board in 2000. As noted in the Pell Institute's findings, the Texas Higher Education Coordinating Board's charge is to expand postsecondary opportunity to the students who historically have lacked college access—the growing number of low-income, minority, and first-generation populations.

Examining the Data

In 2004, EPCC became one of the first community colleges funded by the Lumina Foundation in the program, Achieving the Dream: Community Colleges Count. A premise of Achieving the Dream is to use data to make better decisions about student success—especially low-income, minority, and first-generation students. The purpose is to use data to help EPCC students achieve their dreams by focusing on the desired outcomes of seeing more students:

- Successfully complete developmental courses
- Enroll in and complete gatekeeper courses
- Complete the credit hours for which they enrolled
- Reenroll from one semester to the next
- Earn certificates and degrees
- Transfer to 4-year institutions (EPCC, 2005)

One of the first pieces of data that we gathered and analyzed was the placement exam results of all students enrolling at EPCC for the entire 2003–2004 academic year. Although we realized that a large number of our students were placing into developmental courses, we had never looked at the data to see the percentages. We were astounded! Of all the students taking the placement test for that 1-year period, 97% required remediation in math, approximately 70% required remediation in reading, and approximately 52% required remediation in writing. We then decided to disaggregate the data to see if there was a significant difference between GED recipients, high school graduates less than 1 year out of high school, and high school graduates more than 1 year out of high school at the time the placement exam was taken. The data are shown in Table 7.1. EPCC has multiple levels of developmental courses, depending on the needs of the student. For example, math has four levels of developmental courses. Our next step was to disaggregate the data further by level into which the student placed. For math, the results are shown in Table 7.2.

Table 7.1 Placement Test Results by Academic Background for El Paso Community College: 2003–2004

	% of Students College Ready Vs. Needing Remediation					
	Math		Reading		Writing	
Academic background before test	College ready	Not college ready	College ready	Not college ready	College ready	Not college ready
High school grad < 1 yr.	5%	95%	29%	71%	54%	46%
High school grad > 1 yr.	3%	97%	30%	70%	48%	52%
GED	1%	99%	33%	67%	31%	69%
No high school diploma or GED	1%	99%	16%	84%	26%	74%

Table 7.2 Math Course Placement Test Results by Academic Background for El Paso Community College: 2003–2004

	Math Course Placements				
		Developmental requirement			
Academic background before test	College ready	Highest level 0305	0303	0301	Lowest level 0300
High school grad < 1 yr.	5%	26%	5%	24%	40%
High school grad > 1 yr.	3%	18%	6%	24%	49%
GED	1%	7%	6%	27%	59%
No high school diploma or GED	1%	4%	4%	20%	71%

We then shared these data with several constituent groups. First, we shared with each of the school district superintendents, giving them the disaggregated data in the matrix format for the students in their respective districts. We further disaggregated the data by high school within each district. This was the first time that the superintendents had been presented with these data. Previously, they had focused on high school exit test results, believing that if students passed the high school exit test, then they must be college ready.

Next, we presented the data to our EPCC faculty and staff during a series of campus forums, concluding with a special conversation with the entire developmental education faculty. The third group to receive the data was a community advisory committee established as a part of the Achieving the Dream grant. The advisory committee was composed of the CEOs of the local chambers of commerce, the superintendents of the school districts, the presidents and chief academic officers of UTEP and EPCC, the CEO of the Regional Education Service Center, the CEOs of the local newspapers, and some key business leaders.

In an effort to ensure that the meeting would not involve any finger pointing or blame gaming, I announced that we had several laptops available in the adjoining room with the college placement test loaded on them. If anyone wanted to point fingers, he or she could use those fingers at the key pad of the computer to take the test, and we could find out quickly how many of us would test into developmental math. That set the tone for an engaging dialogue in which all participants became learners in the courageous conversation. This use of data in an open and transparent conversation of the issue may have been one of the most important "tipping points" in the El Paso quest for making a difference in bridging the gap between high school exit competencies and college entrance requirements.

Establishing the College Readiness Consortium

Several critical improvements emerged from this nexus. The College Readiness Consortium was the ingenious idea of Dennis Brown, EPCC vice president of instruction. He and Richard Jarvis, provost of the University of Texas at El Paso (UTEP), cochair the consortium of members including the associate superintendents of instruction from the 12 school districts. This unique collaboration began with the following charge:

> It is the belief of area school districts, El Paso Community College and the University of Texas at El Paso that students graduating from high school having completed the recommended curriculum and the TAKS Test are ready to enter postsecondary institutions without the need for developmental reading, writing or math courses. With this belief in mind, the purpose of the Consortium is to ensure that college-bound high school graduates' initial enrollment is in entry-level college courses. Working in collaboration, the school districts, the university and the community college will identify barriers that interfere with students' transition from high school to college. The Consortium will develop a plan to address these barriers. The goal would be for high school students to test

into college-level courses prior to graduation. Among the issues to be addressed are: assessment/placement testing and re-testing; pre-testing workshops; post-testing preparation workshops; comparison of ACCUPLACER and TAKS tests, and comparison of ACCUPLACER and high school graduation competencies. The chances for student success are greatly increased when the student's first experience in higher education is in the pursuit of college-level degree or certificate programs of study. A report on the Consortium's findings and recommendation will be presented to area superintendents, and the Presidents of the University of Texas at El Paso and El Paso Community College.

The consortium was created in the fall of 2005. The progress and collaboration between the various entities has been phenomenal:

- Approximately 4,000 seniors in six school districts were oriented and prepared for testing on the ACCUPLACER test during spring 2006. Students not passing one or more of the three areas (reading, writing, or math) received interventions and were retested.
- All 12 school districts tested the seniors during fall 2006, and most of the school districts tested the juniors during spring semester 2007.
- The College Readiness Implementation Committee has been developing pretest orientation, test preparation materials, testing processes, score reporting processes, interventions before retesting, and transition processes into higher education.
- EPCC and UTEP co-funded a college readiness research position for greater data sharing with all members of the consortium.
- All students tested in the high schools complete a joint EPCC/UTEP admissions application.
- A Title V pilot was developed to evaluate math intervention processes. Data revealed that as little as 6 hours of math refresher practice led to 49% of students advancing one to two course placements higher.
- Dual credit classes of core courses were increased at all high schools. Students taking dual credit at high schools in El Paso increased from 100 in fall 2001, to more than 2,000 in fall 2006.

EPCC Vice President of Instruction Dennis Brown described the consortium as follows:

As the Consortium moves to full implementation, the number of students whose initial enrollment in college in core curriculum and major courses will increase dramatically. This partnership is an example of the El Paso education community joining together to successfully address a problem that has negatively impacted incoming college students for years. The transition from high school is becoming fully aligned and integrated, and the student is the beneficiary.

DEVELOPING A TEAM—GROWING YOUR OWN

A major ladder in the EPCC climb to success is its ability to develop the team. The college committed itself to growing its own leaders by creating the EPCC Leadership Academy. We began building this ladder by consulting with Cornell University's Institute for Community College Development. In the fall of 2003, staff members from the institute spent 3 days in El Paso interviewing more than 50 employees and conducting two surveys to gauge needs and acceptance of such a program: the "Twenty-first Century Enterprise Questionnaire" and the "Fifteen Leadership Competencies Survey."

Based on the interviews, the recommendations suggested there was strong agreement that both faculty and staff are promoted into positions where they do not have the full complement of skills required to be successful. Unfortunately, this situation creates great stress as people are forced to learn on the job. There was also strong interest in the concept of a Leadership Academy; the employees would like this initiative to be available and accessible to all staff and faculty and the process to be transparent and inclusive. From the Twenty-First Century Enterprise Questionnaire, we learned that the employees believed that the most important organizational competencies included the following:

- Vision directed
- Flexible and continuously learning
- Customer driven and marketing focused
- Creative use of technology
- Innovative

From the Fifteen Leadership Competencies Survey, the employees identified the most important competencies for leadership at EPCC as follows:

- Knowledge of job
- Taking action and making decisions
- Energy, drive, and ambition
- Time management
- Communicating information and ideas
- Coping with pressure and adversity

The recommended leadership and support to ensure a successful academy consisted of three critical elements. The first element was the creation and assignment of a leadership development coordinator. For this critical role, we turned to Shirley Gilbert. The second element was to develop a leadership development committee to assist the coordinator. The committee was composed of entrepreneurial pioneers representing the following:

- Faculty, staff, and administrators
- All campuses
- A mix of gender and ethnicity
- A mix of education backgrounds and experiences

The third element required support from all levels of the administration.

With the three critical elements in place, the coordinator and her team began planning the curriculum and structure of the academy to meet EPCC's unique needs. The committee created two simultaneous tracks: a fundamentals leadership track and an advanced leadership track. Both tracks would be yearlong processes with monthly workshops of 4 hours each, attendance at the Border Learning Conference, a summer retreat, and a graduation ceremony in December. At the culminating graduation, teams from each track would present college application projects enhancing student success. The program components consist of monthly seminars and activities, portfolios, team projects, and individual learning action plans. The targeted size for each track was 30 employees. The first leadership academy year commenced January 1, 2005. The college has celebrated 2 years with 116 employees completing the academy and 70 employees currently participating in the third year.

Since its inception, the academy has been blessed to have Amado M. Peña, Jr., join us during the summer retreat for a program called "Painting with Peña"—bringing out the creative energies in leadership and learning. The success is best described by some of the participants:

> Even though I have been in an administrative position for 25 years at EPCC, I learned new things about leadership in this academy that I am now practicing. The leadership provided me with a wonderful learning experience, which has given me new insight about effective leadership.—Bobby Ortega, instructional dean

> The academy has helped me in many areas of my life. I feel more confident in the way I interact with students, colleagues and administrators. I am amazed that what I have learned through the sessions (ways of speaking to people,

conflict resolution, sharing) has actually remained in my memory! I am more aware of myself and have learned to listen instead of reacting.—Sandra Padilla, reading faculty

The Leadership Academy helps to develop a team by emphasizing the worth of each person on the team and the importance of his/her contributions. Training sessions present the skills needed to recognize and utilize each one's strengths. And, the academy promotes confidence in the participants that their individual efforts are appreciated, and that their team project will be valued.—Gail Shipley, economics faculty

In the Fundamentals Track of the Leadership Development Academy we use the slogan "You don't have to have a title to be a leader." In the Advanced Track we use "Having a title doesn't make you a leader." Each year I watch for the light to go on in the participants eyes, the light that tells me "they got it." For some it comes early in the year, and for others it takes longer; but it always comes. That is when I know that we are doing what we hoped to do, that we have touched their lives and the lives of the people they will touch. That is when I know why I do what I do.—Shirley Gilbert, EPCC assistant to the president

DEVELOPING THE COMMUNITY

The fourth ladder on EPCC's climb to success focuses on serving the community. Four years ago, we had a conversation with the director of the United Blood Services of El Paso. During that conversation, we were told that El Paso did not have enough blood donors to meet the needs of the hospitals for our own community—that is, we were blood importers. She asked for our help. Being a competitive person, I asked how many units of blood the largest institutional contributor was donating. She responded, approximately 500 units per year. I said that our faculty, staff, and students would beat that, and we did. We donated 785 pints in 2003, 1,872 in 2004, 1,682 in 2005, and 2,382 in 2006.

The college has been recognized not only by United Blood Services as its largest donor but also by America's Blood Centers. When passionate, committed people dedicate themselves to such a worthy goal, blessings abound. One of those passionate people is Ron Stroud, director of institutional effectiveness, who has taken this effort on for the college with zeal and a commitment:

In a community of some 16 hospitals needing 150 daily donations of what can only come from people willing to help fellow citizens whom they may never

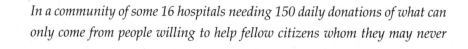

meet, blood donations are nothing less than the donation of life to the community. Since, in the time of need, neither private wealth, nor the most pitiful poverty, can hope to obtain what the community has not already given of its own free will, this ongoing investment on the part of thousands of citizens demonstrates communal responsibility of the highest order. As the number one blood donor of the region, El Paso Community College has taken the lead in this aspect of community development.

Because of these efforts, El Paso is no longer a blood importer.

United Blood Services (UBS), El Paso's nonprofit community blood center, has developed a strong partnership with El Paso Community College, resulting in the improvement of the quality of life of members in our community. Congruently, both organizations have worked together to develop win–win opportunities drawing from both organizations' potential. Through efficient and effective blood drives, El Paso Community College has been instrumental in the collection of over 1,000 blood donations per year. This effort has not only gained El Paso Community College national recognition and a national award from America's Blood Centers, but it has resulted in a positive impact in the lives of many patients at our hospitals requiring blood components … . The partnership between El Paso Community College and United Blood Services is a perfect example of how two solid and reliable organizations can work cohesively to build a better community overall.—Paula Villalobos, executive director of United Blood Services

EVALUATING

An integral step on any ladder to a quality improvement process is evaluating or measuring progress in specific areas of importance. EPCC uses various tools and methods to evaluate the learning and service processes. One of those methodologies—surveys—is especially productive. We rely on three critical elements of feedback from all our survey tools to improve the climate for learning.

The Noel-Levitz Student Satisfaction Inventory measures the importance and satisfaction of 12 student-service clusters on a 7-point scale. EPCC began using this instrument in 2002, administering it to our students in the fall semester of even-numbered years. We use fall 2002 as the baseline year to measure improvements in student perceptions in the 12 cluster areas. Outcomes are shared with the entire college family. Any areas that indicate reduced satisfaction between years or significant gaps between importance and satisfaction are analyzed and incorporated for improvement action plans. These data are not only benchmarked against prior years but also compared with all community colleges using the instrument, as well as a set of peer institutions. A comparison of satisfaction levels between 2002 and 2006 appears in Table 7.3. As the data indicate, students at EPCC believe significant improvements have occurred in all 12 clusters.

Table 7.3 Noel–Levitz Student Satisfaction Inventory Scores for El Paso Community College: 2002 and 2006

Student Service Clusters	2002	2006	Mean Difference
Academic advising/counseling	4.77	5.11	.34*
Service excellence	4.90	5.23	.33*
Registration effectiveness	5.05	5.38	.33*
Admissions and financial aid	4.84	5.17	.33*
Concern for the individual	4.81	5.11	.30*
Campus climate	4.98	5.28	.30*
Student centeredness	5.02	5.31	.29*
Instructional effectiveness	5.11	5.37	.26*
Academic services	5.24	5.50	.26*
Campus support services	4.80	5.05	.25*
Safety and security	4.97	5.13	.16*
Responsiveness to diverse populations	5.34	5.49	.15*

Note. Scores are based on a 7-point scale (1 = lowest, 7 = highest).
*$p < .001$.

The second survey instrument is the Community College Survey of Student Engagement (CCSSE). The college began using CCSSE in the spring of 2005 and conducts this survey every spring. CCSSE measures student perceptions of learning engagement based on five categories:

- Active and collaborative learning
- Student effort
- Academic challenge
- Student and faculty interaction
- Support for learners

As Table 7.4 shows, EPCC was rated as a "high performer" in four of five categories for 2005.

Table 7.4 Community College Survey of Student Engagement 2005 Benchmark Results for All Students at El Paso Community College

Benchmark	El Paso Community College	2005 Colleges Comparison Group Statistics ($N = 257$)	
		Benchmark score	Score difference
Active and collaborative learning	55.1	50.0	5.1
Student effort	55.1	50.0	5.1
Academic challenge	52.6	50.0	2.6
Student–faculty interaction	50.3	50.0	0.3
Support for learners	58.0	50.0	8.0

Note. Data are from the Community College Survey of Student Engagement. Each benchmark score was computed by averaging the scores on survey items that comprise that benchmark. To compensate for disproportionately large numbers of full-time students in the sample, all means used in the creation of the benchmarks are weighted by full- and part-time status. Benchmark scores are standardized so that the weighted mean across all students is 50 and the standard deviation across all participating students is 25. Institutions' benchmark scores are computed by taking the weighted average of their student's standardized scores.

The third survey is the Employee Climate Survey, conducted annually in the spring semester. All full- and part-time employees have the opportunity to participate. We use 2001 as the base year for comparisons and institutional improvement strategies. We believe a positive and supportive employee climate is necessary for the staff and faculty to engage and serve students fully and effectively. The elements measured and a comparison of 2006 to the base year are provided in Table 7.5.

It is essential for colleges to use multiple methods and processes to evaluate and assess learning, services, and effectiveness. With these data and the feedback cycle, we have the opportunity to engage our faculty and staff in courageous conversations to improve the learning environment continually. EPCC math faculty member, Lucy Michael, makes the following observation:

> *Using data in our work towards the goals of Achieving the Dream helped us focus our efforts in a direction that would be more useful. Also, more than giving us information, looking and using data made us realize we needed more data and more ways to gather data. The only data we have been looking at are what happens at the end of a course and not necessarily at factors that create the end result. The data also gave us leverage with supporting the changes we were proposing. With the data, we were able to clearly paint a picture of how a restructure of courses would better address students' needs. An*

example of this is where we had a situation with four remedial courses in our developmental sequence for mathematics. Of all incoming students who were taking placement exams, only 3% were placing into our introductory course. This facilitated and supported our proposal of transitioning the four course sequence into a three-course sequence.

Table 7.5 El Paso Community College Employee Climate Survey Results: 2006

	% Agree or Strongly Agree	
Survey Item	**Base 2001**	**2006**
Well-known mission	69.9%	93.5%
Well-known strategic goals	57.0%	84.2%
Curriculum consistent with mission	72.1%	92.1%
Planning and evaluation consistent with mission	62.7%	86.5%
Financial and physical resources consistent with mission	44.2%	79.4%
Educational programs consistent with mission	84.1%[a]	92.4%
Educational support services consistent with mission	75.6%[a]	86.8%
Administrative processes consistent with mission	67.0%[a]	83.3%
Focus on students in all we do	71.1%	82.2%
Satisfactory communication	52.7%	73.4%
Effective leadership	56.2%	79.4%
Satisfactory shared governance	54.5%	75.9%
Teamwork and collegiality	64.5%	78.9%
Good working relationship with supervisor	86.1%	90.4%
Work satisfaction for me	87.2%	91.9%
Effective hiring procedure	54.8%	65.0%
Salaries and benefits attracting good employees	48.4%	62.0%
Effective grievance procedure (wages, hours, conditions)	73.4%[b]	75.8%
Time allowed for professional development	70.5%	84.2%
Satisfactory staff scholarships	54.7%	78.5%
Physically safe environment	83.4%	90.7%
Well-maintained facilities	64.4%	79.3%
Computer and software adequate for job	70.9%[c]	87.4%
Overall Average	64.1%	82.3%

[a] 2002; not asked in 2001

[b] 2004; not asked in 2001

[c] 2005; not asked in 2001

RESPECTING THE LEGACY AND CULTURE, AND RESOLVING TO MAKE A DIFFERENCE: SALUTE TO THE ARTS

Communities and community colleges have their own legacy, tradition, history, and culture. As leaders of institutions, we must understand a college's and community's legacy and culture to make a difference. In El Paso, the arts are a major part of our culture. The state legislature significantly reduced state funding midyear in 2002–2003 as the result of a state economic decline. Typically, institutions respond by reducing funding in the arts in times of declining revenues. However, because the arts are such an important element of EPCC's culture, we decided to do the opposite—we invested more time, energy, and resources in the arts. We created a year of "EPCC Salute to the Arts," during which we sponsored visual art exhibits for the college and the community.

One of the most successful exhibits, which has now become an annual tradition at EPCC, was the K–12 art exhibit and reception. The first K–12 exhibit resulted in more than 300 pieces of art submitted by several schools throughout the 12 school districts we serve. The exhibit culminated in an evening reception for the artists, their parents, and their teachers. The reception attracted more than 300 people and was embraced passionately by K–12 students, teachers, parents, grandparents, and family members. We realized that this was the first time many attendees had ever set foot on a higher-education campus. The exhibit became an amazing opportunity, not only to celebrate the culture of our community but also to bring the community into the college and create a new ladder to success.

I asked Amado M. Peña, Jr., to be our 2003 commencement speaker. We honored Amado that evening by creating a $25,000 endowed scholarship in his name, awarding him an honorary associate degree, and making him a member of the EPCC family. He has since donated 65 pieces of his original art work to EPCC. Peña stated:

> In my journey through life I have had many experiences with different organizations and institutions. Many have left a lasting impression on me, but not more so than El Paso Community College. The love and respect the College administrators and employees have for each other and for the culture is like nothing else I have experienced. That is why I decided this is where I want to be remembered; this is where I want to leave my legacy.

CREATING STRATEGIC PARTNERSHIPS

The most successful colleges of the 21st century will be those who have created the strongest strategic partnerships within their communities. EPCC is blessed to be aligned with some very passionate and entrepreneurial partners—including

UTEP, the Socorro Independent School District, the City of El Paso, and the Canutillo Independent School District.

Diana Natalicio, president of UTEP, as well as a visionary and impassioned leader, has helped us take collaboration to another level through her leadership and commitment to the partnership with EPCC. The synergy between the faculty and staff of the two institutions has resulted in several new ladders to student success:

- Articulation committee for ease in transfer of courses between institutions
- Joint admissions application process
- Financial aid consortium agreement aiding students concurrently enrolled in both institutions
- Wohlslager EPCC transfer scholarship
- Joint Title V EPCC/UTEP student advisory program
- El Paso Collaborative for Academic Excellence alignment of math and science curriculum K–16
- College Readiness Consortium

Another visionary and impassioned leader, Robert Duron, superintendent of the Socorro Independent School District, helped us create the Mission Early College High School. This early college high school project began in 2004. Through the great team approach of Dr. Duron, his staff, and EPCC team, the Mission Early College High School received funding from the Bill and Melinda Gates Foundation through the Texas Communities Foundation. The doors opened to the first cohort of high school freshmen in July 2006. The high school, located on EPCC's Mission del Paso campus, provides students with a rigorous curriculum, allowing them to graduate in 4 years with a high school diploma in one hand and an associate degree in the other. The numerous challenges in facilities, curriculum design, student admission process, transportation, and food service, among others, were met by the collaborative team with a positive "can do" attitude that never wavered. As Alma Garcia, coordinator of Early College High Schools for the Communities Foundation of Texas, stated at the grand opening,

> *Throughout the entire implementation process, the two institutions worked hand in hand. Normally, when you run into problems between two partners you hear them say, "my lawyer will talk to your lawyer," but in this partnership it was "my plumber will talk to your plumber."*

The cornerstone in the success of this school was found in the principal hired to lead the staff, faculty, and students—Armando Aguirre—an energetic, brilliant, student-focused advocate for accelerated learning opportunities.

In 2001, the Canutillo Independent School District began to look for a location for a new high school, after outgrowing the existing high school and deciding to use it as a middle school. I suggested the idea of a high school colocated with our Northwest Campus in Canutillo. The two boards of trustees met in a joint meeting to discuss the concept, and the result is history. El Paso now has its first collaborative educational campus of EPCC and Canutillo High School. A new library was completed in 2002 on the EPCC Northwest Campus. Previously, the community of Canutillo did not have a public library. EPCC began deliberation with the City of El Paso about a joint city–college library to be located in our new library facility. The city liked the idea because it could serve the population of Canutillo without the enormous expense of building an additional facility. The City of El Paso agreed to fund one full-time librarian and the cost of a children's section of the library to make the EPCC Northwest Campus Library a community library. This collaborative library has now been in operation, serving thousands of underserved, economically disadvantaged citizens of our community, for more than 4 years.

Through conversations with a dear friend of the college, Adair Margo, former member of the Texas Higher Education Coordinating Board from El Paso, we discovered that First Lady Laura Bush's mother, Jenna Welch, grew up in Canutillo. With this information, our librarians researched and located the house in which she grew up and identified some of her dear friends. To honor this influential former member of the Canutillo community and her commitment to reading and learning, the college decided to name the library the Jenna Welch and Laura Bush Community Library. Partnerships are delicate relationships that require commitment, honesty, courageous conversations, and a lot of hard work. These examples of strong partnerships have those ingredients, a result of the leadership and the spirit of collaboration that exists in El Paso.

CONCLUSION

EPCC has seen significant changes over the past 5 years. In spite of the economic challenges facing our population, EPCC has been one of the fastest-growing community colleges in the nation. During the 2003 fiscal year, EPCC was *the* fastest-growing community college in the nation. The college has grown by 41% over the past 5 years. More importantly, numbers of graduates are growing even faster—during 2002–2007, by 78%, almost double our enrollment growth. In 2006, *Hispanic Outlook* magazine recognized EPCC as the community college enrolling the largest number of Latino graduates in the nation.

Even with our tremendous accomplishments and achievements, we realize we are still a learning college. The Ladders to Success framework that exists at EPCC is possible because of the dedicated, committed, and entrepreneurial faculty and staff who have a passion to pursue the shared vision of student success. They are the builders of ladders every single day, student by student, heart by heart, mind by mind, and hand in hand. All seven ladders described here can change the face of higher education, allowing and affording the citizens of our communities the opportunities to continue their journeys to ever-higher levels of success.

REFERENCES

Blanchard, K. (1999). *The heart of a leader.* Colorado Springs, CO: Cook Communications Ministries.

El Paso Community College. (2005). *Achieving the Dream: Community colleges count.* Retrieved August 20, 2007, from www.epcc.edu/achievingthedream

O'Banion, T. (1997). *A learning college for the 21st century.* Phoenix, AZ: ACE/Oryx Press.

Pell Institute for the Study of Opportunity in Higher Education. (2006). *Straight from the source: What works for first-generation college students.* Washington, DC: Author.

Texas Higher Education Coordinating Board. (2000). *Closing the gaps: The Texas higher education plan.* Austin, TX: Author. Retrieved August 20, 2007, from www.thecb.state.tx.us/reports/PDF/0379.PDF

University of Texas at Austin, Community College Leadership Program. (2005). *Institutional report 2005: Community College Survey of Student Engagement.* Austin, TX: Author.

8

The College of Southern Nevada: A Journey Toward a Shared Vision

Richard Carpenter

Remembering that trust is never freely given,
we must make earning it an ongoing priority.

—Richard Carpenter, College of Southern Nevada

The population of southern Nevada has doubled in the last 10 years and is predicted to double again by 2020. The College of Southern Nevada is the only community college serving this immense growth; it is the largest higher education institution in the state. Troubled for years with leadership changes and a lack of accountability, the college needed rapid, creative transformation to meet the overwhelming needs of the population.

Richard Carpenter, president of the College of Southern Nevada for 3 years, helps us imagine the possibilities for the Las Vegas community and shows us that a chaotic situation can become a promise of blue skies for the future. His creative vision required a commitment to hard decisions and a willingness to listen to the data. Workforce training with global outreach, accessible and on-demand online education, multiple campuses with complete student services, new campuses that are mixed use urban villages, and partnerships with the community that help to finance the necessary college ventures are but a few of the transformations at the college within the last few years. Under Carpenter's leadership, the college transformed its culture and public image and is now poised to grow alongside the greater Las Vegas region.

IMAGINE! IMAGINE AN ENTIRE MODERN community college campus built without tax dollars and with minimal private donations. Imagine this college as a public–private partnership—a mixed use self-supporting urban village. Imagine parks and palm-lined avenues. Imagine classrooms, instructional laboratories, and faculty offices intermingled with designer retail stores, restaurants, boutique shops, a $100 million teaching hospital, a hotel and convention center, and more. That is the vision for the next campus of the College of Southern Nevada, and this vision is unfolding.

Each month, almost 8,000 people move to Las Vegas. Consequently, for the past few years, Las Vegas has been touted as the fastest-growing city in the United States. To support this growth, a decade-long construction boom has tapped labor resources from all over the country; still, there are shortages. In this city of 1.7 million people, a vacant parcel of land without construction cranes is hard to find. Proliferating road construction projects snarl traffic. Last year, airport traffic topped 46 million passengers as the gaming industry reached new multibillion dollar profit margins.

PUBLIC EDUCATION IN A CITY OF EXPLOSIVE GROWTH

Clark County School District, the single school district serving Las Vegas, is rapidly becoming the largest in the country. On average, this district opens a new school every month; yet crowding continues, and the 2006–2007 school year began 1,500 teachers short. Skyrocketing housing costs exacerbate the teacher shortage. In 2004, for example, the value of the average home in Las Vegas experienced a phenomenal 53% increase—in a single year!

Like many other parts of the country, demographic shifts are redefining the student population, and a growing number of students lack basic English skills. Nearly 40% of the high school graduates require significant remedial work on entry into college. Due perhaps to the unique economic engine of the city (gaming), education has been undervalued culturally and historically. The pressure on this school district, by all accounts, is unprecedented in U.S. education.

Higher education in Las Vegas is unique. Once a branch campus of the University of Nevada–Reno, the University of Nevada–Las Vegas (UNLV) has evolved atypically. For instance, a drive through this 26,000-student campus would reveal minimal residence facilities and limited building space. As a frequent guest professor at UNLV, I find that the campus has the distinct feel of an urban community college. The student demographics mirror those of the community college, as well. However, UNLV is in the midst of a makeover of sorts as it strives to become more of a research university. Recently, the university raised its admissions standards for entering freshmen, but it has continued its remedial programming.

In 2002, the state opened a new type of higher education institution in Henderson, Nevada, a bedroom community to Las Vegas. Nevada State College's primary mission is the production of teachers and nurses, but the college presses for a broader mission. Almost all of its 2,000 students are from the surrounding community and exhibit the typical characteristics of community college students. Indeed much, if not most, of the growth of this institution has come at the expense of the nearby community college campus. This said, Nevada State College has become a major partner with the community college.

A COLLEGE ON THE MOVE

Long-time residents still refer to the community college as Clark County Community College, although for a decade the official name of the college was the Community College of Southern Nevada. Recently, the board of regents approved a name change for the Community College of Southern Nevada. Effective July 1, 2007, it became the College of Southern Nevada (CSN). This change came at the request of students who generated a 10,000-signature petition for their cause. The college offers a baccalaureate and will continue to explore other niche bachelor's degrees, but it remains true to its mission as a community college. The name change is not expected to alter the institution's community college mission but rather to reflect the extensive role CSN has as a higher education institution in this heavily populated region.

Over the past decade, CSN's prolific growth has rivaled any community college in the nation. Today, CSN is Nevada's largest institution of higher education, enrolling more than 37,000 students each semester. In fact, 64% of all community college full-time enrollments in Nevada are at CSN. Half of all minorities enrolled in the Nevada Higher Education System are at CSN, as are a majority of the state's disabled students. CSN has become the state's largest provider of distance-education programs.

CSN governance is atypical. Unlike community colleges in surrounding states, CSN is not a community college district. Rather, it is a single college with multiple comprehensive campuses and outreach centers. One president is responsible for all campuses (this challenging structure is now under review by the state board of regents). The college has no local board—no dedicated board at all. Instead, it is governed by an elected state board of regents that oversees the universities and the state college, as well. This unique structure has some obvious advantages and disadvantages. A disadvantage is that Nevada's community colleges have few aggressive champions who often are found within the more traditional local board structure. For instance, there is absolutely no participation among the regents and little awareness of the American Association of Community Colleges or the

Association of Community College Trustees. This situation leaves Nevada's community colleges strangely isolated from the national scene. In addition, the board is engaged only minimally in the federal legislative process as it affects community colleges. Without local governance, there is no local tax base to support the community college.

Conversely, this "super board" has made major strides in easing community college credit transfer to the universities, because it has the sole power to do so. Further, it sets capital and budget priorities with the state legislature for both the community colleges and the universities, thereby reducing institutional competition for state-funded projects. In addition, by their nature, super board regents tend to be less inclined to interfere with institutional management than their counterparts on local boards.

REBUILDING A CRIPPLED INSTITUTION: IN THE BEGINNING

In 2004, I left my post as state president for the Wisconsin Community and Technical College System to assume the presidency of the Community College of Southern Nevada. With almost 25 years' experience as a community college CEO, I thought I was prepared for anything. What I found during the first couple of weeks on the job in Las Vegas, however, would unnerve even the most seasoned administrators.

First, I found a shell-shocked institution in need of some serious healing. The last president, popular among faculty, had been fired by the board of regents with an emotionally charged 7–6 vote. Counting all the interim presidents that had been in the position, I determined that I was the college's seventh president in 10 years. Not surprisingly, after only 3 years, I was considered a long-term president at CSN.

As one might expect in such a volatile environment, leadership at all levels of the institution was in disarray. Continuous turnover in numerous key positions had become the norm; what one faculty member dubbed a "lawless culture" had spawned the creation of a vastly bloated and highly paid midmanagement, many with limited credentials. Nepotism was rampant. Dozens of employees were reporting directly to a family member or spouse. Remember, too, that the college was expanding by thousands of students each year.

With the incredible turnover in administrative leadership at all levels, I was impressed to see that, for the most part, the faculty members were keeping the college on course. I continue to have deep respect for the role that faculty leadership played in those dark days of the college. Interestingly, the roles of department chairs and deans had reversed. This proved to be a challenging factor in restoring order and rebuilding the leadership structure of the college; however, in the end, the faculty senate provided the necessary support to do so. I conducted several contentious meetings with our academic department chairs around empirical accountability issues. Although we successfully negotiated written job descriptions for the department chairs, some resigned in protest. We followed a similar process with the deans. Most of the deans had come from the faculty, and little had ever been done to prepare them to be deans. Like the department chairs, they did not have written job descriptions. Formal, written job descriptions were prepared, and approximately half of the deans eventually were replaced with experienced personnel from around the country. Others have benefited from structured and mandated professional development.

Among my first decisions was to freeze hiring at the college for 90 days. The college employs approximately 3,000 people, so this freeze was destined to create an unpopular burden on existing personnel. During this period, we collaborated with the faculty senate to construct a formalized set of recruitment, hiring, and retention policies and procedures. Although continuously being refined, these policies remain fundamentally intact today.

CHARTING A NEW COURSE: THE NEXT STEP

I found several critical leadership positions vacant on my arrival. Others, I intentionally vacated, with an eye toward building a new type of senior leadership team for the college. Deans and department chair job descriptions were rewritten to include specific accountability measures. National searches resulted in replacing four of the college's five vice presidents. All four new vice presidents were seasoned administrators with more than 20 years' experience each. These professionals have become recognized widely in the community, in the state, and by our board of regents, as a top-level, high-performance team.

Taking a lesson from Jim Collins's (2001) bestseller, *Good to Great*, we evaluated who among our management team should retain "a seat on the bus." We were not shy about removing those who had positioned themselves as major and irrecoverable liabilities. Within a few months, $1.3 million in midmanagement positions was eliminated, and the savings were redirected to student and academic support. Several new academic advisors were hired, as were more tutors and laboratory assistants. Morale and pride at the college began to improve quickly and noticeably, and previously hostile editorials in the state's major newspapers began praising our efforts.

CREATING A BLUEPRINT FOR THE FUTURE

Integral to the rebuilding process, the college developed an ambitious "blueprint for the future" and then a formal strategic plan. We all learned that large-group meetings, although efficient, seldom engaged more than a few of the most vocal among our faculty and staff. For this reason, the strategic plan was constructed through countless small-group meetings and online surveys. I led discussions on each of the college's three comprehensive campuses. To ensure a meaningful voice for staff members and students, the college conducted separate and distinct focus group discussions for faculty, staff, and students—on each campus and online. Although laborious, this strategy had the desired effect of greater participation and inclusion of faculty, staff, and students in the process. Eventually, the leadership team engaged the community-at-large in these focus group discussions, typically through breakfast meetings conducted throughout the community.

This intensive information-gathering process culminated in the production of *A Vision of Blue Skies Ahead: A Blueprint for Mapping CCSN's Future* (CCSN, 2005). As the title implies, this product was not only a strategic plan but also a strategic planning framework built around 10 broad goals. These goals, some of which are obviously unique to this college, are as follows:

1. Restoring public confidence
2. Increasing financial support (resourcing)
3. Improving student success
4. Enhancing the college's academic reputation
5. Expanding our role in economic and workforce development
6. Rebuilding distributed learning enterprise
7. Celebrating diversity and multiculturalism
8. Advancing grantsmanship and foundation efforts
9. Planning the future
10. Building campus infrastructure

Next, the college identified specific institutional performance measures (IPMs) that would be used to monitor its progress continuously:

- Institutional support (administrative costs per FTE)
- Academic program costs
- Student/faculty ratios
- Student/administrator ratios
- Average class sizes
- Class size by section
- Faculty workload
- Space utilization
- Student persistence

- Graduation rates
- Student goal attainment
- Posttransfer performance
- Student access
- Student retention
- Student demand
- Student satisfaction
- Employer satisfaction

With the performance measures in place, our Institutional Research Office set out to identify 10 benchmark institutions around the country—institutions that enjoyed a strong national reputation and shared characteristics with CSN—for example, size, growth rates, student demographics, academic programs, funding models, student success ratios, faculty loads. CSN has since partnered with many of these institutions to share performance data. These benchmark colleges are listed here:

- Austin Community College, Texas
- Broward Community College, Florida
- Cuyahoga Community College, Ohio
- Maricopa Community College District, Arizona
- Montgomery College, Maryland
- North Harris Montgomery Community College District, Texas
- Portland Community College, Oregon
- Sacramento City College, California
- Tarrant County College District, Texas
- Tidewater Community College, Virginia

With the groundwork laid and institutional goals delineated, various campus groups were charged with using the strategic planning framework to develop action steps and accountability measures of what would become the college's official strategic plan. Experience has taught us that such plans usually are incremental by nature. Furthermore, my observation is that institutions evolve in a cyclical pattern: advances followed by complacency, relative stagnation, advances, and so forth. Obvious to all was that this institution was at a low point along its evolutionary continuum, and incremental change, although politically expedient, likely would not deliver us to our desired performance level. With this in mind, we kept the following premises before us throughout the development of our strategic plan:

- Guiding Premise 1: The first question we must ask ourselves is not "What are we going to do?" but "Who do we intend to be?"
- Guiding Premise 2: The future belongs to those institutions that become accomplished at continuously reinventing themselves.
- Guiding Premise 3: An institution's capacity to reinvent itself is dependent on several factors:
  - Structure
  - Functional systems
  - Leadership
  - Culture
  - Vision
  - Strategy
  - Measurement
  - Recruiting and retaining talent
  - Hiring, rewarding, and promoting
- Guiding Premise 4: That which gets measured gets done.

THE SLOW PROCESS OF INSTITUTIONAL CHANGE

Most community college planning models are linear—incapable of facilitating quantum shifts necessary for transformational change. Rather, they assume the future to be a natural extension of the past, and, in so doing, they relegate the institution to political timidity, incremental tweaking, and performance lag. The strategic plan that was constructed, ultimately, called for transformational, not incremental, change. We acknowledged that strategic plans often are produced primarily to appease accrediting agencies and governing boards. Seldom do we see these plans used to affect institutional performance. My sense is that this is not intentional. Rather, with the ever-increasing pace of activity at the college, we just lose sight of our institutional goals and, sometimes, our priorities.

In an effort to keep the faculty and staff focused on strategic implementation and institutional performance, the college placed large flat-screen monitors throughout each of its campuses, including all departmental faculty office areas. The multimedia information displayed on these monitors is maintained centrally and updated daily. In addition to general announcements, deadline reminders, and highlight videos, real-time institutional performance data are displayed to track performance against peer institutions. The data serve as constant reminders of who we intend to be and how well we are progressing. In addition, every goal and objective found in the strategic plan has an "owner" who is personally accountable for its achievement. College leaders voluntarily publish periodic report cards for the board.

As we were assigning individual accountability for specific actions outlined in our strategic plan, we observed some significant skill gaps among our faculty and staff. To address these gaps and position the institution for continuous improvement and professional development, we created the Center for Academic and Professional Excellence. With full-time staff and state-of-the-art technologies, this center provides a robust and varied professional development program for faculty and staff alike. For example, with help from this center, the Student Affairs Unit of the college conducted student surveys, followed by intensive customer service training for staff. The center also has provided formalized training for midlevel managers and supervisors.

With ever-increasing student expectations, the public's demand for increased accountability, and the explosive growth in hybrid and Web-based academic programming, the community college Information Technology Unit has become the institution's nerve center. This unit was struggling early on with turf battles, underskilled personnel, and chronic poor funding. This unit was the most complained about entity at the college. I quickly concluded that we did not have the time to rebuild this unit and properly train the staff.

Therefore, I made the most unpopular decision of my presidency—outsourcing! After months of intense negotiations with the Sungard Higher Education Group, we agreed on a multiyear contract that resulted in an almost $7 million savings. Of course, it also resulted in the elimination of approximately 55 information technology jobs, but many of these people were rehired by Sungard. Eighteen months later, we had a model information technology plan and were in the middle of a $6 million technology infrastructure upgrade designed to position the college as the most technologically advanced academic environment in Nevada.

DISTANCE EDUCATION: A COMPLEX ENVIRONMENT

Many community colleges are experiencing the tension between senior faculty members who loathe the idea of entering into the Web-based education arena and the hoards of traditional-aged students who are demanding more Web-based offerings. Many faculty members, particularly in the hard sciences, argue that their courses cannot be delivered online and maintain quality and academic rigor. Others eagerly develop their courses and programs for online delivery.

Nationally, community colleges have been far more aggressive in developing online programs than their university counterparts. One alarming observation, however, is that the student services and student support for which community colleges are famous have not evolved at the same pace as academic programming. In fact, some colleges offer no online student support at all. On my arrival, I found a loose collection of apparently unrelated course offerings, varying widely in scope and quality. Demand for these courses was growing slowly. There was no common user interface, so every course presented its unique navigational challenges. No two courses looked alike, and there was significant faculty resistance to expanding the college's online capacity.

The college's new strategic plan called for the development of a world-class virtual campus, so we hired a full-time distance education director. We replaced the existing faculty-only distance education committee with a combined academic and student services committee. We asked this group to develop a set of quality standards for online offerings and services and to serve as a peer review team for all online proposals. Today, distance education is the fastest-growing program in the college, expanding at a rate of 20% per semester. The program is so popular that last fall semester, 20,500 students attempted to enroll in CSN's online offerings without success. Online courses at the college are like rock concerts—they sell out within minutes of opening, leaving thousands of disappointed students in their wake.

The college has moved toward complete program development and away from isolated course development, currently offering 22 complete online degree programs. Student demand has replaced faculty interest as the most compelling justification for course development. With the introduction of a complete array of high-quality online student support services, including 24/7 tutoring, we are preparing to launch a virtual college. Incidentally, the capacity issue with this program is not rooted in technology requirements, but rather in the extreme shortage of certified faculty.

We have learned much with our approach to developing a comprehensive and high-quality distance education program. Through this process, we learned numerous valuable lessons:

- Lesson 1: Resist the temptation to develop expanded academic offerings faster than the capacity to provide paired online student support systems. Student support should include all aspects of campus-based support. Students enrolling at CSN's virtual campus are provided online academic advising, financial aid assistance, library services, and 24/7 online tutoring services.
- Lesson 2: Consider an online orientation class as a prerequisite to admission to the first online course. Many students are ill prepared for or lack the academic maturity to complete online offerings successfully. Students often think these courses will afford them a less-demanding path to course completion. Anyone who has taught (or taken) an online course knows differently.

- Lesson 3: Move the focus from faculty to student. Most online offerings reflect the faculty's personal interests more than students' needs. Use student-demand data to drive program development.
- Lesson 4: Establish a set of academic standards that must be met before any course or program is offered online. Further, establish a common user interface that will be used for every online offering. This way, once students complete the first offering, they will find it easier to navigate subsequent offerings. Use peer review teams to authorize new offerings.
- Lesson 5: Invest in faculty and staff. The skill set for teaching in an online environment differs markedly from that required in the traditional classroom setting. Do not expect faculty to acquire these skills on their own. At CSN, no faculty members are authorized to teach online without first being certified by the college's Center for Academic and Professional Excellence.
- Lesson 6: Think programs, not courses. The number one complaint among online students is that they cannot complete all or most of their programs online. CSN has committed to launching three new all online programs every year and has a current inventory of 22.
- Lesson 7: Provide incentives for hybrid course offerings. Most of today's community college students are technology savvy. Even for their classroom-based courses, they like to use technology. Students give high marks to faculty who make use of the Web, for instance, to support classroom work. In addition, experimentally, students in some CSN classes are issued iPods so that lectures can be podcast for student review.

OUT WITH THE OLD, IN WITH THE NEW

In February 2005, CSN launched its Division of Workforce and Economic Development. This division combined the former Language Institute, Business and Industry Institute, Hospitality Institute, Corporate and Customized Training, and Continuing Education into an integrated unit. These silos had caused confusion in the business community and duplication within the college. The college immediately realized a $350,000 per-year efficiency savings by eliminating duplicated programs. Today, this new division consists of 10 departments: (1) adult literacy and language; (2) community and personal enrichment; (3) transportation, manufacturing, and construction; (4) education and government; (5) business assessment and consulting; (6) hospitality; (7) apprenticeship and prisons; (8) healthcare and emergency services; (9) retail services, banking, and finance; and (10) occupational safety. A workforce specialist or director heads each department, and a dean administers the division. This new division functions as an entrepreneurial and self-supporting unit of the college. Every member of this division must generate his or her salary and benefits each year to continue employment with the college. Contract receipts already total into the millions each year.

This division generates several large partnerships. For instance, in 2006, it received a $1 million grant from the U.S. Department of Labor to work with several casinos. Currently, it is negotiating a contract for a partner who will hire 12,000 new employees by mid-2009. Yet, another example of its success can be seen in the recently approved partnership with several colleges in Mainland China and on the island of Macau to provide train-the-trainer programs for the gaming industry. The gaming industry there plans to hire 9,000 employees before 2008.

BUILDING A CULTURE OF TRUST

Much has been written about transformational change and organizational dynamics. We sometimes fail to recognize, however, that the degree of difficulty in transformational change is dictated more by institutional culture than just our natural aversion to change. For example, because I was the seventh president in 10 years—and the previous president was popular among faculty—most college employees were reticent to change. They assumed I would be gone within a year anyway, so why bother? The departure of the previous president created hostility, cynicism, and apathy. The institution had been mired for years in a sea of corruption, taking an immeasurable toll on morale and collegial trust.

Such an environment creates ideal conditions for an endless flow of wild, and often absurd and baseless, allegations of wrongdoing. These situations affect institutional image, which in turn affects faculty and staff morale. Low morale manifests itself in mediocre performance, and the cycle continues. This cycle had a chronic negative impact on trust within the institution, and trust is arguably the most critical component of any successful transformational change effort. Changing the culture of CSN will be a long process, but significant movement is already evident. Trust is never freely given; we must make earning it an ongoing priority.

RECOGNITION FOR HARD-WON CHANGE

The Community Responds

As the college began to reinvent itself with a keen focus on measurement and accountability, the community took notice. First came a series of positive newspaper articles. As president, I quickly became a regular on television and radio talk shows. I never turned down an opportunity to be on the screen, even the late night, live television shows. Editorials lauding the college's efforts appeared in every major state newspaper. *Community College Week* and *Community College Times* gave us national exposure. *The Chronicle of Higher Education* published a two-page article on the rebuilding of the college (Evelyn, 2005). The Nevada Board of Regents (CSN's board) took note and began to champion the cause, becoming supportive and generous with the authority granted me to launch several bold and innovative initiatives. Private funding from the community increased dramatically, and seemingly everyone wanted to partner with the college. In the fall of 2006, during the college's 10-year accreditation review, the Northwest Commission on Colleges and Universities commended the college leadership for developing an atmosphere of stability and confidence within the college and the community.

The State Legislature Responds

In the midst of all the media attention, the biennial Nevada legislature went into session. As a new president in the system, I made getting to know legislative leadership a priority. As a newcomer to the state, I was burdened with some disadvantages, but the continuous statewide media coverage of the college afforded me opportunities to mitigate my outsider status, at least partially. I lobbied aggressively for $20 million in capital funds, and I argued that CSN's faculty members were paid less than their counterparts at other Nevada community colleges. At the end of the session, the college came away with $41 million in capital funds and $9 million for faculty salary increases, breaking all previous records for legislative support. As might be expected, these gifts generated a major boost in confidence and morale among faculty and staff.

Where's the Money? Partnerships Lead the Way

Due in part to its size, CSN receives dramatically less money per student than any other public college in Nevada. One community college in Nevada, for instance, is state-funded at a rate exceeding $11,000 per FTE, compared with $5,300 at CSN. This reality places a huge burden on the college. Most of the state's non–English-speaking students attend CSN, as do most of its disabled students. Moreover, the cost of living in Las Vegas is far greater than living in rural communities. An independent legislative study in 2003 discovered this inexcusable funding disparity, but little has been done to address it. The board of regents is asking the 2007 legislature for a $31 million budget infusion for CSN to begin closing the gap, but few people believe these funds will be allocated.

In spite of these budget difficulties, the college has some big plans. In the past 3 years, the college has celebrated the opening of three new facilities. Two more are currently under construction, all totaling some $100 million in expanded infrastructure. Yet, the college needs more. New facilities are filled to capacity immediately on opening. In addition, the college is investing $6 million in technology infrastructure, making it the most technologically advanced institution in Nevada.

Creative Financing

As part of a centralized state system of higher education, CSN enjoys no local tax support. Virtually all support—except tuition—comes from the state coffers, both for operations and capital. Although the state has been relatively generous in addressing the college's ever-expanding physical plant needs, student demand continues to outpace state-funded construction. Some unmet needs include parking structures, a student center for one campus, and a new fourth campus.

To fill these gaps, the college is pursuing public and private partnerships aggressively. For example, CSN has entered into a partnership with a major apartment complex developer to build a 360-unit luxury apartment complex on the Henderson campus. Leveraging 20 acres of its prime real estate, the college will become 50% owner of this complex, with no cash investment. The college's share of revenues from this project will generate a dedicated cash flow for bonding to build the new student center immediately—at no cost to taxpayers. Over time, this project will fund at least three construction projects for that campus. In addition, 10% of the apartments will be subsidized for college faculty and staff, easing national recruitment into Las Vegas' high-priced real estate market.

Improved public confidence led the city of Las Vegas, in 2006, to donate $60 million in prime real estate to the college to build a new fourth campus. This 60-acre parcel fronts the city's busiest freeway and is surrounded by new residential development, a new mega mall, a new hospital, and numerous other projects. In partnership with developers and retail specialists, the college plans to build an entire campus with little or no taxpayer funds.

This new northwest campus is described in the opening paragraph to this chapter. Before building each phase of this park, the college will enter into long-term, binding agreements with retail and service providers that will generate the revenue stream to pay for construction. College facilities will be integrated into each project and will be paid for from lease revenues. The master plan for this campus envisions a 12,000-student capacity at build-out. Construction plans for the first phase are nearing completion. Now the college is pursuing an additional parcel of land to develop a similar project in the southwest quadrant of the city.

Partnerships and More Partnerships

Due perhaps to the constant short-term turnover of leadership at the college, the college's foundation was active only minimally and had lost some of its members. Private giving had dwindled considerably; for a college of CSN's size, the foundation was achieving quite limited results. This foundation had never engaged in a capital campaign, and previous presidents had taken a hands-off approach to this work. The foundation has since been revamped, adding staff,

129

replacing the director with a trained and accomplished fundraiser, adding several new board members, raising membership contribution minimums, and installing modern computer hardware and software management tools.

Acknowledging limited finances as the number one barrier for community college students, the foundation created the First Course program, which provides free tuition for the first course in which a student enrolls at the college. With significant contributions from the faculty, the program has recently expanded into the First Course–First Book program. At all community speaking engagements, I now carry event-like tickets for a free course and a free textbook, and the popularity of these tickets has been astonishing.

In 2006, the CSN Foundation hosted a community gala and silent auction at the famous Caesars Palace Hotel and Casino on the Las Vegas strip. The purpose of the event was to raise funds (and friends) for needs-based student scholarships. Six hundred people attended the black-tie event; by evening's end, more than $350,000 had been raised for needy students. In its second year, the now-recurring annual gala featured community achievement awards with endowed scholarship funds named for the award recipients; proceeds matched those of the first year.

Revitalizing the foundation forged a much better link between the trustees and the institution. Indeed, many of the foundation trustees are now avid community advocates for the college. With strong community support and restored public confidence, the foundation is in the initial stages of its first-ever capital campaign—with a goal of some $50 million, destined to be among the larger community college campaigns in the country.

More Partnerships: The K–12 Connection

Part of the effort to restore public confidence in the community was an ambitious new K–12 partnership initiated by the college. During a decade of constant leadership turnover, sadly, the college had neglected much of its responsibility with the public school system while the school district had exploded into the fifth largest in the country. As in many states, the need for remedial education for recent high school graduates had prompted increased public scrutiny. Nationally, some 34% of high school graduates need remedial preparation on entering college, most often in mathematics and English; in Las Vegas, it is 37%. This need continues to leave lawmakers scratching their heads, arguing that they are paying twice for basic education. To some degree, they are right.

Many high school seniors become part of our fastest-growing number of part-time students. Many of these students complete most of their graduation requirements by the end of their junior year, leaving only two or three courses for their senior year. Some of these students fill the balance of their schedules with general education courses at the community college. Many other students simply waste much of their senior year, only to discover that on entry into college, they are required to take remedial courses before enrolling in college-level work.

In an effort to stem this tide, CSN and the Clark County School District entered into a partnership. The community college now tests public school students during their junior year for college placement. Those in need of remediation will be identified, and remedial courses will be offered at their high school during their senior year. The cost to these students will be minimal as the college and the school district will cover most of the expense.

As with many of the nation's community colleges, CSN's scope and breadth have expanded dramatically in recent years, although many high school juniors and seniors do not know about these positive changes. To counter this reality, CSN entered into another partnership with the school district. The college is installing kiosks in each of the high schools; the first will always be installed at cafeteria entrances for high-traffic visibility. Each kiosk is equipped with advanced technology and academic program information and has flat screen monitors that display short video clips about featured programs, available jobs, and anticipated wages. The college provides a career coach at these kiosks during school hours.

Partnerships: The Global Connection

CSN currently enrolls students from 72 countries and 48 states. Its international student program is recognized widely. International partnerships and faculty exchange did not develop until 2007, but now the college is in partnership discussions with colleges in several countries. Most recently, the college launched its China partnership with Jilin University. The first faculty assignment to China occurred in the spring of 2007. Another partnership is being developed with the University of Guadalajara Medical School in Mexico. This program aims to produce more bilingual nurses and promote CSN as a portal for entry into the University of Guadalajara Medical School.

CONCLUSION

Imagine a college that overcomes its troubles to unite in partnerships with the community, the schools, the state, and the world. Imagine a college that puts its blueprint for the future in front of every student and takes its information to the public schools, emphasizing the possibility of college for all. Imagine a college that publicly broadcasts its own data in contrast with the data of similar benchmark institutions. Imagine the broad vision behind true transformation and the commitment to achieve a sustainable, thriving educational culture in the face of monumental area growth. CSN has achieved these things and more.

REFERENCES

Collins, J. (2001). *Good to great.* New York: HarperCollins.

Community College of Southern Nevada (CCSN). (2005). *A vision of blue skies ahead: A blueprint for mapping CCSN's future.* Henderson, NV: Author.

Evelyn, J. (2005). A Las Vegas makeover. *The Chronicle of Higher Education, 51*(48), p. A22.

9

Cuyahoga Community College: Building One College With Second-Generation Technology

Jerry Sue Thornton

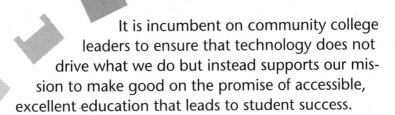

It is incumbent on community college leaders to ensure that technology does not drive what we do but instead supports our mission to make good on the promise of accessible, excellent education that leads to student success.

—*Jerry Sue Thornton, Cuyahoga Community College (OH)*

133

Cuyahoga Community College is the largest community college in Ohio, serving more than 50,000 students each year in the Cleveland area. With three campuses, two corporate centers, and 50 other off-campus sites, maintaining a singular identity could prove difficult. However, Tri-C, as the college is called, works hard to maintain a "one-college" vision.

Tri-C succeeds at being one college through technology, using it to unite rather than alienate students, faculty, and staff. The college leverages technological innovation to simplify communication processes, offer students the best classroom and curriculum technology, and streamline data management. Jerry Sue Thornton, the president, praises Tri-C's technology teams for their careful strategic planning and recognition that new technology requires nimble decision making, adoption, and adaptation. Combining "high-tech" with "high-touch" makes the perfect mix for student success.

TECHNOLOGY, PARTICULARLY THE INTERNET, HAS transformed higher education. The most significant shift over the past decade is the influx of the so-called technology generation. Having grown up with technology, this generation of community college students is extremely tech savvy. It is commonplace for one student to carry a menagerie of electronic gadgets—(e.g., cell phone, laptop, iPod, PDA)—or a single, integrated device consisting of several technologies. Often, students are more competent technologically than faculty members are, and their expectations change constantly. For example, faculty who e-mail students might encounter resistance from students who consider e-mail to be outdated; instant messaging is the preferred communication method for today's young people.

For community colleges, keeping up with this generation and the increasing complexity and pace of change presents many opportunities and challenges. As new technologies appear on the horizon, sifting through them and choosing those that are most appropriate presents a formidable challenge. Too often, unforeseen effects of new systems negatively affect an institution's effectiveness. Adding to this challenge, the rapid pace of technological change requires us to evaluate, select, and implement technologies quickly; to be effective, we must find new ways of working through bureaucratic systems that can slow decision making. Once we determine which technologies will add value, we must find creative ways to make the sizable investments in financial and human resources required to purchase, install, and support new systems. In addition, we must devote additional resources to training and development to help faculty stay abreast of new technologies.

Like most community colleges, Cuyahoga Community College (Tri-C), a large, multicampus district serving northeastern Ohio, must deliver high-quality educational and value-added services with dwindling financial resources, while serving a diverse student population and responding to increasing demands for information technology. Technology allows us to improve access to educational programming and academic support for our students. Technology allows us to enhance learning by accommodating differences in learning styles, reaching an increasingly diverse range of students, engaging students in new and compelling ways, increasing students' technical competencies through experiential learning, and preparing students to use technology in the workforce. Each year, we give projects that focus on learning and the student experience top priority for technology funding.

Technology also offers convenience and access. Blackboard technology and virtual office hours improve communication between students and faculty. Online registration (used by 70% of Tri-C students in the spring 2007 semester) eliminates the hassle and time involved in standing in line on campus, and distance learning or hybrid courses (combined online and traditional classroom) enable a wide range of students to participate in higher education. Because technology can reduce the number of students' face-to-face interactions with faculty and administrators, one might think that it also reduces the quality of personalized service we provide. Paradoxically, the reverse is true. Technology enhances our ability to connect with students and improves the overall student experience. For example, advisors can give thoughtful advice on the spot because they have instant access to students' transcripts and records.

Tri-C's technology successes include a new one-stop portal for students, faculty, and staff; smart classrooms designed to enhance interactive learning; patient simulators in the nursing laboratories; an expansive distance learning program; a leading-edge "institutional intelligence" data and analysis system; and a robust knowledge-management function. These technologies help us fulfill our vision of being one college across several campuses and make it easier for students to succeed.

TEACHING AND LEARNING

Community colleges are undergoing a significant change in their approach to education: a purposeful shift to student-centered learning. The instructor's role is changing from a dispenser of knowledge and information to a facilitator of student learning. Technology is a catalyst that makes this shift possible. Tri-C faculty use technology to support and promote student-centered learning and to satisfy the demands of students for high levels of interaction. Most faculty communicate by e-mail and instant messaging. Some faculty experiment with blogs, wikis, and net meetings; others hold virtual office hours using software that allows for real-time conversation with white board and chat capabilities.

Faculty members also use software applications to support classroom and distance learning. The most common applications include Blackboard for course development, teaching, and course management; Respondus for customized course assessments; Adobe Presenter (formerly Macromedia Breeze) for video-enhanced and voice-annotated PowerPoint presentations; Adobe Connect Professional for interactive web-conferencing; and Docutek E-Reserves for online management of course materials. In addition, Tri-C faculty experiment with a variety of new technologies and educational delivery methods to enhance learning. With podcasting technology, students receive and review classroom lectures anytime on their MP3 players; they also use their MP3 players to download supplemental instructional content such as e-books, articles, course packs, poetry, and music.

In a pilot program funded by a $5,000 Tri-C technology mini grant, several biology instructors took podcasting a step further and developed "vodcasts" (video-on-demand or VOD) to enhance site observations in the plant laboratory.

As students move from station to station observing bryophytes and angiosperms, they watch and listen to supplemental instructional videos on their MP3 players. VOD technology enables students to review instructional materials in a library, in a campus learning center, or on their own computers.

Tri-C's Academic Excellence Centers are housed on each campus to help instructors enhance their skills in integrating technology into classroom learning. At the centers, some faculty members are exploring the use of a student response system called "Instant Feedback!" With this application, students use clickers to record and present their responses in large lecture classes, much like on the television show, *Who Wants to Be a Millionaire?* This methodology provides instant feedback for the instructor and promotes interactive, participatory learning.

LEARNING STUDIOS

In the fall of 2007, students began taking classes in three "learning studios" or smart classrooms, which Tri-C is piloting on each campus. These flexible learning spaces are equipped with wireless connectivity, state-of-the art projection technology, and multimedia presentation tools such as movable SmartBoards. The studios are designed to facilitate the integration of an array of personal portable devices; each seat features a "docking station" into which students plug laptop computers, iPods, and cell phones for use during class. The studios are reconfigured easily for individual work, small-group discussions, or large-group presentations. Learning studios facilitate easier classroom scheduling and eliminate the frustration of having to schedule technology carts for use in the classroom; everything is already built in.

Cross-functional teams of faculty from each of Tri-C's three campuses, as well as representatives from faculty development, academic administration, and student affairs, helped to develop the studios. They conducted best-practice investigations and an appreciative inquiry visioning process to imagine the possibilities for a learning experience enhanced through interaction and collaboration. Then they were challenged to design fully integrated classrooms. The project began with classrooms for developmental English and math—emphasizing improving completion rates for students to move into college-level courses.

This design process can be applied to every area of the college campus, so students will have instant access to wireless connectivity and digital media the minute they step onto campus. In addition to creating learning environments, the design teams will work together to develop assignments and activities that engage students in collaborative projects, active research, case studies, shared authorship, and more.

We expect the learning studios will transform the way we teach and interact with students. As class discussions develop, instructors can take advantage of teachable moments by showing Web sites, audio/video clips, and graphics that bring a new dimension to the discussion. Students can use their laptops to look up additional information on the Internet as the lecturer speaks. Instructors may expand this activity to include the entire classroom. In a cutting-edge practice called "Google jockeying," for example, the instructor appoints a student "jockey" to conduct targeted searches on the Internet, supplementing the lecture as it is happening. The jockey's screen is projected so that the class can see the search results.

PATIENT SIMULATORS

In health-care education, there is no substitute for hands-on experience in a controlled environment, especially when mistakes with real patients can result in loss of life. This is where the magic of simulation comes into play. Tri-C's nursing laboratories are equipped with state-of-the-art simulators—much like those used to train aviators—that allow students to practice repeatedly until they achieve mastery in complex tasks, and high-quality health care becomes second nature. Data show that simulator use improves nursing students' success rates.

Controlled by intricate PC-based platforms, the simulators are almost as complex as the human body. For example, the human patient simulator (HPS) is a full-sized adult mannequin that breathes, has a heartbeat and pulse, blinks, has seizures, and displays human responses to procedures such as cardiopulmonary resuscitation, intravenous medication, catheterization, intubation, and trauma. The Emergency Care Simulator, a more portable simulator designed to train emergency healthcare responders, is as lifelike and authentic as the HPS (METI, 1995a, 1995b).

Both models are connected to medical gasses; can be connected to intravenous fluids, catheters, cardiac monitors, ventilators, and more; and can be outfitted with an array of traumatic injuries. They are equipped with a data recorder and a drug recognition system, employing a bar-code system to read the labels on syringes of administered medications so that a record is kept of the time, drug, dose, and appropriateness to the situation. The laptop-driven simulator can be connected to a variety of multimedia tools to enhance learning, and faculty can choose prepackaged scenarios or integrate customized scenarios into the curriculum. To decrease anxiety around using the HPS equipment, open-laboratory hours provide an opportunity to practice with operator assistance.

Simulators provide cognitive and procedural testing based on professional standards of practice, generating an evaluation report every time a student proceeds through a case. This report can be viewed by the student and instructor to monitor progress and highlight skills that need improvement. Students are videotaped while interacting with the mannequins, providing immediate feed-back about their performance. After reviewing the tapes, faculty members lead a debriefing to facilitate learning.

DISTANCE LEARNING

Distance learning aims to expand opportunity and access to education. It allows community colleges to serve multiple audiences, including students who want to supplement on-campus classroom learning with online learning, students whose schedules are too erratic to attend scheduled on-campus courses, local students who are serving overseas in the military, students who travel regularly, students who return from other colleges or universities during the summer and want to continue taking courses, and students in niche fields of study who may be nationally or internationally dispersed.

Not surprisingly, interest in distance and hybrid (combined classroom and online) learning opportunities is on the rise. In a 2006 study of more than 1,000 colleges and universities in the United States, online enrollment grew 35% from the previous year, from 2.3 million students in 2004, to 3.2 million in 2005 (Allen & Seaman, 2006). According to the study, the online enrollment growth rate is more than 10 times that projected by the National Center for Education Statistics for the general postsecondary student population. The perception of online learning is changing, with an increasing number of academic leaders viewing online educa-tion as critical to an institution's long-term strategy (Allen & Seaman, 2005).

In line with this trend, Tri-C has experienced rapid growth in distance learn-ing and has the second-largest online enrollment in the state of Ohio. Distance learning at Tri-C started in 1975, with one telecourse and 123 enrollments. In fiscal year 2006, Tri-C offered 536 courses and 818 sections with approximately 19,000 enrollees, representing more than 11% of the college's full-time enrollments. Tri-C's distance learning offerings consist of the following:

- Web-based instruction: full course delivered via the Internet
- Hybrid courses: combining online with face-to-face classroom instruction
- Telecourses: professionally produced, prerecorded video programs broadcast on the local PBS affiliate station
- Cable College: students view lectures live on cable television and participate in classroom discussion via telephone from their homes
- Interactive video: one course offered simultaneously on all three campuses and selected off-campus sites; students and faculty interacting with each other in real time

- Independent learning courses: students using a variety of instructional components (e.g., online, video, texts) to work independently on a course

Tri-C's distance learning group was selected for the 2005–2006 Innovation of the Year Award from the League for Innovation in the Community College, for developing two technology applications to enhance student success.

The first, LearnBB, is a customized application that facilitates the scheduling of classes, maintenance of enrollment information, and support for retention strategies such as student progress follow-ups for distance learning students who participate in an asynchronous Blackboard Web-orientation course. Data collected with this application indicate that students who participate in the orientation session are more likely to complete Web-based courses than students who do not.

The second is an application designed specifically for court reporting and captioning courses. This application allows faculty members to upload digitally recorded materials, which students use to practice dictation. This technology supports students to be more successful and enhances the quality of this competitive program.

As technology becomes more infused in all aspects of higher education, the lines between traditional classroom learning and distance learning are becoming blurred. For this reason and because demand for distance learning is growing so rapidly, it is imperative for community colleges to develop a strategy, devise a long-term plan, and invest in infrastructure to manage growth and quality concerns related to distance learning. Recognizing the importance of a one-college perspective on distance learning, Tri-C initiated a seven-committee distance-learning strategic planning process in summer 2006. The committee is charged with prioritizing distance learning initiatives, identifying preferred modalities, and recommending guidelines for best practices.

If we are to fulfill the promise of distance learning, we must meet several challenges. We must find ways to modify assessments appropriately for distance learning students, address intellectual property issues for distance courses, and enhance online learning communities to promote critical thinking and reflection. We also must institutionalize a campus culture of distance education and ensure that online courses are equivalent to classroom-based courses. Moreover, we must replicate traditional student services in online and self-service formats. This last point is a priority at Tri-C and is described in detail in the following section.

At Tri-C, our leadership team is laying the groundwork that will enable us to address these challenges. In 2006, we engaged faculty and administrators in a distance learning planning process. Working together on seven special interest group task forces, we explored the current state of distance learning at Tri-C, the national landscape regarding distance learning, and opportunities to expand and improve our distance learning offerings. In town hall meetings, we engaged others in the conversations about distance learning. Distance learning was a topic of our American Association of University Professors faculty negotiations this year and has led to the development of a faculty and administrative joint committee to explore issues around academic quality and distance learning policies.

STUDENT SERVICES

Like many community colleges, Tri-C will be working over the next decade to improve and expand student support services (e.g., applications, registration, and tuition payment systems, as well as value-added services such as degree audit systems) via fully integrated online student information systems. Enhanced offerings such as online advising and counseling and virtual student associations will begin to take hold over the next couple of years. In the fall of 2006, Tri-C deployed a new portal, "my Tri-C space," for 3,500 faculty and staff. In April 2007, we deployed it to 40,000 credit and noncredit students; approximately 25,000 credit students received college-supported e-mail accounts for the first time.

The portal is a necessary investment to ensure student success and the ongoing collaboration of faculty and staff in our one-college vision. Operating on a single-user-ID and password, the portal is a virtual front door to resources that students and employees use on a regular basis, including links to registration, grades, financial aid, library, academic services, Blackboard, personal and group announcements, campus news, and federal government sites. Students can customize portal pages to fit their needs and interests.

The my Tri-C space home page is personalized, with information pushed to a student's account on logging into the system. Here, current course schedules, financial aid awards, and account balances are displayed automatically, giving students easy access to information and improving communication between students, faculty, and administrators. The my Tri-C space student e-mail account has become the official communication method between the college and students. In addition, my Tri-C space provides access to degree-audit software that provides students with the ability to track their own progress toward a degree. In the spring of 2007, more than 70% of Tri-C students registered online. We anticipate that this percentage will increase with the increased usage of my Tri-C space.

For faculty and staff, the my Tri-C space portal reduces the need for global e-mail messages and allows for more targeted announcements. Employees also are using my Tri-C space to complete their timesheets, submit student grades, and register for staff development programs and training sessions. In addition, the human resources department has devised a way to give new employees a warm welcome to the college. The department posts photographs of all new employees every 2 weeks.

BEHIND THE SCENES: ADMINISTRATION

Institutional Intelligence

In today's world of accountability, a public institution of higher education must be able to facilitate and evaluate student success by asking questions such as, How do we know that students are learning? and What impact does distance learning course delivery have on students, faculty, costs, facilities, image, and the like? What expenses are associated with adding a new program? What is the consequence of flat or declining enrollment?

Typical metrics such as annual compliance reports, 5- to 10-year accreditation reviews, or enrollment headcount reports are not sufficient for today's leaders. This is especially true in the community college environment, where a timely and collaborative response to economic and civic changes is expected. We need a comprehensive system to convert data into information, information into knowledge, and knowledge into wisdom—empowering decision makers to respond rapidly and effectively to student, faculty, administration, college, and community needs.

To this end, Tri-C is an early pioneer among higher education institutions in the application of "business intelligence." Business intelligence software (e.g., SAS, Cognos, or Business Objects) provides the tools for gathering, storing, analyzing, and providing access to data to facilitate decision making based on accurate, current, and relevant information. To distinguish the differences from corporate applications of business intelligence and infuse the approach within the college environment, Tri-C renamed the methodology "institutional intelligence." Further, to support our one-college vision, we branded the initiative "One Institutional Intelligence." One Institutional Intelligence will allow college leaders to summarize data into multidimensional views for querying and reporting and to create and track performance metrics. Ultimately, our goal is to create a comprehensive system of analytics that will support decision making that is proactive, focused at multiple management levels, and improves institutional performance and accountability. In addition, it will help us to

- Perform repeatable compliance reports with ease
- Enhance access and service for faculty and staff
- Leverage technology assets for expanded access and service
- Unify the digital campus

Committing to and organizing around this vision requires support and sponsorship from all parts of the organization, notably executive involvement. This should not be viewed as a technology project to develop reports. Institutional intelligence is a transformative initiative that puts enormous knowledge directly into the hands of decision makers at all levels of the organization. Combining personal experience with this knowledge leads us more quickly to the top of the institutional intelligence pyramid—for example, data, information, knowledge, and wisdom.

The challenge of corralling all the data is daunting. At Tri-C, our data warehouse that feeds the institutional intelligence analytics engine that comprises our enterprise resource planning system, our curriculum management system, and more than 20 other separate applications and databases that are used and maintained by more than 40,000 people across six locations. The institutional intelligence software sits "on top of" these many software applications and allows us to organize the data sources, reach into them, and perform advanced analytical operations. The potential applications are endless, from student retention to employee recruiting, from alumni analysis to financial projections. In addition to these internal software applications, institutional intelligence technology can access external data sources (e.g., school district enrollment demographics, labor market data), allowing us to collaborate more effectively and rapidly with our partnering community organizations and leaders.

The first specific institutional intelligence application for Tri-C involved implementing a financial intelligence solution. In August 2005, the college's executive leadership identified needs and opportunities related to financial reporting and budgeting functions. At that time, these processes were deemed cumbersome within the existing enterprise resource planning environment; they offered limited financial reporting capabilities and were time-consuming, labor intensive, and prone to human error. College managers could not access the financial information they needed about various functions or individual lines of business by course, program, campus, or other specific budgetary unit. Furthermore, the reports were driven by historical metrics and performance and were not forward focused.

To respond to these challenges, Tri-C implemented the institutional intelligence solution in December 2005. Initial implementation focused on financial reporting functionality for the auxiliary and quasi-auxiliary operations—the college's Work Force and Economic Development Division (WEDD)—as well as the bookstore, food service, and other auxiliary operations. Through this effort, the detailed operating income statement for WEDD, all other auxiliaries, and quasi-auxiliaries is now available in a matter of moments at the close of the financial period. Before implementing institutional intelligence, this specific compilation was extremely labor-intensive, requiring several full-time employees working for nearly a week. Now these reporting functionalities have been applied to other financial reporting areas collegewide, with data available for analytical purposes going back several years.

The next steps for Tri-C involve moving beyond these reporting functions into more elaborate forecasting, metrics, and enhanced analytical research efforts. We are pleased that the organization is embracing institutional intelligence, as evidenced by the sophisticated requests our Office of Institutional Research receives from campus presidents, academic deans, and other college leaders. Once we have built the necessary capacity, we intend to use institutional intelligence to conduct research that links internal data with external sources such as census data, labor market projections, state enrollment reports, and K–12 demographics to carry out a variety of forecasting functions. With these tools, we hope to answer questions about the interest and intentions of prospective students, reasons for student attrition, ways to improve course scheduling, and strategies for advising students on course selection to improve progress toward graduation. We also aspire to generate more sophisticated analyses of financial trends and patterns, cost analyses, and revenue projections.

We will continue to implement One Institutional Intelligence through 2007 and 2008, moving to the academic and student affairs areas, followed by finance and human resources. Ultimately, our goal is to embed a culture of analytics and advanced decision making into the fabric of the college's collective thinking.

KNOWLEDGE MANAGEMENT

Tri-C also has been a pioneer in bringing knowledge management (another corporate practice) to higher education. For the past 7 years, we have worked to leverage and share knowledge to improve our ability to collaborate, learn, and innovate. The purpose of knowledge management is to

- Know individually what we know collectively and apply it
- Know collectively what we know individually and reuse it
- Know what we don't know and learn it together in community (Havens & Knapp, 1999, p. 27)

Knowledge management (KM) is "the creation, capture, organization, access and use of knowledge" (Logan, 2006). KM is as much about people as it is about technology, and it does not happen without collaboration. KM encompasses explicit knowledge found in databases and shared drives, as well as tacit knowledge found in the experiences of people who have made sense of information and made it actionable, thus enabling learning and innovation to take place.

Tri-C leverages knowledge through "communities of practice, a method of connecting people with common needs and interests about a particular topic to share ideas, insights and information; address challenges and advise each other; learn and laugh together; create processes, frameworks, templates, etc.; and own and maintain content" (Reis & Eugene, 2006). Each community identifies the critical data, information, and knowledge needed to improve and innovate, then stores the knowledge on a team Intranet site, or portal. These collaborative team sites include document libraries, lists of key contacts or subject-matter experts, online discussion forums, and meeting spaces.

The technology team site includes information related to all current and past technology projects in the college. It is used largely by our Executive Technology Steering Committee to monitor projects. In addition, users throughout the college can learn about current and past technology innovations. The curriculum development team site documents the curriculum development life cycle, organized according to phase and step within the cycle. The content on this site is maintained by a knowledge coordinator and subject matter experts whose job duties include conveying and sharing curriculum development knowledge. Since 2000, Tri-C team sites have increased in number from 2 to more than 70. Our strategic initiative to become one college has created a vision for sharing what we know and collaborating, and our communities of practice are engaged actively in manifesting that vision. The team sites currently average 75,000 hits per month from an average of 550 users.

Other areas in which KM has proved effective include organizing and maintaining shared computer drives using Microsoft Office SharePoint Portal Server technology; streamlining surveys and forms; and managing our Internet presence through a collegewide, cross-functional Web Council, which sets the tone, strategy, and standards for the institutional face we present to the community at large. In the future, we intend to develop an expanded content-management system, an expert directory in which people can identify colleagues with specific expertise, an Extranet where we can collaborate with third-party partners, and more efficient records-management and inventory-control systems.

The Funding Challenge

In a world that is "turned on" 24/7 and is pushed to do increasingly more with less, organizations across all industries struggle with increasing technology costs, despite the promise that technology can make our lives more efficient, with reduced costs. Across the board, technology costs are rising by 10% to 12% annually. Tri-C s information technology budget funds the following:

- Capital improvements
- Hardware (servers and PCs/laptops)
- Networking and communications
- Software licensing
- Staff

In addition, funds are dedicated each year for initiatives that address software improvements and new technologies.

Technology is important and necessary in meeting our educational and training mission, but the cost often is prohibitive. For example, the human patient simulator used in our nursing program costs $235,000. The high cost makes it difficult for most community colleges to purchase technology that could affect the quality of their programming.

The my Tri-C space project was a large initiative that required additional hardware, software, and outside services for the initial implementation in mid-2006; it will incur significant additional costs within the first 2 years, with some big-ticket items remaining to be covered by other budgets. Although the most expensive components of this project were the hardware and software, indirect items for the portal—data storage (which will need to increase by 8 times) and help desk support (which will need to increase by 10 times)—also were costly.

The implementation of the One Institutional Intelligence project involved an initial significant investment for software, hardware, and consulting services. In addition, numerous internal staffing resources dedicated to the program must be considered in the total cost. Also contributing to the increasing cost of technology is the investment we must make to keep existing equipment running smoothly. Flashy implementation projects aside, the bulk of the information technology department's work lies in maintaining and upgrading existing systems, upgrading databases, fixing desktop and laptop computers, supporting phone systems, and installing software patches.

For a community college to leverage effectively the opportunities technology offers, it must accept the responsibility to fund them appropriately. Tri-C has established explicit governance practices that ensure transparency of all technology spending and provide a mechanism to educate the decision-making bodies on emerging technologies. Our objective is to integrate an authoritative—and thus nimble—approach to funding technology initiatives with a collaborative approach to decision making. The college's executive technology steering committee, the body that makes decisions around technology resource allocation, regularly invites experts to its meetings to discuss emerging technologies. This group includes leadership across all units of the college. All discussions regarding information technology include aligning funding with institutional priorities. Specifically, project funding is tied to measurable examples of how the project will promote the mission, vision, and values of the college. The executive technology steering committee approves budgets for technology initiatives but, more importantly, guides the college in continuous dialogue about the strategic use of technology, emphasizing transparency of the project approval and management process.

Agility is essential, as well. Because technology advances at a rapid pace and often involves a shorter time for approval and implementation, it is not always possible to anticipate innovative technology projects several months in advance. We must be more responsive to the dynamic nature of innovation in today's rapidly changing environment. Our leadership team stays current with technology by tapping into the many pockets of knowledge and expertise inside the college. Beyond the Tri-C campus, our involvement in the League for Innovation provides many opportunities to share information and ideas with other community colleges. We discuss how to use innovative technology, and we visit one another's campuses to see technology in action.

At Tri-C, we assess classroom technology needs annually and fund them through the capital budgeting process. However, because staying current with the latest classroom technologies is a strategic necessity, the college is considering a permanent allocation for this expense in annual operating budgets. This would be a major structural change in the college's budgetary process, reflecting the need to recognize a variety of technology costs as fixed, regularly recurring, and essential to fulfilling the organization's mission.

At Tri-C, we endeavor to find creative solutions to our technology funding dilemmas. In the my Tri-C space example previously mentioned, we partnered with OneCommunity, a nonprofit Internet service provider consortium, to purchase raw storage capacity on an as-needed basis. This strategy allowed us to forego a significant up-front cost for storage that may have gone partially unused until the full e-mail deployment had been completed. In another example, we consolidated a variety of telephone service plans into one converged communications network; this move allowed us to optimize design, infrastructure, and buying power across numerous facilities, locations, and departments across the college.

CONCLUSION

In the years ahead, technology systems that are adaptable, flexible, multifaceted, and highly interactive hold the most promise for effective student-centered education in community colleges. At the same time, providing high-tech at the expense of high-touch could have detrimental effects for faculty and students. Seldom does technology stand alone. We have learned the importance of determining what we hope to accomplish with a particular type of technology before making a decision to allocate significant funding to it. Although it is good to be on the leading edge, being on the "bleeding edge" can be time-consuming, frustrating, and expensive and can affect return on investment negatively. Another lesson is to know that the organizational culture is ready to embrace a new technology before adopting it; if it is, success requires that we invest significant resources in education and training.

Given these considerations, community college leaders must make sure that technology does not drive what we do but instead supports our mission to make good on the promise of accessible, excellent education that leads to student success. If we are successful with the efforts described here, in the next few years, Tri-C will have achieved its mission to provide access to quality higher education in an interactive learning environment to anyone who truly wants it by removing the barriers of time, geography, and inconvenience. In our vision for the future, our students will be able to learn anytime, anyplace, and at their own pace, while collaborating with other students.

Colleges will offer flexible or virtual learning environments in a variety of technical fields that previously would have required on-site training. Our use of instructional technology will have matured to be almost completely transparent. All students—on campus and off—will learn in a rich, immersive educational setting that offers effortless navigation and use of services and resources. Faculty will employ a variety of technologies that enable them to adapt the learning environment and curriculum to their preferred pedagogical style or their students' preferred learning styles. All faculty and staff will have easy access to relevant content that is transferred easily to the compatible digital devices of their choice. Furthermore, our use of technology resources will set the standard for our students' expectations of technology in the private and public sectors.

If we realize this vision, we will leverage technology fully to increase student success as defined by the traditional measures such as retention, course completion, and graduation. We will improve the ability of our students to succeed in ways that transcend those traditional definitions. With access to global information, communication, and collaboration, students will understand better the world in which they live and work. They will be able to use technology better in all aspects of their lives, and they will have a competitive edge in the workforce.

REFERENCES

Allen, I. E., & Seaman, J. (2005). *Growing by degrees: Online education in the United States.* Needham, MA: Sloan-C.

Allen, I. E., & Seaman, J. (2006). *Making the grade: Online education in the United States.* Needham, MA: Sloan-C.

Havens, C., & Knapp, E. (1999). Easing into knowledge management. *Strategy & Leadership, 27,* 4–9.

Logan, D. (2006, February 3). *Using technology to create and capture knowledge.* Retrieved May 15, 2007, from www.gartner.com

Medical Education Technologies, Inc. (METI). (1995a) *ECS user guide* (6th ed.). Sarasota, FL: Author.

Medical Education Technologies, Inc. (METI). (1995b). *HPS user guide* (4th ed.). Sarasota, FL: Author.

Reis, F. W., & Eugene, A. C. (2006). *Knowledge management in practice: The Cuyahoga Community College experience.* Phoenix, AZ: League for Innovation in the Community College.

10

Community College of Denver: Triumph Over Challenge

Christine Johnson

A community college president's insight comes from living with the institution 24/7, thinking about and analyzing every aspect of what does and does not and what will and will not create greater institutional effectiveness. Every day, students, faculty, staff, community, colleagues, and educational leaders provide the answers for those who lead community colleges.

—*Christine Johnson, former president of Community College of Denver (CO)*

The Community College of Denver (CCD) recently celebrated 40 years of success. Its accomplishments illuminate a strong belief in the people of Denver and their potential to learn, despite challenges. CCD has not only survived the ups and downs of Colorado's crippled state funding system but has also continued to grow during the leanest years. During Christine Johnson's presidency, CCD became a college where belonging to a minority group and testing into developmental education classes became predictors of graduation, not failure. Each person's success continues to be the primary focus of staff and faculty. The diverse programs offered by CCD make higher education more accessible to ever more people while relying on less state funding than ever before.

Johnson believes that community support is the key to CCD's success. Creative partnering reinforces CCD's ability to create success stories, new programs, and scholarships at a time when other colleges in Colorado are fighting to keep their doors open. By thinking globally about serving a community and educating the whole student, Johnson and her collegiate family have made Denver an example of success in the hardest of times and places.

Author's Note. Credit for innovation and progress at CCD is owed to many, but I would like to specifically acknowledge Elaine Baker, Gary Cooper, Ramzi Munder, Rafael Rodriguez, Ken Swiney, and Wei Zhou for strengthening CCD every day through their commitment and contributions to the college.

A S THE COMMUNITY COLLEGE OF Denver (CCD) commemorated its 40th anniversary in 2007, it celebrated its abundance of successes while boldly embracing the daunting challenges of its future. One of 13 two-year institutions under the auspices of the Colorado Community College System, CCD is an urban commuter college. It shares the 127-acre downtown Denver Auraria Campus with the University of Colorado at Denver Health Sciences Center and Metropolitan State College of Denver. Auraria is the higher-education base for more than 42,000 students annually. This unique partnership includes shared classrooms, faculty, and some academic and student support programs; a 700,000 volume regional library; physical education and recreational facilities; an historic student union; and opportunities to structure creative transitions between the college and its 4-year campus partners. CCD also operates four branch campus locations within the city and county of Denver.

CCD is a comprehensive, learning-centered college, with the most ethnically and socioeconomically diverse student population in all of Colorado higher education, a distinction it has held for nearly two decades. The student population in FY 2006 totaled nearly 14,000 (headcount), and there were more than 5,000 full-time equivalent (FTE) employees. Its composition mirrored that of the City and County of Denver service area: 26% Hispanic, 15% Black, 6% Asian/Pacific Islander, 2% American Indian/Alaskan Native, 44% White, 6% international students, and 1% unknown. Sixty-one percent of the total population is female, 57% are the first in their families to attend college, and 50% of all CCD students qualify for financial aid. The average age is 28 years, with 47% older than 24. CCD is the only Hispanic-serving institution (HIS) in the seven-county metro-Denver area.

In 40 years of increasingly rapid change, CCD's mission has reflected a steadfast belief in its institutional power to transform lives through a solid foundation of learning programs and strategies that promote access and success for underserved and, more recently, academically underprepared students. The college character is focused on overcoming challenges and beating the odds. Respecting diversity and expecting student success remain the college's core values. Coupled with enhancing faculty teaching skills to serve a diverse student population and a long-range commitment to eliminate differences in outcomes for students of color, CCD became a pioneer among the nation's community colleges.

Creating and maintaining a premier education for students in the context of the changing political climate, fiscal constraints, expectations of the workforce, and increasing accountability are constant challenges that require commitment, flexibility, and an ongoing commitment to quality. The college achieved these goals one step at a time, building on the expertise created and lessons learned at each step, beginning with the creation of a nationally recognized developmental education program, case management system, and the Teaching Learning Center professional development program. Through Title III grants, the college implemented a first-of-its-kind learning laboratory for the developmental education program; developed critical instructional and student support interventions to increase retention, and systemically improved the collegewide cultural climate, with an emphasis on using outcomes and data to measure effectiveness. With an HSI grant, CCD focused on improving Hispanic, low-income, and first-generation student retention, graduation, and transfer. The college implemented the first learning communities in the state; created an individualized educational case management team approach to retaining and promoting students into science, technology, engineering, and math (STEM) majors; and developed a computerized database system for tracking student progress and measuring student and college success.

In the last few years, the college continued to build on this integration of educational case management and instructional excellence with new programs that take on the next set of challenges: (1) reducing the time that students spend in developmental education by using acceleration strategies and (2) increasing the success of low-skilled students who enter the college through adult education and GED programs. With funding from the Lumina Foundation for Education and the Mott Foundation's support in Breaking Through, a joint project of National Council of Workforce Education and Jobs for the Future, CCD continues to adapt and refine its expertise and chart new territory in the challenges that face today's students.

CCD modeled learning-college practices and created change strategies to realize its workforce mission: linking demand-side labor-development principles and integrating college programs with workforce and economic development policy and priorities. Efforts included the Essential Skills partnership (to connect those eligible for Temporary Assistance for Needy Families, the college and employers) to create career pathways to move participants from public assistance to employment. Another effort was Quick$tart Careers that matched Workforce Investment Act customers with certificates and degrees for high-demand occupations that pay a living wage. As the focus of workforce efforts shifts to regional economic strategies, CCD has continued to be at the forefront of innovation with a recently funded career-pathway initiative, supported by the Metro Denver Workforce Innovation in Regional Economic Development (WIRED) project.

Years of countless efforts by numerous faculty, staff, students, and external constituencies have boosted CCD's percentage of minorities among graduates and transfer students to more than 50%. Cohort tracking indicates no significant difference in student success on the basis of race, ethnicity, age, or gender. The historical evolution of CCD continues to ensure and increase access and success, eliminate the performance gap between groups, and ensure CCD's reputation as an equal-opportunity college.

ENVIRONMENTAL FACTORS DEFINE THE 21ST CENTURY

The military phrase, "VUCA world," refers to a time of international volatility, uncertainty, chaos, and ambiguity. The phrase aptly describes the last decade in Colorado higher education, especially for community colleges. VUCA forces in Colorado arose from an economic decline that began in 2000, and grew exponentially after the terrorist attacks of September 11, 2001. The downturn crippled higher education budgets and brought institutions to their knees. Ambiguity from policymakers and Colorado citizens promoted the uncertainty of community colleges' survival. Unpredictable annual state budgeting caused chaos and uncertainty among higher education employees, from classified staff, to faculty members, to presidents (e.g., what programs, what departments, who would be cut?).

Cuts were made to keep the doors open. With every program or service closure and subsequent layoffs, those remaining personnel felt the pain through added responsibilities, longer working hours, and no or minimal annual pay increases. Every disruption in college programs, personnel, and services generated chaos among students. Uncertainty, which has been the watchword for low-income, first-generation, and immigrant students in Colorado for years, became more pronounced. Uncertainty about access to the American dream and moving up the economic ladder was their reality. Without an education, their ability to provide for themselves and their families was in doubt.

So far in the 21st century, external forces colliding with community colleges nationwide have been sweeping in scope, speed, and direction. To detail all of the forces is beyond the scope of this chapter. However, some of the most obvious standouts include leadership and educational vision modifications at all levels, demography, competition, fiscal crises, technology, technological and generational learning divides, constant redefinition of accountability, human resources, and organizational capacity. Beginning in 2000, as the presidential leadership changed at CCD, the leadership and educational vision also changed in the top posts in the federal, state, and city governments; in the Colorado Community College System's president's office; and Denver Public Schools (DPS). Accountability in education became a focal point nationally with the new federal administration. Colorado's new governing body quickly followed suit, putting greater emphasis on standardized quality indicator measures to meet the state's goals and expectations. However, through standardization, the governor and the Colorado Commission on Higher Education made the playing field even more uneven. Urban and rural community colleges were pitted against one another and against state colleges and universities.

Between 1982 and 1992, Colorado passed significant taxpayer relief legislation. Although this legislation was successful initially, beginning in 2001, migration into the state leveled off and even declined in some areas. This caused severe budget shortfalls in the state. The crises worsened as the effects of Amendment 23, approved by voters in 2000, required the Colorado General Assembly to increase base per-pupil funding for K–12 education annually, by inflation plus 1 percentage point through 2010 and by inflation thereafter.

CCD counteracted the budget decreases of nearly 30% from 2001 through 2004, with increased enrollments of more than 30% during the same period. Two years running, the college claimed top honors for increased enrollment among all 28 institutions of higher education. Although unfilled vacancies diminished full-time staffing, and increased tuition and fees put a greater financial burden on students, perseverance created greater educational access. The 2004 Colorado General Assembly recognized CCD for its efficiency, its innovation, its partnerships, and its standards of excellence.

State funding for higher education dropped from 20% in the late 1990s to 10% by 2006. Colorado now ranks 49th among the states for funding to higher education (Colorado Succeeds, 2006). In 2005, the state legislated and implemented the College Opportunity Fund (COF). COF supports higher education by paying a per-credit-hour stipend to the institution for students attending, rather than a set amount for FTE accounting. Students must apply for COF and designate a home institution. The stipend amount, legislated annually, comes directly to the school but appears as a tuition credit on student bills.

TRANSFORMATION BEYOND TRADITION

Tradition, along with a compelling vision and a passionate belief in its mission and values, are the keys to CCD's success. CCD is a place where ordinary people do extraordinary things. With the advent of the 21st century, however, it became clear that tradition could no longer sustain the college: CCD faced a $1 million deficit and zero-balance state-required reserve, declining enrollment, and continued state budget cuts.

But beginning in March 2001, a transformation began to take place. CCD began evolving beyond its traditions by strengthening existing programs and creating new programs to meet anticipated community, state, and national needs. CCD realized that it would have to raise consciousness about its value among all constituents, internal and external to the college: the college; public schools; local, state, regional, and national education boards; commissions; taskforces; and work groups. To fulfill the role, CCD would have to

- Reach into the high schools and provide a bridge to achievement and to college
- Create transitions and collegewide support systems for students who normally would not make it through the educational continuum
- Understand the economic role of the college and build strong connections to the workforce.

Shaping state and national educational policy quickly became the norm at CCD. The president and members of the administrative team, faculty, and staff helped to advance an external dialogue on the importance of community colleges in Colorado. College representatives participated on the Governor's Blue Ribbon Panel on Higher Education; helped the Colorado Commission on Higher Education shape a new accountability system; and worked with, not against, legislative processes to ensure city officials and state legislators recognized the economic role of community colleges.

COLORING OUTSIDE THE LINES: MAXIMIZING OPPORTUNITIES FOR GREATER STRENGTH

In executive orders in 2001, the college was expected to show a zero deficit and progress toward building a reserve within 2 years, in addition to meeting new and more stringent accountability measures. From that time forward, it was no longer business as usual. CCD's administration needed to work with faculty and staff to combine their extraordinary talents, uphold core values, preserve the learning-centered experience, and design the CCD vision to advance the city and state's economic future. In short, the college would need to create magic. The college established three goals:

- Increase student learning and success
- Change organizational culture to support learning
- Attain and maintain fiscal stability through increased enrollment

All three goals carried the same weight; none was more important than another was. In fact, the goals were interdependent. Increased enrollment meant increased FTE funding from the state. Increased funding would allow maintenance and creation of programs to support access, learning, and success. Changing the culture to support learning would enable and ensure greater student success through academic and student services support.

Strategic collegewide, team-based planning helped realign limited resources and drive the change. The staff redefined its work and relationships to better integrate and leverage public and private resources, align educational sectors, create greater student personalization for learning, and engage multiple communities and publics to expand its reach. Fiscal year 2002 was a year of magic! Hard work and sacrifice, enrollment growth of 7%, and renewal of community commitment enabled CCD to beat the state budget mandate by 1 year. The emphasis for growing enrollment was not on numbers but on creating programs of access to higher education for those people within the college's service area who did not know, or did not believe, that continued education was necessary or within their reach. Reaching out to diverse populations of prospective students was essential to CCD's access strategies. Populations included public school students and dropouts, GED students and graduates, adults (aged 21 and older), displaced and laid-off workers, and incumbent workers who required upgraded skills to keep up with the changing workforce.

Changing the organizational culture to support learning and meet the established goals was the mandate. As a whole, CCD underwent a process of exploring what was working well. The next step was to connect and expand successful strategies to create a shared vision of the future. Through introspection, the college was able to meet an internal need for cultural continuity, institute efficiencies to do more with less (funding and staff), and build new systems to meet external change forces.

Instructional reorganization came first. Learning centers replaced the historic higher education departments. Academic deans became responsible for multiple centers, encouraging systemic implementation of the educational plan. The centers included business and technology; educational advancement; health, math, and science; language, arts, and behavioral sciences; and learning outreach. Greater educational access was accomplished by expanding and promoting evening, weekend, online, accelerated, open-entry/open-exit, and FlexLearning (one third online and two thirds in classroom) learning options. Greater student success was accomplished through assessment of enrollment and proper placement. Outdated programs were discontinued, and new programs that addressed 21st-century workforce needs were created.

Innovation within student services followed to support the new learning paradigm. Decision making was devolved, and teams of employees (faculty, staff, and administrators) closest to students were empowered to make customer-service decisions to promote student retention and success. The Student Tracking Committee (now the Student Success Committee) was created to identify and remove barriers to student access, retention, and success. The cross-representational group of faculty, staff, and administrators met monthly as a whole and semimonthly in special teams to study and plan in-depth solutions and quick fixes to student access and success issues and to make recommendations to the president's executive staff for implementation. Tracking data advised the process, from the Community College

Survey of Student Engagement and scholarly publications, to institutional research, student success outcome measures, and student focus groups.

Goal-oriented solutions were implemented immediately. Student and enrollment services shifted funding to create a recruitment and student outreach program, student orientation programs, and express enrollment to promote access and success. The institutional advancement department began oversight of an expanded, bilingual customer call center that supported student access, recruitment, retention, and success. A three-tiered student services and instruction-integrated advising and early-warning program, coupled with an enhanced, collegewide educational case management system, helped ensure student access, retention, and success.

Institutional insight focused on the college's ability to change and provided motivation through inclusive activities. The president's executive staff was expanded to include the executive directors of human resources and institutional advancement along with the vice presidents of instruction, student services, and administration. The weekly executive staff meetings, open to all employees, were hosted by the deans within their various centers. An executive staff summary was included in weekly electronic *Inside CCD* newsletters.

Semiannual convocations became opportunities for the college community to learn from state and national educational leaders, study outcomes to make data-directed decisions, and set annual goals, and, in 2002, to draft the application for the Academic Quality Improvement Project (AQIP) from its accrediting organization, The Higher Learning Commission of the North Central Association of Colleges and Schools. After acceptance into AQIP, a cross-sectional group of more than 40 college employees developed and recommended strategic priorities to meet CCD's established goals (listed previously). The priorities were as follows:

- Develop an early- and middle-college model
- Create strategic campus and venue expansions
- Develop a model planning process, incorporating AQIP criteria as touchstones
- Strengthen community by building relationships and partnerships that target regional labor markets, focus on employment sectors, and combine education, training, and on-the-job learning opportunities
- Ensure Colorado's economic stability and enhance and protect our nation's tenets of freedom through educating today's workers for tomorrow's workforce

Finding resources to achieve these objectives became a consequential priority. Led by institutional advancement, collegewide grant-writing teams increased grants and contract revenues from 27% in 2000 to 41.4% in 2006 and a dollar total of $17,461,560. In 2001, a revitalized and expanded foundation began fundraising in earnest to develop partnerships with private and public organizations and to secure and invest resources that contribute to the well-being of CCD students and the community. Between FY 2002 and FY 2006, the CCD Foundation Inc. more than doubled its scholarship endowment to $838,436, and resolved to break the million dollar mark in FY 2007.

CCD has maximized opportunities for students and leveraged resources by building alliances, establishing funding coalitions, and promoting growth in all its relationships. Internally, the college supports faculty and staff through professional development opportunities, shares institutional and community data to encourage creation of new programs across all disciplines, and advocates innovation in its student services and support programs. Externally, CCD is methodical and unceasing in its efforts to forge partnerships with and among K–12 school districts; government agencies at all levels; state and regional institutions of higher education; local, state, and national foundations; and the business and industry sectors. For example, between 2001 and 2003, 12 different learning initiatives took place—involving more than 25 government, business, and industry partners—with a 2-year goal of tripling the number of CCD nursing graduates. CCD surpassed the goal in 2003, increasing program enrollment by 25% and graduating 356 nursing students. Since then, additional training options and partnerships have helped expand educational access and retention to maintain and increase the number of nursing graduates each successive year.

Quick$tart Careers, sponsored by the Denver Mayor's Office of Workforce Development (now the Denver Office of Economic Development—DOED), leveraged Workforce Investment Act and government training dollars and provided CCD's certified nurse aid and licensed practical nurse (LPN) training to displaced and laid-off workers. Exempla Healthcare, CCD, and DOED partnered in training entry-level employees to move into next-level health careers. CCD provided worksite education; Exempla provided employee tuition through a DOED grant. CCD, the University of Phoenix, and Meridian Retirement Communities leveraged training, marketing, and program public relations activities to enroll students into CCD's LPN program. LPNs who continued to earn an associate degree in nursing (ADN) to registered nursing (RN) degree transferred all credits to the University of Phoenix to complete a bachelor's degree in nursing. To meet CCD's nursing instructor shortage, Meridian and University of Phoenix provided several tuition-paid scholarships to students in the University of Phoenix master's program, who, in return, contracted to teach CCD undergraduate nursing courses for 2 years.

By means of collaboration between CCD and several other entities (e.g., HealthONE, the U.S. and Colorado departments of labor, and the Colorado Office of Workforce Development), CCD condensed the traditional 24-month ADN program into a 16-month ADN program. The Colorado Community College Online program created the state's first online health academy with CCD's advanced placement online nursing program. CCD provided worksite nursing training, and Rose Medical Center provided 20 full scholarships for Rose employees to enter the nursing program. CCD, Regis University, Presbyterian/St. Luke's Medical Center, and HealthONE formed an educational partnership to prepare HealthONE employees as bachelor's degree nurses: CCD provided the required prenursing and ADN courses, and Regis University provided the additional 60 credit hours toward the students' bachelor's degrees. HealthONE provided employee scholarships, tuition assistance, and other incentives for future contracted service at HealthONE facilities.

Since 2001, the demand-driven workforce model for learning has set the course for CCD. Current and future programs are based on national, state, regional, and local job surveys and economic indicators. It is a "field of dreams" theory, supported by a supply-side equation. If CCD provides educational training today for tomorrow's workforce, students will come. Government, business, and organizational partners will come. Funders will come. Thus, the cycle of maximizing opportunity is perpetuated.

NEXT-GENERATION INNOVATION NARROWS THE GAP

Between 2001 and 2004, CCD grew enrollment by more than 30%, taking top position among all Colorado institutions of higher education in 2003 and 2004. By 2006, its community nexus numbered more than 200 partners. Inclusive educational strategies allowed a greater number of people to participate in the American dream. Nevertheless, if statistics were predictors, CCD should have a high dropout rate, given the challenging population it serves. Instead, its in-semester retention rate in special population support programs averages 80%, and the college's persistence rate from fall to spring semester for first-time, full-time, degree-seeking freshmen is nearly 70%. The FY 2006 1-year retention rate (fall to fall) for first-time, full-time students was more than 56% for CCD's total minority cohort.

More can be done to increase student success and create a workforce that can broadly share the gains of economic growth. The starting point is to narrow the skills gap for people between the top and the bottom rungs of the economic ladder. Because technology, labor laws, minimum wage, immigration, and globalization affect the skill gap, greater efforts are needed to address these issues. A conceptual economy is the future, and U.S. employment will need more people trained to do intellectually oriented work. Education is key, but not the run-of-the-diploma-mill education. Insight and ingenuity are the United States' strengths, and community colleges, which are historically at the vanguard of educational transformation, should not be afraid to put innovative and experimental education to the test. Leveraging existing funding and garnering resource partnerships can make it happen.

The numbers of unprepared and underprepared first-time college students entering CCD have risen steadily over the last decade. Reaching into the high schools to provide a bridge to achievement and college and creating transitions and collegewide support systems for students who normally would not make it through the educational continuum became a priority. CCD began discussions early in 2001 with DPS administrators, staff, and instructors to develop a programmatic bridge from high school to college.

CONCURRENT HIGH SCHOOL ENROLLMENT

The first step toward building that bridge was to revitalize CCD's postsecondary enrollment options (PSEO) high-school concurrent enrollment program, which allows high school students to take college-level courses for both college and high school credit, at the expense of the local school district. In FY 2002, only 47 students enrolled in CCD's PSEO program. The goal was to create a PSEO delivery model that provided a variety of learning options for high school students, based on the unique needs of the community. In the CCD model, students can take college courses on any one of its five college campuses and may take courses at six DPS high schools. Working with DPS high school counselors and administrators, CCD identifies specific courses that fit within the high school culture.

Developmental and ESL courses are offered at a high school with a high percentage of nonnative–English-speaking students. College core courses are offered at traditional and alternative high schools to introduce college as an option to students who are not necessarily college bound. A certified nurses' aide preparatory program was developed in partnership with a high school to introduce alternative career tracks to low-income students with few college options. CCD also offered on-site, college-level courses in health, fire science, criminal justice, and computer information technology that complement and extend the high school program offerings at a DPS alternative high school that focuses on preprofessional, career-oriented academic programs.

In 2003, CCD and DPS launched the state's first middle college: the Fred N. Thomas Career Education Center's Middle College of Denver. Within this alternative school, the middle college offers students a seamless educational track from completion of a high school diploma toward matriculation into an associate degree (AD) program at CCD. Case management of all middle college students provides a comprehensive introduction to college through orientation programs and campus tours, enrollment and registration assistance, and transportation to and from the college campus for their courses.

The Southwest Early College, a DPS Charter School, opened and became CCD's postsecondary partner in 2004. Located on the CCD West Campus, the early college partnership encourages higher academic achievement in the junior and senior years of high school to the 90% Hispanic student population and provides individualized support and guidance to students in the early years of college. The goal is for Southwest Early College students to graduate in 5 years or less with a high school diploma and an AD. The partnership granted its first high school diplomas and ADs in May 2007.

With private funding from donors and from the Piton Foundation, Janus Fund, the Denver Foundation, and DOED's Division of Workforce Development, in 2005 CCD created additional academic momentum for underserved, low-income, first-generation DPS students through Bridge to Achievement Labs at Abraham Lincoln and Emily Griffith High Schools. The mission is to increase the basic academic skill levels of DPS high school students as measured by the ACCUPLACER skills assessment and placement instrument. Its objectives are to increase the number of high school students who are college ready, particularly in math and English, before graduation; encourage participation in PSEO while students are in high school; and increase the number of students entering college after graduation. The overarching Bridge Lab goal, however, is to develop parallel, rigorous curriculum. Partnering with Lincoln's math department, and using CCD curriculum, the Bridge program implemented a teacher-initiated tutoring referral system that resulted in nearly 1,000 hours of individual and small-group tutoring for 516 students.

In 2006, CCD and DPS joined forces to launch the district's first Freshman Academy Summer Institute at Montbello High School. The program academically indoctrinated 350 new ninth-grade students through an accelerated secondary schooling process. In the fall, CCD and DPS furthered the partnership to create the Montbello Early College Academy. Montbello Early College is the product of an extensive school revitalization effort, merging community needs with the missions of DPS and CCD. The academy currently has 500 students from 10th- through 12th-grade, of which 100 are enrolled in college classes.

Today, CCD has nearly 800 high school concurrent enrollments, totaling nearly 2,000 credit hours of study. Hundreds more high school students participate in college-experience activities sponsored by grant-funded programs. In 2006, CCD provided ACCUPLACER precollege testing services to more than 1,000 DPS students. The results are promising, especially for the population of DPS students served. Spring 2003 grade analyses of high school concurrent enrollment students indicated that approximately 84% passed their college course with a C or higher grade, and high school students who took at least one college course before graduation were 50% more likely to matriculate as a regular degree- or certificate-seeking student at CCD. Regular DPS math teachers at Lincoln have acknowledged that "something is working" in the Bridge to Achievement Lab classes, where approximately 65% of the MAT 030, MAT 60, ENG 30, and ENG 60 students at Lincoln are passing with a C or higher.

DEVELOPMENTAL STUDIES

Well-designed and strongly supported developmental education programs are bridges to bring unprepared and underprepared students to college level, success, graduation, and productive lives. The next generation of CCD's nationally recognized developmental education is concentrated on increasing access to college and narrowing the skills gap. Nearly 40% of CCD entering students are assessed as unprepared or underprepared for college-credit course work and must enroll in developmental courses in reading, writing, and math. In many colleges, students who do poorly on an assessment test in one subject find themselves in developmental courses for all of their subjects. At CCD, students in developmental courses may take college-level courses for which they are prepared, allowing them to tap their strengths while supporting their weaknesses.

A 2003 cost analysis of CCD's Essential Skills, TRIO, and First-Generation Student Success programs addressed access and success of economically disadvantaged students and the cost of supportive academic programs. The analysis was conducted by the Education Foundation and the Colorado Community College System, supported by the Bridges to Opportunity initiative of the Ford Foundation, to understand the fiscal and programmatic strategies needed to expand postsecondary access for this student population. The study confirmed that information on differential costs and services for specific populations can aid in the design of programs for all disadvantaged populations, helping administrators map a continuum of costs and services necessary to promote access and success.

The three CCD programs, although serving different populations and targeted outcomes, shared common strategies (e.g., integration of developmental and academic functions, tutoring and academic support, personal and educational case management, mentoring, administrative oversight, and student tracking). Although the categories of services were the same, the costs of services per participant varied by program, based on the staffing patterns required to deliver these services successfully. The differences pointed to the need for flexibility in program design and implementation. From the perspective of using the cost-differential model as a strategic planning tool, colleges can identify a target population, or several target populations, and design programs to address the needs, strategies, and ratio of students to staff in each of the service areas selected to bring the programs to scale with available resources.

As a direct result of the cost analysis study, the Lumina Foundation for Education teamed with CCD through the Colorado Community College System in a project to increase the rates of college retention and success for more than 300 underserved students through institutional change at three other Colorado community colleges. As the project's lead institution, CCD offers its expertise in preparing academically unprepared students to the colleges through peer-learning and consultation. In addition, CCD shares its successful developmental education curriculum designs and student support service strategies and program details with these colleges.

FastStart@CCD, supported by external funding, is one of the most exciting new initiatives to emerge from this interplay of a strong foundation in developmental studies. It is an accelerated developmental education learning community, with the goal of accelerating the movement of students with precollege skills needs through the developmental education sequence. FastStart, built on the strong foundation of the Center for Educational Advancement, combines CCD's learning community concepts, academic support services, educational case management model, college orientation, contextualized curriculum, career guidance, and flexible instruction delivery.

With funds from the Lumina Foundation for Education and, more recently, from Breaking Through—a joint project of the National Council on Workforce Education and Jobs for the Future—CCD integrated developmental courses into an accelerated format, giving students the opportunity to complete two levels of developmental English and reading or two levels of developmental math in one semester. Students are grouped in both day and evening cohorts and are supported by educational case management, career-guidance activities, and supplemental tutoring. Using cohort tracking and methodologically rigorous evaluation, including qualitative evaluation techniques with students and project faculty and staff, the college demonstrated statistically significant increases in retention for FastStart students. This, in turn, led to a second Lumina-funded project phase to conduct a cost–benefit analysis of the FastStart model.

Closely monitoring outcomes continues to drive FastStart adaptation and improvement. Through student interviews and observation of patterns of persistence in the first cohort, the FastStart staff added a career awareness and guidance focus into the curriculum and project activities in Year 2. In the short term,

THE CREATIVE COMMUNITY COLLEGE

these types of program improvements are dependent on both data and external resources. In the long term, data help create the case for the institutionalization of best practices through increased student persistence and success. Now FastStart is serving approximately 100 students per semester. Preliminary data for the cost–benefit analysis indicate that revenue from increased retention exceeds program costs. As grant funds end, the program is being institutionalized, giving more students an opportunity to complete their education in a shorter period of time in a way that is cost-effective for the college.

Another effort that works to reduce the time that students spend in developmental course work is College Connection, an 8-week transition program piloted in the summer of 2007. The program targets GED completers, focusing on strengthening math, reading, and English skills. The approach orients students to college programs and services; offers relational opportunities for students, instructors, advisers, and peers before the fall semester; and starts the process of career exploration and educational planning. College Connection curriculum was developed through comparative competency analysis of Colorado developmental courses (a three-level, three-semester curriculum), the National College Transition Network competencies, and Florida GED+ curriculum. It combines whole-class, small-group, individualized instruction, and integrated reading and writing instruction. Students undergo pre- and post-ACCUPLACER tests and enroll in a 1-hour career planning course (AAA 101).

STUDENT SUPPORT SERVICES

AAA 101 has become a predictor of retention over its 2-year existence. Sponsored by Student Life, the 1-hour elective course covers the basics of college life at CCD, including advising, scheduling, registering, financial aid application, time management, and note- and test-taking skills. Between the spring of 2004 and the fall of 2006, 948 students enrolled in the course; 794 completed the course. An average of 83% of those completing were successful, receiving a C or higher. The average semester-to-semester enrollment for AAA 101 completers is 62%, compared with 38% for all students' persisting from semester to semester.

CCD continues to enhance support services for developmental studies and all students through the Learning Success Services' (LSS) Academic Support and Technology Centers. The programs, housed in an 11,613 square-foot area, serve more than 5,000 students each academic year. LSS offers labs for reading, study skills, writing, ESL, math, and GED, using systems that include faculty-led and computerized courses, faculty one-to-one and group tutoring, and peer tutoring and mentoring.

Formerly funded by the state through an FTE formula, LSS is now a course-for-fee service. Considering COF stipend funding for higher education, CCD created a 1-credit lab course that would allow access to the support services. All students registered in a developmental studies course must register for AAA 175, the enhanced learning support lab. However, any CCD student may pay a semester fee of $80 for unlimited access to LSS.

The Center for Academic Support and Achievement (CASA) is a consolidation of academic and personal support services and resources, primarily for first-generation and low-income students and students with disabilities, served by TRIO and First-Generation Student Success programs. CASA support mechanisms include advocacy, mentoring, tutoring, computerized classrooms, drop-in labs for supplemental support and enrichment, and social and cultural activities. CASA also houses the new Title V Denver Transfer Initiative, created by CCD and the University of Colorado at Denver Health Sciences Center.

The pipeline goal is to increase the number of CCD graduate transfers to and graduates from bachelor's degree–granting institutions. The project is creating joint developmental, transfer, liberal arts, business, and technology learning communities and is offering combined professional development activities that promote instructional techniques and technologies to ensure student success. Denver Transfer Initiative services encompass career and educational planning, tutoring, financial aid assistance, and links to the University of Colorado at Denver Health Sciences Center support programs through faculty, project staff, university student ambassadors and peer learning coaches. An educational case management model is the common denominator for all CASA programs, which, in turn, touches all areas of the college. Case managers direct students' college retention and success, using a holistic approach of direct access or referral to a wide array of services to address any and all factors that may impact a student's ability to succeed.

CCD adapted and pioneered the human services model in its technical education centers in the early 1990s. The educational case management model was adopted into CCD's developmental education and Title III Hispanic-serving institution programs by the mid-1990s. In 2000, it was adapted by the Title V HSI Access and Success grant, which placed educational case managers within the STEM major disciplines to ensure retention and graduation of STEM majors. Title V was integral to the 2001 establishment of a collegewide integrated advising and educational case management academic retention strategy that starts when a student enters CCD and follows through to graduation, transfer, and beyond.

STEM PARTNERSHIPS

Student access, retention, and success in STEM disciplines have been at the forefront of CCD endeavors since 2001. U.S. competitiveness in a forward-thinking global economy is dependent on STEM education. CCD is well aware that the links between awareness, desire, and ability to complete a STEM education, especially for minority, low-income, and first-generation students, begin long before college. It takes a holistic K–16 education to build foundational skills and acquire specialized knowledge, followed by a well-orchestrated plan to land a job in these fields. CCD is creating the links among K–12 school districts, institutions of higher education, and employers, by reaching students early, especially minority students, and sustaining their engagement along the educational pathway and into the workplace. Two examples include the new Aerospace Engineering Technology (AET) and Emerging Technology (ET) programs.

Two initiatives support AET, including the Access to Collaborative Education in the Sciences (ACES) program, funded by the National Aeronautics and Space Administration, and the WIRED enterprise, funded by the U.S. Department of Labor through the Metro Denver Economic Development Corporation and the Denver Office of Economic Development. AET is building a partnership among local K–12 school districts, regional institutions of higher learning, local economic and workforce development organizations, associations of minority groups, and the regional aerospace industry. Targeting underserved populations, ACES and WIRED will include a high school-to-college summer bridge project, 9–16 high-school to college-level parallel-curriculum development, and experiential learning applications. AET has a significant focus on real-world applications and industry-related methodologies, including project management modalities that will be institutionalized collegewide in the near future.

In response to Colorado's recent Bioscience Cluster Profile and study, CCD developed and is implementing the AET program, which is strategically focused on biotechnology and nanotechnology. Collaborating with the University of Colorado at Denver Health Sciences Center, the program will develop an interdisciplinary educational strategy and integrate academic curricula with project-based learning, employability skill-building, and continued advanced educational opportunity in biotechnology and nanotechnology.

The AET and ET programs will enable the college to incorporate current advances in science and technology into the undergraduate learning environment, facilitate students' exposure to potential careers in STEM-related fields, build capacity and connections through a state-of-the-art interdisciplinary associate of science degree program, and cement the pipeline between CCD and 4-year STEM programs of excellence. Providing role models that represent all students will increase participation rates of minority students in math and science majors. Currently, 40% of CCD's math and science faculty is minority, including Blacks, Asian Americans, and Hispanics.

INTERNATIONAL PERSPECTIVES

CCD's foray into the international arena, historically university territory, is aimed at advocating a twofold role for community colleges: preparing people to function successfully in the world village and providing world-class, worldwide education and training. CCD has created a bridge partnership with North High School to advance its International Association for Astronomical Studies students through the educational pipeline and into an aerospace engineering systems technology degree. Fifty predominantly minority students participate in the premier DPS Aerospace and Astronomy program each year. On program completion, the participants have advanced by two to three grade levels and set their sights on college. The program has a 95% completion rate. The pipeline project includes a CCD summer bridge program and a 2 + 2 degree partnership with Metropolitan State College of Denver on the Auraria Campus. The 8-week summer conduit provides precollege classes and workshops to prepare students for college-level math and science courses at CCD. Students become acquainted with CCD and Metropolitan State College of Denver faculty, engage in experiential learning in the new Metropolitan State Space Lab, and visit with engineers and scientists at local aerospace industries.

The college's Center for International Languages and Cultures is fostering student competencies in world languages and cultures and preparing global business citizens and partners. CCD's newly established Confucius Institute is a global partnership with China's government and universities. CCD is providing collaborative ADs and faculty–student exchange programs through several Chinese institutions of higher education. Beijing has sent several delegations to the Auraria Campus to visit with CCD, Metropolitan State, and University of Colorado at Denver constituents. The Auraria Campus personnel hope to deliver 2 + 2 degree programs in China soon.

CCD'S FUTURE THROUGH THE LOOKING GLASS

Community colleges are pivotal to global workforce competitiveness and key to the diverse social and economic fabric that is this country's framework. It is not easy from the vantage point of a community college president to understand why these institutions are not well-funded, well-understood, or highly regarded. It is difficult to imagine a United States without community colleges; yet it is critical that community college leaders recognize the imperative to change the assumptions that lower costs mean lower quality or that discounted tuition leads to discounted dreams. The challenges facing CCD are not dissimilar from those faced by other urban 2-year institutions. CCD has made progress toward increasing student access and success; however, even greater progress must be made to double graduation and transfer rates.

A community college president's insight comes from living with the institution 24/7, thinking about and analyzing every aspect of what does and does not and what will and will not create greater institutional effectiveness. What could have been done better? Was the problem caused by a failure in or lack of communication? Were support measures adequate? Every day, students, faculty, staff, community, colleagues, and education leaders provide the answers for those who lead community colleges.

Talent, insights, rigor, and courage from all constituents internal and external to a community college are necessary for a community college to take bold action in a sea of change. A willingness to explore blue ocean strategies, to take calculated risks in altering even tried and true practices to yield greater productivity and greater quality, is essential to continued growth and improved performance. Community college presidents must lead and encourage change—and admit failure and chart a new course, as is necessary.

CCD has set successful examples of redefining and creating relationships in overlapping sectors of education that are engaged in the business of learning. Role modification of K–12, 2-year, and 4-year groups has formed new linkages, produced parallel thinking, and created educational channels for student success. Building strategic partnerships has been and still is a major initiative at CCD. The sole purpose of building partnerships is to strengthen the college's role in the community—educationally, financially, and politically—by influencing policy decisions at all levels. The approach started with allies—organizations and people that shared the same goals, needs, and strengths. Making the case to the college community for genuine collaboration was the easy step. Gaining internal support from two or more external organizations was more complicated. Sustaining the relationships over time was and is the difficult and necessary work.

The 21st century is here, and there is no turning back. Demographic, social, and political challenges to community colleges will not cease. Retaining and graduating underserved students will be the most important work. Providing students with the needed level of support, personalization, and guidance to overcome barriers to their education will keep the community college on its toes. With continually constricting resources, holding on to a talented, forward-thinking, and overworked staff will be challenging, as will providing monetary encouragement or upward mobility. By the strength of its values in action and a collegewide conviction that education empowers people for the rest of their lives, CCD continues to transform itself.

REFERENCES

Colorado Succeeds. (2006). *Higher education in Colorado: An economic engine running on empty.* Denver, CO: Author.

Editors' Note. The editors gratefully acknowledge the pioneering work of former CCD president Byron McClenney and the entire CCD team for their early commitment to student success. CCD received national recognition during the 1990s for establishing a learning-centered institution. In 1996, Henry Cisneros, then-secretary of Housing and Urban Development, documented CCD's successful business partnerships and collaborations in Hallmarks of Best Practices in Urban Community Colleges. CCD's successes were also noted in *Embracing the Tiger: The Effectiveness Debate and the Community College* (Roueche, Johnson, & Roueche, 1997) and *A Learning College for the 21st Century* (O'Banion, 1997). Other publications highlighted CCD's developmental education program as a successful model for improving student success, and CCD was featured twice (1997 and 1999) by the Public Broadcasting System's Adult Education program, *Author Author,* a program showcasing successful higher education books through interviews with their authors. In 2000, CCD was awarded the Hesburgh Award for the outstanding professional development program in American higher education. The foundation laid by McClenney and his team has obviously yielded continued success for CCD into the present, as this chapter attests.

11

Florida Community College at Jacksonville: Institutional Advancement Through Change, Agility, and Innovation

Steven Wallace

Florida Community College at Jacksonville responds to mission-related changes on behalf of the citizens and organizations of Northeast Florida with fierce determination and unrestrained enthusiasm.

—*Steven Wallace, Florida Community College at Jacksonville*

The tale of Florida Community College at Jacksonville (FCCJ) is a story of awakening and metamorphosis. Located in the northeast corner of Florida, FCCJ serves more than 65,000 students from 120 countries. Until the mid-1990s, the college was traditional in its mission and attitude. Then came a change in leadership.

As an impassioned leader took hold of the college, life and perspectives of the future changed. President Steven Wallace and his newly developed leadership team envisioned a future never before seen in Jacksonville. They removed standard service district boundaries. "Create a new vision" became the expected attitude. If they saw a need, they built, created, and designed whatever was necessary to make a learning-centered solution come to life.

The traditional community college mission, funding streams, and behavioral expectations have changed dramatically at FCCJ under President Wallace. Possibility, attitude, and determination are as important as funding, technology, and teaching strategies. A bold shift in their values and the way they viewed change turned roadblocks into what Wallace described as "an entrée of extraordinary opportunities."

Author's Note. Edythe Abdullah, Carol Byrd, Maggie Cabral-Maly, Don Green, Rob Rennie, Carol Spalding, and Denis Wright contributed portions of this chapter relating to the initiatives under their administrative authority.

COMMUNITY COLLEGE LEADERS ARE FACED with challenging enterprise as they attempt to craft the creative college. The increasingly rapid and complex changes faced by community colleges are manifested in three primary domains: operational, mission, and macro strategic. Operational changes involve ongoing interests such as capitalization of requirements and initiatives, as well as quality enhancement. Mission-related changes relate to essential responsibilities in the areas of access, economic development, and community education. Macro-strategic changes engage the college in complex endeavors to improve the positioning and capacity of the community it serves to perform well in an increasingly competitive global knowledge economy.

Florida Community College at Jacksonville (FCCJ) responds to these changes on behalf of the citizens and organizations of northeast Florida with fierce determination and unrestrained enthusiasm. The difficulty of the changes notwithstanding, we believe that the United States has evolved into the era of the community college. Accordingly, we see unprecedented opportunities to serve our region in highly consequential ways. We take seriously, however, the responsibility to pursue these opportunities and overcome the inherent challenges through distinctive innovation, resourcefulness, and an unwavering commitment to excellence. Our responses to important changes across the three domains faced by Florida Community College at Jacksonville include heretical approaches that are well tolerated, if not actively encouraged.

OPERATIONAL CHANGES

The historic funding model for community colleges is becoming inherently unsustainable at a level of operational sufficiency. State legislatures encounter too many demands to provide colleges with the capital required for significant levels of growth, quality, and innovation—and improved funding is not on the horizon. Our response has been to take charge of our own financial destiny by securing substantial funds in new national markets. Three examples—the Military Education Institute, our strategic alliance with Anheuser-Busch, and the SIRIUS Academies initiative—illustrate how college operations can be capitalized in new and substantial ways. The examples involve the application of thought processes and financial strategies not typically found in higher education. Therein lies their creative potential.

Military Education Institute

Building on FCCJ's 40-year history of serving the military on local Navy bases, the Military Education Institute (MEI) was established in 1999 as an advancement of the college's education and training programs to military service personnel, their family members, and federal government employees globally. These were a logical extension of our highly successful program delivery experience to support multiple strategic ventures. The underlying strategy has been to exploit unique and distinctive capabilities in a high-yield, sustainable niche market profoundly underserved by traditional higher education. Consequently, in 2007, MEI managed 37,000 enrollments in credit and noncredit programs in multiple states and $17 million in contract annual revenue.

We are proud to serve those dedicated people who protect our nation. MEI's faculty and staff are made up almost entirely of retired service members, employing a staff with more than 800 years of active duty and reserve military service from all military branches. They have a professional orientation toward adult learning and workforce development and are highly experienced in the requisite aspects of basic skills, leadership, management, and technical and information technology training and degree programs. Most members of the MEI management team have at least master's degrees and are familiar with military "school houses." This broad understanding has enabled MEI to respond quickly to the educational and training requests of the U.S. Armed Forces and has positioned the college as a national leader in adult learning with the military services.

MEI won its first national competitive Navy training contract in 1999, in support of the Navy's concept of Homeport Training. MEI used the Navy curriculum to train sailors in culinary arts and as disbursing clerks to receive their Navy designations. In response to the terrorist attacks of September 11, 2001, FCCJ was awarded a $15 million, 5-year Navy contract to provide force protection and antiterrorism and law enforcement training to more than 2,000 sailors each year. Extensive connections and relationships within the military education community led to Navy inquiries about our capabilities in this area. Ultimately, five different courses were created, including a 6-week Navy Enlisted Classification school ("A" School). The courses involve extensive weapons and tactical training and boast one of the highest pass rates in the nation. The award of college credit for these courses is evaluated using American Council on Education guidelines and is articulated internally into college associate degree programs in criminal justice.

As a result of its experience and performance, in September 2007 the college was awarded a competitive instructional services contract at Naval Station Great Lakes, Illinois, valued at $44.9 million over 5 years, with projected enrollments of 15,000 per year—the largest contract in the college's history. The college now provides qualified personnel, supervision, management, and materials to perform training and other educational services to sailors, including instruction of courses and content, award of college credit, remediation, and testing support.

In October 2006, FCCJ was awarded an instructional services contract at Naval Air Station Pensacola, Florida, valued at $22.2 million over 5 years with projected annual enrollments of 20,000. The college provides instruction and services similar to those in Great Lakes, as well as technical training in areas such as aviation, air traffic control, and personal financial management. The complex human resource requirements attendant to both the Great Lakes and Pensacola contracts have been met through an innovative contractual relationship with a well-positioned national staffing agency. The approach provides great flexibility and allows the college to be responsive to the Navy's needs.

The college awards 1 credit hour toward a degree to every sailor successfully completing the personal financial management class at Great Lakes and Pensacola. In addition, sailors earn additional credit for several classes in their "A" and "C" schools and are on their ways to completing their degrees using one of the several college degree road maps designed for the military. After the sailors conclude training, the college's extensive online program is available for sailors to complete their associate of science degrees and to prepare for promotion in the Navy and high-wage occupations.

Open Campus, the administrative home of MEI, operates other highly successful institutes, as well. For example, the MEI force protection and antiterrorism contract positioned the college to provide security training to a nonmilitary population after the terrorist attacks of September 11, 2001, resulting in the college creating the Florida Security Institute (FSI). The expanded needs met by FSI for security included customized training for the Miami Super Bowl and contracts with the Jacksonville Port Authority. The net gains from these activities have included elevated visibility, valuable relationships, financial resources, and additional future opportunities.

Anheuser-Busch National Training Initiative

Since 2004, FCCJ has been under contract with Anheuser-Busch to provide the leadership and administration for a consortium of community colleges, technical schools, and universities in the implementation of the company's Process Support Technician Development (PSTD) program. Process support technicians provide production equipment maintenance services for Anheuser-Busch. This initiative involved one of the college's first large-scale efforts to respond to the education requirement of a major corporation on a national scale. It resulted from a long series of discussions among the senior leadership personnel. Now, FCCJ serves as the coordinator between the Anheuser-Busch Training and Development Group, the individual breweries, and the participating educational institutions for this innovative workforce educational program.

Currently, 10 different educational institutions are under contract. One of the many unique facets of this program is that the participating institutions are contracted with FCCJ—not Anheuser-Busch. FCCJ is responsible for managing the quality and content of all instructional delivery under the contract. The innovative concepts of this program are evident in the approach and methods FCCJ uses to monitor and manage training implementation. The FCCJ Program Coordinator works directly with all new institutions from the time they are accepted into the consortium until the program at each location is completed. The program coordinator counsels and assists new institutions coming into the program by performing a site analysis, negotiating contractual issues, and helping to prepare the college's key personnel for the program. The site analysis evaluates the instructor's qualifications and experiences, classroom facilities, and laboratory equipment.

FCCJ's primary responsibility is to ensure quality, consistency, and standardization in the training. FCCJ provides continuous program review and interagency communication. The communication consists of conference calls at three critical points during training and involves representatives from each educational institution. The precourse conference call attempts to identify any potential problems in the delivery of training and ensures that the instructor is prepared and the necessary equipment is in place. The second call is made at midterm and is designed to resolve any issues hindering student success. The final call, or postcourse conference call, reviews student evaluations, makes recommendations for improvement, and anticipates needs for the next class.

Instructors are required to submit electronic weekly reports to the FCCJ program coordinator. These reports identify potential problems, verify participant attendance, and identify grade anomalies. In this report, the instructor must define class activities and equipment issues and recommend training improvements. In addition to the weekly reports, students evaluate curriculum and the instructor at the third, sixth, and ninth week of each course. Constant interaction between FCCJ, the partnering institutions, the Anheuser-Busch Training and Development Group, the local brewery, and the curriculum developers ensures that student outcomes are standardized and are of the highest quality.

Even though the PSTD program is noncredit training delivered through other colleges, FCCJ has articulated this training to award college credits. It registers all students, maintains historical records, and oversees the curriculum to ensure alignment with articulated credit courses. Training participants are provided certificates of completion, and transcripts are provided to those who request them. Every August, Anheuser-Busch conducts a train-the-trainer program for site coordinators, instructors, and brewery training managers. This training program has two basic objectives: to provide administrators with the ability to refine procedures and standards and to provide an opportunity for all program instructors to review curriculum changes that occurred throughout the years, based on student evaluations and learning outcomes. After more than 2 years of operation, the program has proven to be so successful that Anheuser-Busch has extended the FCCJ's contract for 3 years and plans to increase the number of participating institutions.

SIRIUS Academics

The increasingly competitive environment in which we operate online and hybrid courses demands extraordinary and uniform enhancements to instructional quality. Nowhere is this more important than in the delivery of our highest-enrollment courses, particularly those taught by adjunct faculty. Another competitive consideration is the impact of the cost of textbooks on the total cost of courses. Accordingly, we have addressed the needed changes in both of these interests through the SIRIUS project.

SIRIUS is both a development process and a product. The development part of SIRIUS consists of an instructional development assistant. The instructional development assistant is software that uses a systems theory approach to lead groups of faculty through an outcomes-based process of material development. Furthermore, the methodology used in the instructional development assistant is based on grounded theory because it uses a structured approach. It considers both the learning environment and content; focuses on providing a learning experience that is relevant, engaging, and interactive; and provides frequent and comprehensive feedback. Faculty adoption of SIRIUS materials has been excellent and is expanding to faculty in community colleges across the country.

The materials or products produced through SIRIUS can be used in traditional, hybrid, or online classes. All materials are digitized and conceptualized to provide a text, CD/DVD, and online materials. Instructional manuals are produced for each delivery method. Foundation course materials can be individualized by the teacher and should be considered to be in a constant state of development because faculty will be adding components of new materials on an ongoing basis. We intend for these materials to be sold to students at a greatly reduced price, thereby addressing the number one student complaint: the high cost of textbooks. The process of developing these materials provides faculty with the opportunity to engage in the scholarship of producing teaching and learning materials—an important activity unavailable to most community college faculty. In addition, because the materials are owned by the institution, derived funds provide a source of revenue for continuing enhancements, student scholarships, and faculty development.

An important consideration in ensuring the success of the project is maximizing faculty adoption of the material. By forming the International Academy for the Scholarship of Learning Technology, a structure has been put into place that encourages, by invitation only, new faculty members to become part of the ongoing development team. Faculty from new institutions will be contacted by their colleagues to join the project. When new faculty is recommended for a development team, calls are made to supervising deans inquiring about instructional quality, teamwork, and other selection criteria. Joining the project requires the adoption of the materials and participating in enhancing the materials by adding text, learning objects, and exams.

The SIRIUS project has provided positive outcomes for the college (e.g., the faculty development program). Teams of faculty from every discipline have studied learning and motivation theory, worked in collaborative groups, produced a product using best thoughts on instructional design, and produced a product made specifically for community college students. One faculty member said, "My students have responded very positively to working with SIRIUS course materials. They actually use words like 'engaging' and 'interactive,' but most just say, 'This is cool stuff.' They also say things like, 'I like learning this way.'" Attendance in classes that use SIRIUS materials has improved. Students are focused and involved with the subject matter. Feedback from students has been very positive, and results on exit exams show improved student learning. Most importantly, the data reveal that SIRIUS courses are accomplishing their goals of increasing student class performance and retention.

MISSION CHANGES

In 2006, FCCJ stretched its mission dramatically in response to compelling employer and community needs. The traditional role of the community college in education and social change severely suboptimizes the extraordinary impact our college is capable of having in many essential areas such as economic development, equality of opportunity, and quality of life. The confines of the associate degree are too restrictive to allow us to respond effectively to the emerging needs in the knowledge economy, of our students, employers, and community. We chose, therefore, to begin offering bachelor's degrees and to establish a charter high school. In addition, we decided to play a significant role in resolving a critical teacher shortage in our local school districts.

It has been clear for several years that the next logical evolution of the community college in a knowledge economy is the extension of selected highly successful associate in science degrees to the baccalaureate level. Preserving the essential community college mission requires strict discipline in determining which upper-division programs should be added. Our carefully considered rule requires practitioner-oriented bachelor's degrees to meet significant employer demands and exceptional career opportunities for graduate careers.

Bachelor's Degrees

Politically, authorization for the first such degree is the toughest. Therefore, we chose a bullet-proof option. For more than 20 years, FCCJ and the Jacksonville Fire Rescue Department (JFRD) have sustained a strong partnership to provide training for firefighters at FCCJ's Regional Fire Training Center. The Regional Fire Training Center was built through funds provided by both FCCJ and JFRD. The facility is on college property at the South Campus and maintained by college staff. The facility currently provides training to fight aircraft, structural, rail, and vehicle fires. Plans have been approved recently for the acquisition of a shipboard firefighting trainer that will allow marine firefighting training through state funds. In addition, FCCJ is seeking federal funds for an Air Force Rescue and Firefighting simulator in the interest of expanding the regional (and, perhaps, national) impact of the center.

FCCJ has used this exceptional facility and its close relationship with JFRD to develop the college's first bachelor's degree program; the bachelor of applied science (BAS) in fire science was approved by the state of Florida and the Southern Association of Colleges and Schools. After many years of associate degree education in fire science technology, FCCJ accepted its first BAS class in the fall of 2007 and will begin to offer baccalaureate-level course work in fire science. The Regional Fire Training Center will become the most extensive and sophisticated of its type in Florida. The ongoing development of the Regional Fire Training Center and the new bachelor's degree program are evidence of FCCJ's commitment and comprehensive view of fire science training and education. The required professional courses for the new BAS degree will provide students with the necessary knowledge and skills for advanced practice in areas such as hazardous materials, counter-terrorism, urban search and rescue, and interagency coordination during catastrophic events.

The JFRD has responded by developing a new set of requirements for employment with the fire services department and advancement in the professional management ranks. Not surprisingly, FCCJ's programs in emergency medical technology and its associate and bachelor's degree in fire science education, play integral parts in this advancement system. Consequently, the collaboration involved has elevated the scope and quality of the training programs of both organizations.

FCCJ has been accredited as a bachelor's degree–granting institution, and new bachelor's degree programs in nursing, computer network administration, and business have been developed. These new degrees are applied, practitioner-oriented degrees. This strategy is consistent with our belief that new demands within some careers will require applied baccalaureate preparation in addition to upper-division course work to provide a foundation for graduate school. It will be important for universities to consider the evolving interests of employers and students in deciding the admission of BAS degree holders to graduate programs, particularly because they can expect to see many more such applicants in the future.

Charter High School

More than 3,000 students drop out of FCCJ's local high schools each year. People without high school diplomas have few economic opportunities and frequently become serious problems for the community. High school dropouts are a significant source of crime and social problems. Increasing the number of high school graduates has been the most effective means of reducing societal costs for public assistance and the criminal and prison systems. In addition, it increases tax revenues and produces a workforce that will attract new and growing industries.

Through our work in the community, we have become convinced that effective programs for high school dropouts—citizens at risk of having no real economic opportunity—are absolute imperatives. FCCJ has developed intensive and focused "rescue and turn around" programs to retain, reattract, engage, motivate, and inspire high school dropouts to achieve the academic and career skills necessary to lead productive lives. The college, in partnership with the local public school district, the regional workforce board, and businesses, has created three unique high school programs: (1) an adult high school program that emphasizes secondary and postsecondary academic and career preparation for students ages 18 to 72; (2) a partnership with the local public school system that allows students, at risk of dropping out and whose performance has placed them in an alternative high school instructional program, to attend high school for the first half of a day and participate in postsecondary course work the second half; and (3) a charter high school that focuses on 16- to 20-year-old high school dropouts with intensive intervention services, such as mentoring and case management, to help students focus on earning secondary and postsecondary credentials.

Institute for Teacher Preparation and Development

In August 2005, FCCJ was authorized by the Florida Board of Education to be an Educator Preparation Institute, providing a comprehensive alternative teacher certification program for postbaccalaureate students. The program, Teach First Coast (named after its highly successful pilot in 2003), offers preparation for all state certification exams, seven competency-based instructional methods courses leading to professional certification, and mentoring support through the first teaching year.

More than 100 teachers were prepared through Teach First Coast in its first year, and approximately 200 students were expected to graduate in 2006–2007. With the addition of Teach First Coast, FCCJ redefined its education department and renamed it the Institute for Teacher Preparation and Development (ITPD). ITPD works with local school districts to develop additional programming, as needed, for teachers, substitutes, and paraprofessionals. FCCJ also has established a clear academic pathway for teachers of young children. Housed under ITPD is the Career Ladder for Early Childhood Educators, which includes all precollege certificates for the child-care industry and the associate of science (AS) degree in early childhood management. Enrollment has grown by nearly 1,000% in child-care certificate programming and by 300% in the AS degree in the last 2 years.

In the last 2 years, ITPD has been awarded three state-sponsored grants totaling $380,000 for teacher preparation. Wachovia Bank has donated $150,000 to support teachers who are pursuing certification at FCCJ in the critical shortage areas of math, science, exceptional student education, reading, and ESL. In addition, the Early Learning Coalition of Duval, the North Florida Partnership for Professional Development, Headstart Urban League, and Bank of America have contributed tuition scholarships to students enrolled in early childhood programming. ITPD is an ongoing initiative, and its focus will vary depending on the needs of the school districts and early learning centers it serves. Plans include the creation of additional courses and training for teachers who are seeking certification in the most critical shortage areas, additional grant proposals to seek funding to support the professional development of teachers, training programs to provide options for teachers seeking specialized endorsements, the expansion of ITPD to all college campuses and centers, and, finally, the pursuit of additional articulation agreements with partnering universities and colleges.

MACRO-STRATEGIC CHANGES

Aggressive leadership sometimes is required to deal effectively with major challenges and to take full advantage of extraordinary opportunities. Three examples of innovative change aligned with key FCCJ strategic interests are offered here. The first involves direct action in improving the quantity and quality of high school graduates continuing into higher education, and the others relate to unique approaches to leadership in the critically important area of information technology, particularly advanced academic technology.

Early College High School

The Early College High School (ECHS) is a unique initiative involving a partnership between Duval County Public Schools and the college, designed to serve underrepresented students who statistically are the first to drop out of school. ECHS seeks to identify students who typically might not pursue higher education after high school and offer them college-level curriculum and instruction under a distinctive, nurturing, and rigorous dual enrollment model. The goals are to encourage students who would otherwise forgo higher education to attend college and provide them with the background and skills needed to succeed in that environment. As part of a comprehensive articulation agreement with Duval County Public Schools, ECHS offers a rigorous collegiate general education curriculum to high school students in grades 9–12, simultaneously satisfying some high school graduation requirements through dual enrollment. Those students who succeed have the potential to earn an associate in applied science (AAS) degree from FCCJ, concurrently with high school graduation. The first ECHS cohort was established in the fall of 2003, and graduated its first students with a high school diploma and an AAS in December 2006. A second ECHS program was established in another part of the college's service area by its North Campus.

Initial funding for the ECHS program was provided by the Bill and Melinda Gates Foundation. The grant funded a strategic alliance that partners schools, universities, industry, and government to renew and strengthen the professional capacity of K–12 educators, motivate and mentor students, and empower parents and communities so that all young people will learn and achieve at higher levels. The program now is supported fully by the partnership between Duval County Public Schools and the college, with the school district investing significantly in the operation of the program.

The Information Technology Leadership Academy

FCCJ has become a technology leader in American higher education, in large part because of its early adoption of technologies with particular educational promise and its commitment to thinking differently about the application of technology. One example of an innovative program resulting from the concept of thinking differently is the Information Technology Leadership Academy (ITLA). The concept for ITLA began as an idea to give back to the information technology industry, that is, to build next-generation technology leaders. It was clear that the capacity to mentor the necessary volume of new technology leaders, as well as a large corps of alpha technology leader role models and mentors, simply was not available.

Although this may appear more like a problem befitting a university-based solution, FCCJ saw the synergistic potential to leverage the college's extensive and substantial professional network to craft a solution that would accomplish the following:

- Support economic development by bringing key industry leaders and decision makers to Jacksonville and introducing them to the area, its economy, and its lifestyle benefits
- Provide professional development to the college's information technology leadership team as well as information technology leaders from local business and industry
- Keep up-to-date on key technology and business issues and trends
- Create a rich source of research and professional expertise in support of the construction of a technology leadership curriculum and repository of related learning objects
- Provide content for national publication, further increasing awareness of ITLA, FCCJ, and the Jacksonville area
- Do it all at no expense to the college and at minimal expense for attendees.

Once the concept was approved, a business plan established specific financial targets whereby the program would start with college seed money but be self-sufficient by the end of the second year and have a full-year's operating budget (the equivalent of the start-up funding) in reserve by the end of the third year. The program met each of its fiscal targets 1 year early. The key component of the success of the new venture was the leadership secured to build ITLA. Leveraging personal and longstanding professional relationships and networks resulted in the employment of a world-renowned futurist and technology thought-leader to serve as executive director and dean of ITLA. This person not only had the draw of his reputation to attract interest and support for the program but also the benefit of being a regularly published author and keynote speaker in the technology landscape. These factors, in combination with his professional network of hundreds of technology leaders from around the world, provided a solid foundation for building the ITLA programs and brand.

In addition to having met its fiscal goals, ITLA, in its initial 20 months of operation, brought more than 200 Fortune 500 technology executives from around the world to Jacksonville, Florida. The program consistently receives rave reviews from attendees and sponsors and has had national coverage in *Computerworld* and *CIO Decisions*. It has developed links with executive education programs at major universities around the country and has earned its place among premium technology leadership programs. It has contributed to the development of a new perspective on the part of significant business leaders about the range and depth of what community colleges can and should do.

Technology Enablement Model

In 1997, FCCJ was a well-respected institution with a history of traditional instruction and a small distance-learning program. It operated in what could be described politely as a technology-free environment. There was no network, there were few acceptable computer labs for students, and few faculty members had computers or access to any technology resources.

Historically, approximately 72% of the college's total technology expenditures and nearly 90% of staff effort went into administrative computing; the majority of the remaining balance went into libraries and instructional support, with academic computing and technology receiving few dollars and almost no staff attention. As part of a broad-based technology agenda for the college, the new chief information officer recommended reversing the trend immediately and dedicated all possible technology resources toward faculty and students. A series of implementation plans was immediately approved by the college president and went into effect. These were built on a foundation of philosophies that formed an "enablement" model. The model was simple and based on the following framework:

- Provide 100% of faculty members with the best technology available. They will develop new and creative ways to use technology for the improvement of teaching and learning, but they must have the technology first.
- Provide a robust college-wide infrastructure and 100% access. Ubiquity and connectivity add value; access to electronic resources of scholarship is essential, and a rich network supports collaboration.
- Create a best-of-class academic computing resource for students. Computer labs and classrooms had to include all of the tools necessary to scholarship and a consistent user-experience at all college locations.
- Build a capable and committed technology leadership team and staff. The existing team was perfectly skilled to meet the demands of the past. Creation of a new team built on pure intellectual horsepower rather than a specific skill set was critical. Focusing the team on the core business-education was also essential.
- Develop a new model of technology as a "value creation engine" with a deliberate focus on enabling new businesses, new processes, and new opportunities for the college. Every technology initiative had to expand collegewide capabilities as well as build or strengthen a positive brand.

The results of this innovative approach to thinking about technology have been significant and impressive. The college is viewed as a leader in technology, having been ranked first in the United States in technology programs and services by the

Center for Digital Education for 3 of the past 4 years. The college has grown its distance-learning programs and improved teaching and learning, largely because of the technology position achieved through this enablement model.

CONCLUSION

The profound and compelling changes required of community colleges can—if approached with innovation, resourcefulness, and effective leadership—provide an entrée to extraordinary opportunities in each of the three domains of change. Organizational, mission, and macro-strategic changes may appear cumbersome, but this is not the case in practice. We at FCCJ are energized on a continuing basis by the kinds of positive change responses described here. Going forward, we plan to build on this capacity to use change strategically on behalf of our students, our college, and our community.

12

Kentucky Community and Technical College System: Building a New System

Michael B. McCall

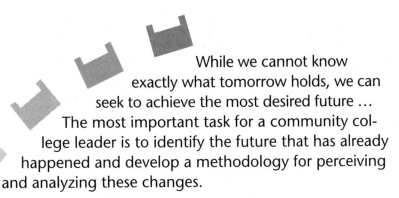

While we cannot know
exactly what tomorrow holds, we can
seek to achieve the most desired future …
The most important task for a community college leader is to identify the future that has already
happened and develop a methodology for perceiving
and analyzing these changes.

—*Michael B. McCall, Kentucky Community and Technical College System*

The founding of the Kentucky Community and Technical College System (KCTCS) is a story of a divided state transformed into a united system. Integrating an ailing technical college system with a poorly managed community college system was just the beginning for System President Michael McCall. His mission was to forecast the future of education and the needs of the state and craft a plan detailing how a comprehensive community and technical college system could fill this void.

The road was not paved with bluegrass; in some cases, it was not paved at all. Forging through the countryside, McCall worked tirelessly with community members, legislators, and business and industry to remove resistance. Community leaders saw the vision he placed before them, and they, too, understood its value to the state.

KCTCS leadership created a system that exceeded expectations. Now, nearly 100,000 Kentuckians are educated and trained at one of the 65 campuses statewide. Kentucky is beginning to see that its investment in this newly created system is paying off in one of the most productive workforces in the state's history.

FOR MORE THAN 100 YEARS, community colleges have handled changing economic, social, cultural, demographic, and political forces while serving their communities, growing in numbers, and becoming more competitive in postsecondary education. However, economic indicators and social and cultural trends are creating a set of conditions that may produce unintended consequences. Although we cannot know exactly what tomorrow holds, we can seek to achieve the most desired future.

As the founding president of the Kentucky Community and Technical College System (KCTCS), I had the honor and opportunity to lead this new system into the 21st century as a strong, united system. The motto of the Commonwealth of Kentucky is "United We Stand." Today, that could also serve as the motto of KCTCS. The Kentucky Postsecondary Education Improvement Act of 1997, which changed the system to the current consolidated, seamless system of higher education, allows students to move easily within the system and on to 4-year colleges and universities. KCTCS serves more than 87,000 Kentuckians at 65 campuses, allowing them to transition easily between programs and institutions as they pursue academic and technical degrees and workforce training.

Internal and external environmental scanning are keys to proactive planning and responsiveness. To create its preferred future, KCTCS constantly scans both the external and internal forces that affect the system. It places a high priority on the flexibility and adaptability to deal with change. KCTCS values strong leaders, talented faculty and staff, high performance standards, and a will to be exceptional. With these traits, the system can meet student, community, and business and industry partner needs.

Since 1997, KCTCS has negotiated college consolidations, accreditation conundrums, and community partnerships. It has recognized and responded to organizational internal needs while simultaneously creating supportive, collaborative, external relationships presented challenges and constant change. Through responsiveness, flexibility, and adaptability, the new system met the challenges of its first decade. KCTCS is prepared to continue to work toward a vision of national excellence.

Strategic planning is crucial to facing future challenges creatively and successfully. The strategic plan guides your change effort and your business. It continuously detects changes in the outside world, deciding how to deal with them and translating these needed changes into programs that produce desired results. Yesterday's generation of leaders would blanch at what we accept as a way of life: accelerating change in our markets and customer needs, increasing competitive pressure, shortening product life cycles, increasing foreign competition, and creating innovative technologies. Such a pace demands that organizations quickly detect and respond to shifting needs in the outside world. Just keeping your head above water requires fast, imaginative anticipation of market changes before the competition has a chance to respond.

KCTCS was created from two distinct separate systems: community colleges and technical schools. As administrative, financial, and technological challenges were recognized and met, projects, programs, and plans were structured to respond to both short-term and long-term goals and objectives. Parts of the KCTCS story are provided here to offer our friends, partners, and constituents the opportunity to celebrate our successes as well as to recognize the long road ahead.

BACKGROUND

The first community college system in Kentucky was created with the passage of the Community College Act in 1962. This legislation mandated the formation of a statewide system of community colleges, administered by the University of Kentucky. The system began operation July 1, 1964. Over time, 14 community colleges were established across the commonwealth.

The community colleges were separate from the technical colleges. Kentucky had a long history of vocational and technical education. Over the years, state-operated technical schools were founded to support high school programs and provide adult occupational training. Until 1990, the Kentucky Department of Education operated these schools. In 1990, the Kentucky legislature created the statewide Kentucky TECH System of technical schools, operated by the Department for Adult and Technical Education, Cabinet for Workforce Development.

TRANSITION TO THE KENTUCKY COMMUNITY AND TECHNICAL COLLEGE SYSTEM

In May 1997, the community college system entered an exciting new era when the Kentucky General Assembly enacted the Kentucky Postsecondary Education Improvement Act of 1997. One of the most significant changes resulting from this legislation was KCTCS, composed of community and technical colleges. The General Assembly declared on behalf of the people of the commonwealth the following goals to be achieved by the year 2020:

> *(a) A seamless, integrated system of postsecondary education strategically planned and adequately funded to enhance economic development and quality of life ... (e) A comprehensive community and technical college system with a mission that assures, in conjunction with other postsecondary institutions, access throughout the Commonwealth to a 2-year course of general studies designed for transfer to a baccalaureate program, the training necessary to develop a workforce with the skills to meet the needs of new and existing*

*industries, and remedial and continuing education to improve the employ-
ability of citizens; and (f) An efficient, responsive, and coordinated system of
autonomous institutions that delivers educational services to citizens in quan-
tities and of a quality that is comparable to the national average. (Kentucky
General Assembly, 1997, p. 2)*

As required by the act, the University of Kentucky Board of Trustees delegated
management of 13 of the 14 community colleges (excluding Lexington Community
College) to the KCTCS Board of Regents, effective January 14, 1998. Simultaneously,
15 postsecondary schools in the Kentucky Tech System moved from the Workforce
Development Cabinet and joined KCTCS, effective July 1, 1998. Six years later,
Lexington, the remaining community college, was brought under the KCTCS
administrative umbrella. Geographic overlap encouraged colleges to collaborate
on enrollment management, advertising and marketing, strategic planning, and
advancement and development. Collaboration reflected geographic, cultural, and
industrial diversities of each region. Out of collaboration came consolidation, and
16 KCTCS colleges emerged, serving 86,475 students in fall 2006.

LEADERSHIP SUCCESS

As with any organization, success is only as strong as the leadership. Leadership
does not apply to one person but refers to the people and systems that make the
campus, college, and system effective. For me, success comes from hiring first-rate
people and creating meaningful community partnerships. Ingredients to KCTCS
leadership success have focused on the following:

- Creating a leadership and oversight structure
- Aligning the colleges into a united system
- Incorporating a healthy leadership philosophy
- Encouraging continual professional and leadership development
- Creating mutually supportive external partnerships
- Developing and deleting programs
- Promoting technology
- Ensuring fiscal resource development

Addressing each of these issues takes time and commitment—it does not happen overnight. Since my tenure began, we have focused intensely on each of these
areas with great results.

LEADERSHIP STRUCTURE

The KCTCS board of regents has full legal authority and responsibility for the governance of KCTCS. The KCTCS president is the CEO of the system with broad authority delegated from the KCTCS board of regents. As the CEO of KCTCS, the KCTCS president recommends to the board of regents policies to be considered for adoption, carries out policies determined by the board of regents, and has full authority and responsibility over the administration of the academic, business, and fiscal operations of KCTCS. These responsibilities include all official communication with the board of regents, the council on postsecondary education, and governmental and external agencies and specific responsibilities for the policy, planning, and development functions of the system.

In January 1999, KCTCS began a strategic planning process that led to identification of the KCTCS vision, values, goals, and priorities. The *KCTCS Strategic Plan 2000–2005: Building Unity* (KCTCS, 2003) was adopted by the KCTCS board of regents on October 8, 1999. The board directed me to lead the system to establish 1-year objectives, develop action plans, and identify accountability measures. The 2006–2010 strategic plan (KCTCS, 2005) uses goals, performance indicators, and targets.

The KCTCS environment promotes energy, creativity, and passion. Leadership in this culture takes both skill and practice. Leaders must develop collaborative relationships—getting results by involving and committing people to develop strengths within and across work teams. More importantly, leadership is valued and admired most when it supports teamwork, customer focus, innovation, and organizational vision. Leadership is more about enabling people than promoting individual achievement. Leadership is like duct tape—an odd but appropriate analogy because it is the fabric and glue that hold an organization together.

In the past, hierarchy, rules, and policies were used to exercise organizational control. However, because of constant change, traditional structures and controls are a liability. Structure once served to create order and control; it now inhibits the organization's ability to respond to change in a rapid, focused way. KCTCS emphasizes staying centered in the midst of change; organizational structure deemphasizes hierarchy and distributes leadership by distributing authority, knowledge, and information throughout the organization. Through a structured network and open communication, faculty and staff were resilient and capable of coping with difficult and challenging new realities. The focus on providing them complete and current information was important.

It is scary business to make full disclosure, which is why most people in management do not. They do not know what is going to happen and often feel that their own motives or earlier decisions will be questioned. It simply opens up a Pandora's box when you involve people. Nevertheless, if you do not involve people, Pandora's box opens up in other ways—in an atmosphere of low trust, in spawning more cynicism, and in accusations and hostility (Collins & Porras, 1997, p. 214). Creating a structure with high participation of faculty and staff in decision making—while focusing on processes to achieve our mission and vision—meant aligning the system's network of teams, committees, and task forces.

ALIGNMENT

KCTCS strives to achieve an organizational structure that focuses on alignment, a self-sustaining culture that distributes leadership and energy throughout the organization. Alignment gives organizations the power to get and stay competitive by uniting previously unconnected parts into an interrelated, easily comprehensible model. Alignment gives organizations the power to create a culture of shared purpose.

Alignment refers to several areas that promote the integration of key systems, processes, and responses to changes in the external environment: (1) connecting faculty and staff to the mission by turning intentions into actions, (2) linking teams and processes to the changing needs, and (3) shaping strategies based on real-time information. Creating a culture in which these elements work together seamlessly requires a network of relationships that offer flexibility and high performance. By integrating internal culture and external demands with the mission, vision, and leadership expectations, alignment provides the system the power to achieve consistent, defined levels of growth and peak performance.

Alignment is an ongoing process that requires constant, rapid realigning. Like flying, where the failure to make continuous heading corrections results in drift, organizations also wander from one side of their intended course to another. That's why frequent checking and realigning are so important. With the right gauges and a crew that knows its business, you can stay on course (Labovitz & Rosansky, 1997, p. xiv).

HEALTHY STATEWIDE LEADERSHIP TEAMS

Often during the early days of building KCTCS, we made an analogy about building the airplane as we flew it. It became all the more important to share where we were headed and how we planned the journey. The KCTCS leadership team is founded on a network organizational structure. In addition to the chancellor and the vice presidents, the system office includes professional staff members who provide system administrative services, support, assistance, and coordination for the colleges. State peer teams focus on strategic issues. Each team has a charter that outlines membership and responsibilities. Each team and charter are approved by the president's leadership team.

I established annual initiatives to address the most pressing needs facing the system. In 1999 to 2000, it was ASK—a three-phased leadership approach to begin the process of examining the current status and reviewing options for the future. The initiative included these goals:

- Assessment: Assess the functions, leadership, internal information and system processes
- Support: Seek political and external support for the system
- Knowledge: Acquire the knowledge necessary to meet the mission of the system

This initiative began KCTCS's way of aligning administrative objectives with the needs of the colleges to form the system's strategic plan. The 2000 initiative was based on an inclusive method of problem solving—RSVP (responsive solutions through vigorous planning)—and was designed to ensure that employees at all levels have opportunities to participate in the decision-making process. Six strategic priority teams (which were refined to five in the summer of 2003 and renamed strategic planning teams in the summer of 2004 to assist with the development of the 2006–2010 strategic plan goals) were established to address strategic priorities that involve one or more functional areas. The President's Leadership Team ensures that the goals of the system are achieved; college presidents and CEOs work on RAMP (resources, accountability, marketing, and programs) teams. Twelve peer teams, composed of people responsible for key functional areas (such as chief academic officers, chief business officers, and chief student officers) assist in implementing strategic priorities. Workgroups are formed, as needed, to make recommendations on specific operational functions.

The system focus was designed to respond to the internal and external environmental challenges in each new year. The 2006–2010 KCTCS goals focused on the following:

- Promoting excellence in teaching and learning
- Increasing student access and success
- Expanding diversity and global awareness
- Enhancing the economic development of communities and the commonwealth

PROFESSIONAL DEVELOPMENT

KCTCS has created a series of programs to grow skills and leaders. Each program reflects significant input from faculty and administrators across the system and addresses the needs of college personnel. During the early 1990s, the concept of the "learning college" emerged as a way for community colleges to position ourselves effectively in the marketplace by capitalizing on student- and teacher-centered values. The learning college's premise is to place learning first and provide educational experiences for learners any way, any place, and any time. This customer-based approach is necessary for survival in today's marketplace. Just as colleges have become "learner centered," so has KCTCS adopted a learning organization environment.

Strategies for Teaching Excellence and Professionalism (STEP) is a statewide, three-tiered, comprehensive professional development model. In the first two tiers, the STEP program provides professional development for new, mid-, and late-career faculty. The third tier provides an integrative approach, bringing together faculty and staff as learning facilitators and leaders. This tier is defined by the New Horizons Teaching and Learning Conference, Faculty and Staff Excellence Awards, and the President's Leadership Seminar programs. These programs offer professional development opportunities for all faculty members—classroom and online, experienced or new to the field.

The first tier of the professional development program focuses on new faculty. Programs designed to provide professional development for new faculty include the New Faculty Institute and New Faculty Mentor programs. Each program can meet the needs of individual colleges. As the colleges develop and implement these programs, the professional development coordinators distribute and gather best practices for continued improvement.

The New Faculty Seminar (NFS) is designed for faculty members who have little or no teaching experience and for discipline-specific teachers who may have taken courses in teaching and learning strategies for community and technical colleges but who may now need a more focused instructional plan. The NFS content, written by KCTCS faculty who also serve as seminar trainers, is available via the KCTCS Web site and is adaptable to new faculty training programs at the colleges. The program operates from a train-the-trainer model at the statewide level. Teams of experienced faculty from each of the 16 colleges attend a 1-day seminar during which the orientation program is reviewed and best practices are highlighted. The core elements of the training are disseminated annually to representatives from the colleges in a train-the-trainer model.

The New Faculty Mentor program was developed in 2003 at Madisonville Community College, and it serves as the model for the other colleges. The New Faculty Mentor program pairs less-experienced faculty with more senior colleagues (6 years or more). Academic deans and trained mentors at each college facilitate the mentoring relationships. Each of the KCTCS colleges adapts the program to the needs of its faculty. Ideally, mentors build on the initial NFS training by facilitating the campus and academic orientation of new faculty. Although most often aimed at serving new faculty, the mentor programs also extend to faculty who have taught for several years. The mentor–protégé relationship builds and reinforces a collegial culture. Mentor programs include activities such as mutual classroom visits and informal discussion sessions.

Another program, piloted fall 2005, dovetails with NFS. The online Learning Scenarios project, offered in partnership with Valencia Community College, takes new faculty members through a 6-week online training as they follow the regular activity of a fictional new faculty member. Guided by a trained online facilitator, new faculty members interact with their colleagues at other colleges who face similar situations. In addition, faculty receive a wealth of practical teaching and learning resources available via the Internet.

The second tier of the STEP initiative emphasizes early- to mid-career faculty development. One program is the individualized, confidential, and client-driven Teaching Consultation Program (TCP), which promotes lifelong learning. TCP offers faculty personalized interaction with trained faculty consultants who address various issues that faculty members face at different points in their careers. KCTCS faculty members may request consultations aimed at helping them improve basic classroom strategies or test instructional innovations in a low-risk setting.

The Master Teacher Seminar is an annual 3-day retreat for two faculty members from each KCTCS college. The faculty participant must have at least 3 years of full-time teaching to qualify for the Master Teacher Seminar, and each college may develop additional screening criteria. The session follows the national model and is facilitated by a faculty development professional consultant. Emphasis is placed on reflection and discovery regarding the teaching and learning process. The peer relationships established during the Master Teacher Seminar are long lasting and cut across both colleges and teaching disciplines.

The Lumina Foundation recently funded a faculty development program developed by the Collaboration for Teaching and Learning. In this program, teams of seven faculty members from four colleges will engage in intensive content-literacy training over the course of 2 years. Emphasis is on developing instructional strategies which accommodate a variety of learning styles. In the second year of the grant project, a subset of this cohort will design an introduction to college learning course for new students.

The third tier of the faculty development program is more integrative. TCP and the Master Teacher Seminar continue, targeting more senior faculty. The goals with each of these initiatives are to provide an opportunity for renewal.

The New Horizons Conference on Teaching and Learning, established in 2002, is an annual gathering of faculty and staff systemwide. The conference serves as a significant professional development experience where learning-centered principles are the guiding theme. The conference sessions cover a wide range of topics relevant to the KCTCS strategic goals.

Popular as an accessible professional development opportunity for faculty and staff, the conference has grown substantially over the past 4 years and has become a hallmark event for KCTCS. More than 100 faculty and staff members present to nearly 700 of their colleagues in this 2-day event. The culminating conference event is the awards ceremony. The annual Faculty and Staff Excellence Awards, established in 2002, recognize individual achievement at each college, as well as at the system level. One faculty member and one staff member are selected by each college to receive this prestigious award. From among the college awardees, two are chosen by a panel of their peers as the systemwide award winners. With that recognition comes an award of $1,000 to each for a professional development activity of their choice during the next year.

With our impending leadership shortage and the changing nature of the skills and aptitudes needed by our leaders, one of the most effective professional development initiatives is to grow our own leaders. The President's Leadership Seminar integrates faculty and staff as active leaders in the colleges and addresses leadership development throughout the system. It is a competitive professional development experience directed toward leadership succession. This selective group of faculty and staff from throughout the system gather in the fall for an intensive seminar with the most notable practitioners and scholars in community college education throughout the nation. In the spring, the activities focus on the participant's individual leadership style.

EXTERNAL PARTNERSHIPS

The most important task for a community college leader is to identify that the future has already happened and to develop a methodology for perceiving and analyzing these changes. A challenge for KCTCS was to use the opportunities presented through the college consolidations to serve our communities, business and industry, and government agencies. With 16 colleges serving Kentucky, KCTCS is positioned to help its business partners compete in today's global economy, in part because of our distribution and flexible programming strengths. However, to do this, we had to develop clear understanding of the external changes and how they affected our customers' operations.

At KCTCS, we intend to keep our community colleges in the forefront of national economic and workforce development planning. An agenda for economic development must be made at the local level. Some communities emphasize skills training for highly technical jobs, whereas others focus on partnerships for business and industry training. Increasingly, community colleges must respond to the need to develop entrepreneurship in our communities to foster economic development. This is true in rural colleges, especially. For many small and rural communities, entrepreneurial programs offer the best approach to economic development. Their greatest success has been in providing economic independence to people, cultural enrichment for their communities, and economic development.

We worked with our colleges to emphasize that the global economy is here and that it has far-reaching impact. We communicated to the members of our staff and faculty that world-class excellence is the new standard by which all products are judged. If a company is going to succeed in today's global economy, it must adopt a fast and flexible culture. If community colleges are going to maintain their positions as the leading trainers of the U.S. workforce, they must embrace this same mentality when designing and delivering curricula and programs. Community college leaders need to begin asking ourselves how we can help our business partners learn faster.

In Kentucky, we have had firsthand experience with the need for reducing the learning time in our automotive manufacturer and automotive supplier partnerships. The industry's competitive environment has required auto manufacturers to redefine their just-in-time philosophy to include fast and flexible processes for new technology adoption. We work with our institutions to create curricula and teaching environments that replicate the environment that current and future workers will find in the new green factories. We are reengineering our training delivery model to recreate the environment that our students will experience in the workplace, basing achievement on industry skill standards, and using new visualization and simulation technologies to reduce learning gaps. We adopted a learner-centered approach by retooling our program delivery model to include "chunking" curriculum, multiple entry and exit points, and a reduced learning time cycle. We see the impact of these changes in our partnership with Toyota, which is redesigning its approach to training while working with our institutions to create curricula and teaching environments that replicate the environment that current and future workers will enter.

KCTCS initiated the development and implementation of an Interactive Digital Center of Excellence, hosted by Gateway Community and Technical College. The center provides display, development, and training capacity for three-dimensional visualization technologies, software, and display systems. The center develops custom business and industry training and supports application development for college programs.

The legislation that created KCTCS outlined the importance of workforce development activities for future economic growth in Kentucky. KCTCS institutions were identified as the primary driver of all workforce and economic development initiatives. Economic efforts include entrepreneurial training, small business assistance, grant writing, revolving fund pools for small business owners, and hiring and selection assistance for employers. Training and development efforts include technical training, mathematics, organizational change, management and leadership development, continuous improvement, computer science, communication, problem-solving, apprenticeship, and regulatory training.

Some of the 1999–2006 KCTCS initiatives supporting external collaboration included the following:

- KY WINS (Kentucky Workforce Investment Network System): Funded 364 projects, providing training and assessment for more than 46,000 people
- Kentucky Center of Excellence in Automotive Manufacturing: Provided state-of-the-art training to Kentucky's automotive industry
- Workforce Alliance: United KCTCS, the Cabinet for Workforce Development, the Economic Development Cabinet, and the Council on Postsecondary Education to coordinate workforce education and training services provided by Kentucky's workforce development agencies
- Lean Manufacturing and Lean for Service: Initiated the development of the Center for Excellence in Lean Manufacturing in 2001 in the Madisonville area to serve as the focal point for the development of new programs and to provide consulting services to other KCTCS colleges
- Telephony Program: Developed the BellSouth Project Opportunity in eastern Kentucky to provide training programs for service technicians
- Kentucky Public Power Authority (KPPA)/Tennessee Valley Public Power Authority (TVPPA)/KCTCS Online Training Project: Signed an agreement with KPPA and TVPPA, in cooperation with Kentucky Virtual University, to develop online training
- Empower Kentucky, Department of Transportation: Customized training program for managers and supervisors to improve their coaching skills
- Kentucky Manufacturing Skills Standards (KMSS): Provided administrative support for KMSS and issued and tracked the individual certifications
- Kentucky Adult Education Workforce Alliance Grant: A $200,000 grant from the Kentucky Adult Education provides training and assessment in workforce essential skills, focused on incumbent worker training.

Two partnerships for which we have received particular attention are the North American Racing Academy and Career Pathways. Each, innovative in their own way, provide training that is specific to the needs of our state.

201

KCTCS NORTH AMERICAN RACING ACADEMY

The KCTCS North American Racing Academy (NARA) began offering the first jockey training program in August 2006. NARA is the first thoroughbred racing education program in the United States. This program was developed in conjunction with the thoroughbred racing industry, including The Jockey Club, Keeneland Association, Churchill Downs, Kentucky Horse Park, National Horsemen's Benevolent and Protective Association, Inc., and National Thoroughbred Racing Association. Initially, the academy trained jockeys. As part of their educational experience, students from all areas of the United States meet other thoroughbred industry professionals at Keeneland and Churchill Downs. The program's long-term goal is to build associate degree and certificate programs as career pathways for people interested in working in all areas of the racing industry. At its March 2007 meeting, the board of regents approved an associate in applied science in equine studies that responds to the needs of this industry.

CAREER PATHWAYS

October 2003, KCTCS launched the statewide Career Pathways initiative. With the support of the Ford Foundation, we began laying out a vision for career pathways and requesting proposals from each of our 16 colleges. Career Pathways target regional labor markets, focus on employment sectors, and provide a framework for workforce and economic development. It is important to recognize, however, that career pathways cannot be developed in a vacuum. It is crucial that multiple partners be engaged fully in the process.

Career pathways integrate the programs and resources of community colleges and other education providers, workforce agencies, and social service providers. The pathway offers an open-entry, open-exit educational format; accelerated academic programs and interactive, hands-on learning opportunities. Industry partners use the career pathway to recruit new workers and enhance current workers' skills. Industry partners develop and participate in technical training programs, and they recognize project credentials in employment and promotion practices.

KCTCS committed more than $3.5 million toward the implementation of the Career Pathways initiatives in our 16 institutions. This was matched with more than $3 million in contributions from more than 100 employers and other partner agencies. The Career Pathways initiative requires that strong relationships be developed and nurtured among the partners. Thus, businesses, community colleges, and other stakeholders may be responsive to ongoing changes in workforce needs. These efforts require strong existing relationships and an in-depth knowledge of the industries we serve.

Two regional Career Pathway initiatives in Kentucky have been of particular interest to business and industry partners. The first is the manufacturing career pathway at Gateway Community and Technical College in Northern Kentucky. Gateway's initiative has linked the college's manufacturing programs vertically, from secondary schools to 4-year institutions. Simultaneously, the initiative has engaged manufacturers, ranging from small local businesses to Global 500 companies, by identifying their requirements that will drive curriculum and program development. A key addition to completing the pathway was the development of an associate of applied science degree in manufacturing engineering technology. This degree serves as the link between an associate degree at Gateway and a bachelor of science degree at the local 4-year institution.

The second program is the Manufacturing for the 21st Century model at Owensboro Community and Technical College. This is a multiphased approach that offers people an opportunity for employment through certifiable skills enhancement in the field of industrial maintenance. The pathway uses WorkKeys job profiling to identify the skills present in entry-level manufacturing positions. People are assessed with WorkKeys and are required to earn a Kentucky employability certificate as the first step in the pathway to continued learning. Postsecondary curriculum in the area of industrial maintenance has been enhanced to increase participant access and flexibility of delivery.

The Career Pathways initiative serves as an important bridge between our past efforts to serve and our present efforts to succeed in the new marketplace. The future will require us all to work beyond our present boundaries to embrace the many variables in our new economic equation—education and training, public and private, business and government. Creating opportunities for people to develop and market their talents is another innovative and promising strategy. For many areas of our country, competing for a manufacturing facility or expanding a service business is an elusive goal. Yet, those same areas offer some of the most beautiful and exciting forms of art and culture. In rural eastern Kentucky, Hazard Community and Technical College's School of Craft is one example. To preserve its heritage, the college has created a program of entrepreneurial education for artisans. The result is strengthening a creative community that will harbor a strong tourism economy. Although these programs add one dimension to the role of community colleges, they also provide innovative examples of responsiveness and creativity in developing their local economy. Such local efforts and will contribute to community colleges serving as the nation's engine in promoting workforce and economic development.

PROGRAM DEVELOPMENT

All organizations need to know that virtually no program or activity will perform effectively for long without modification and redesign. Eventually, everything becomes obsolete; and today, the cycle of obsolescence gets shorter and shorter. However, the inability to stop doing anything is a common disease of higher education. Compare ourselves to the automobile industry. In 1913, Ford took weeks to build a single model car with an extremely simple design and no options. Today, automotive makers produce cars with a high level of technological sophistication and a wide variety of options in a single day. So, how do we measure up? In 1913, it took 16 weeks to teach Physics 101 or English 101, the same time that it takes today. In fact, the majority of our country's high schools and postsecondary institutions are following a hopelessly outdated educational model. We must embrace "fast-and-flexible" change if we are going to help our business partners learn faster. To do this, we need to develop tests and yardsticks that measure our performance. We must rid ourselves of the obsolete to avoid becoming obsolete.

We must practice growth by substitution—a much more difficult concept to master than simply adding new programs onto old. To survive, we must reengineer ourselves into becoming customer or end-use focused instead of subject focused. This customer-based approach is necessary for survival in today's marketplace and for meeting the workforce needs of the business community.

Passage of the act creating KCTCS and the delegation of program approval authority to the board of regents engendered an innovative spirit in the college program-approval process. New programs approved by the board of regents included four associate of arts programs, four associate of science programs, 169 associate of applied science programs, 37 associate of technology programs, 140 diploma programs, and 2,052 certificate programs. At the same time, the system has eliminated 159 (unduplicated count) low-productivity programs, including associate degree, diploma, and certificate programs. In addition, we have developed policies for cooperative efforts between KCTCS colleges, ensuring that collaborative program development processes meet criteria specified by the accrediting bodies of the respective community and technical colleges and the Policy for Consortial Relationships and Contractual Agreements (Credit Courses or Programs). This ensures that agreements meet the accreditation requirements of both the Commission on Colleges of the Southern Association of Colleges and Schools and the Council on Occupational Education.

In 2002–2003, KCTCS participated in several collaborative initiatives with 4-year institutions, including Northern Kentucky University, University of Louisville, and Murray State University. The collaborations allow students who complete a KCTCS associate degree program to transfer seamlessly into one of several baccalaureate programs, including criminal justice, communications, training and development, organizational leadership, business and telecommunications, public administration, and independent studies. In addition, KCTCS is partnering with the Kentucky Department of Education and the Department of Technical Education to develop and deliver a Medicaid nurse aide online course to include a statewide network of clinical locations

A Working Connections project in the amount of $300,000 was awarded to KCTCS by the American Association of Community Colleges (AACC) and the Microsoft Corporation. This statewide initiative partners with the business and industry community to expand information technology offerings, develop new modes of delivery, train faculty, offer scholarships for traditionally underserved populations, and seek funding to develop computer laboratories in nontraditional locations (e.g., public housing facilities). This project reaches the largest urban centers, cities, towns, and the rural and Appalachian regions of the state. In addition, KCTCS received Microsoft software at a retail value of $11.4 million to support the activities of the project.

KCTCS was named a Microsoft Regional Information Technology Academy in 2003. KCTCS received a MentorLinks grant from AACC in 2003 to develop a geographic information systems curriculum. The National Workforce Center for Emerging Technologies, Microsoft, and AACC awarded Kentucky a second Working Connection Grant for $37,500 to develop a faculty institute (1 of only 12 nationally). Additional awards in geospatial technology were received in 2005 as part of the MentorLinks program to mentor faculty in Springfield, Massachusetts, and San Francisco, California. The Kentucky Division of Geographic Information awarded a Remote Sensing–Geospatial Information Technology Grant to KCTCS to offer remote sensing classes.

In 2002, Cisco awarded KCTCS a Cisco Academic Training Center for Sponsored Curriculum. In the fall of 2004, KCTCS joined Cisco in a blended distance learning program in networking. Funds for the project were received from the Kentucky Virtual University (now Kentucky Virtual Campus).

In May 2004, Jefferson Community College and the University of Louisville received a grant from the Council on Postsecondary Education to develop a block transfer in information technology and networking. This project provides a seamless 2 + 2 + 2 program with an articulation agreement. KCTCS has information technology articulation agreements with Western Kentucky University, Murray State University, and University of Louisville. KCTCS has quarterly meetings of the Business and Industry Information Technology Advisory Committee and works with secondary partners for curriculum integration.

TECHNOLOGY

Although serving our community is at the heart of our mission, the role of technology in delivering educational programs has expanded the definition of community to include far more than a geographical boundary. Technology has opened the gateway for access to higher education. Technology is revolutionizing our lives, including what we learn and how we learn it, where we work and how we work, and how we create wealth. Nowhere is this transformation more evident than on the campuses of community colleges. Our students are demanding that technology be a key component of their learning experience, and businesses are requiring that we train workers using state-of-the-art equipment.

Today's new technology embraces and feeds off the entire array of human knowledge. This is having tremendous ramifications on all colleges and universities because the search for knowledge and the teaching of knowledge have been dissociated from application traditionally. KCTCS was structured early as an advocate of using technology in the administrative systems, student services, and academics. We recognized the inherent challenges in the innovation, implementation, and expense of technology and the essential and beneficial role technology plays as a tool for transforming our colleges.

From an internal operations perspective, building a sound technological infrastructure made sense. Administrative systems enable colleges to critically assess accountability issues and provide the critical data processing required by our institutions. For most of us, information technology has become part of our necessary, daily operations. A high-speed, statewide network links computers at the colleges and the system office. The network supports both administrative and academic activities. The administrative traffic focuses on the PeopleSoft database and processing modules, including financials (budgeting and financial records), human resources (payroll and employee records), and student administration (student records). An integrated library management system is also in operation. The network traffic includes Internet access, distance education, e-mail, interactive video, and library catalog and circulation access.

KCTCS colleges have made tremendous progress in combining resources to respond to the need for online student support services. Kentucky, as well as several other states, has adopted a comprehensive approach to offering students a method for navigating the entire state higher educational system. Using a comprehensive one-stop Web portal, students easily examine the various educational programs available to them, research financial aid opportunities, and apply online. In addition, outsourcing services (e.g., college bookstores) have provided many colleges with online customer service resources that would have been unthinkable under normal budget constraints. These collaborations make it possible for public entities with limited funding to provide the state-of-the-art services that student customers have come to expect.

The biggest technological payoff, however, is in the area of teaching and learning. The shift from geographic markets to cyberspace, made possible by the digital communications revolution, opens up new ways to organize human relationships. Students now enter our campuses with a high level of expertise using many different types of technologies. Referred to as the plug-and-play generation, today's high school graduates demand an active learning experience using technology in all aspects of their college experience. Fortunately, many faculty members have become technology advocates by seeking out methods to infuse new technologies into their courses. Blending Web-based courses, blogs, wireless computing, and the Socratic method of teaching, students and faculty are finding ways of keeping the high tech–high touch theory alive. The challenge is using technology in appropriate ways to meet student needs and industry expectations, which are changing as a result of technological advancement.

In July 2001, a Regional Information Technology Center grant from the National Science Foundation (NSF) Advanced Technology Education Program established the Kentucky Information Technology Center (KITCenter). The total initial award was $2 million for a 3-year period. A fourth year was funded for an additional $750,000. An additional $1.3 million was received from NSF to continue the project for 3 additional years. Along with matching funds, the project will exceed $6 million during the 7 years. The KITCenter provides professional development for both secondary and postsecondary faculty as well as resources for teachers to use in the information technology field. In addition, the center works with business and industry in helping them meet their training needs and developing appropriate curriculum. The KITCenter will become self-sustaining by 2008.

KCTCS has been working with partners and community colleges in applying new cutting-edge applications of technology that provide for higher levels of student engagement such as three dimensional visualization, simulations, and real-time assessment. The KCTCS Visualization and Immersion Center is developing a teaching and learning environment designed to reduce the learning cycle in both traditional education and workforce development. Replicating real-world situations in a virtual environment allows training to occur in a controlled, safe environment, and facilitates a quick understanding of technology and procedures.

In Louisville, Kentucky, a KCTCS–Ford Louisville Assembly Plant project will use new technology to connect the Internet and the training sites. Students will communicate via computer in real time. Another project with Toyota uses simulation technologies to shorten the learning cycle while holding high standards for skills development, safety awareness, and substantial cost savings. Both of these projects required the collaboration of faculty, administrators, and workforce partners.

Much effort and spending have improved communications, enhanced network computing capability, and upgraded student computer lab facilities. The development of a Network and Information Systems Technology (NIST) curriculum has been an important outgrowth of a 1996 to 1998 NSF grant. Fall 1997, a second NSF grant, A Network Systems Administrative Program for Kentucky, was funded for 1998 to 2000. Delivery of NIST core courses via a distance learning format and summer workshops for faculty were provided. In the summer of 1999, seven KCTCS institutions collaborated to deliver the NIST program. By 2005, all colleges had faculty who had attended workshops sponsored by the NSF grants.

FISCAL RESOURCE DEVELOPMENT

The passage of the Kentucky Postsecondary Education Improvement Act of 1997 served as the foundation from which the colleges individually and the system collectively have strengthened their financial health. As evidence of resourcefulness and preparedness for uncertain economic times, in fiscal year 2001 the colleges began the implementation of a long-term goal of keeping a portion of their public funds budget as an operating budget reserve (public funds are defined as tuition and fees, plus state appropriation). The system has built toward this goal with all colleges having a current public funds budget reserve of at least 4.0%; several colleges have achieved even greater financial health. This achievement has occurred in spite of KCTCS and its colleges withstanding a 2.0% reduction of state general funds in FY 2002, an additional 2.46% reduction in 2003, a 2.4% recurring, and 3.0% nonrecurring reduction in FY 2004.

In June 2006, Moody's Investor Service assigned KCTCS an AA rating based on the general credit quality of the system's sound financial health. This high-quality rating was based in part on KCTCS colleges' unique strategic advantage within the commonwealth—a measure reflective of their increasing financial position, ability to adapt and develop programs desired by business and industry, and geographic location throughout the state, providing substantial enrollment growth with a positive outlook for the future.

Financial stability of community colleges has depended traditionally on public funds, federal funds, and auxiliary enterprises. As KCTCS was established, it was critical to secure additional funds through the private sector. The board of regents recognized the importance of establishing a sound advancement program and authorized the establishment of a statewide foundation. The KCTCS Foundation, Inc., was established in 1999, as the not-for-profit 501(c)(3) fundraising arm of

KCTCS. Under the leadership of an independent board of directors, the primary purposes of the KCTCS Foundation, Inc. include the following:

- Advance the vision, mission, goals, and objectives of KCTCS
- Catalyze, lead, and coordinate the private-sector resource development programs and activities of KCTCS
- Raise private funds for systemwide initiatives and needs
- Seek support from state, regional, and national corporations and foundations
- Provide oversight and guidance for the management and investment of private funds
- Support college foundations
- Advocate and serve as a system friendraiser
- Counsel and advise the KCTCS president

Complementing the KCTCS foundation, each college established or created a local foundation as the official fundraising arm of KCTCS. The system immediately launched a major gifts campaign. Today hundreds of people, businesses, and organizations invest in Kentucky's future through the Fulfilling the Promise Campaign, under way by KCTCS. This statewide fundraising project provides much-needed support for educational programs and services at KCTCS colleges across the state. In addition to the system-level campaign, each of the 16 KCTCS colleges is conducting a campaign to meet the needs of its own communities. Contributions from the private sector support a variety of initiatives, including state-of-the-art training facilities, new occupational and technical programs, student scholarships, faculty development, and technology and equipment.

CONCLUSION

In summary, the individual colleges and the system have built on the initial financial foundation begun in 1997, with cogent effort marked by sound financial measures for success. We have an incredible opportunity to take the lead in preparing Americans for a society in which knowledge is the central energy and driving force behind all that we do. It is an exciting time to be a part of a community and technical college system, but it is a challenging time, as well. Our nation and our community colleges are at a critical crossroads. At no other time in our nation's and in our world's history has learning been as important as it is today. Today's workplace requires a constant upgrading of skills. In fact, most U.S. workers will change careers at least three times during their lifetimes and hold an average of nine jobs between the ages of 18 and 34. This changing environment demands that we embrace lifelong learning in our role as learning facilitators and prepare to fill the leadership gap created by our changing demographics. Serving our communities is the core of the community college mission. To respond quickly to these challenges, how do we create a culture that is customer focused and quickly meets the needs of the marketplace? We must embrace a new leadership challenge for the learning college to thrive. The cultural change we face will take years to realize fully.

How do we keep our nation's implicit promise of equal opportunity to learning in a society more diverse, more complex, and more divided than ever before? Community colleges must answer the call for higher achievement and greater accountability. The role of our community colleges in providing a trained workforce has never before been more critical and more challenged. In addition to the skills gaps and the changing demographics of the workplace, we increasingly see the impact of globalization. The rapid rate of change and the evolution of technology call for a different kind of worker—one who is multifunctional, able to problem solve in a team environment, and is highly adaptive.

On a national level, our colleges' roles in economic development continue to be a hot issue. The primary purpose of President Bush's new Community-Based Job Training Grants program is to build the capacity of community colleges to train workers to develop the skills required to succeed in high-growth–high-demand industries. The Center for Workforce Preparation and AACC (2004) developed a CD, *Working Together: Creating Market-Responsive Workforce Solutions.* It offers "practices and tactics to help develop the capacity of community colleges in responding to local employment needs."

The dilemma for community college leaders is that although they may be intuitive enough to recognize all that must be done, they struggle to do it. It is critical that we remain on the cutting edge and not the trailing edge by advocating the use of technology in all areas of our operations. Through effective advocacy and collaboration efforts, we can overcome the economic challenges associated with the rapid pace of technological change to achieve our goal of being the gateway to the American dream. Community colleges have an incredible window of opportunity, but this window will not stay open for long. We must create a culture in our colleges that aligns knowledge with application. We must create a culture in our colleges that places the customer at the core of all decisions. We must create a culture that rewards change and innovation at every level of the organization.

REFERENCES

Center for Workforce Preparation & American Association of Community Colleges. (2007). *Working together: Creating market-responsive workforce solutions* [CD-ROM]. Washington, DC: U.S. Chamber of Commerce.

Collins J., & Porras, J. (1997). *Built to last, successful habits of visionary companies.* New York: Harper Business.

Kentucky Community & Technical College System (KCTCS). (2003, July). *KCTCS strategic plan: 2000–2005.* Retrieved from www.kctcs.edu/organization/strategicplan2003.pdf

Kentucky Community & Technical College System (KCTCS). (2005, July). *KCTCS strategic plan: 2006–2010.* Retrieved from www.kctcs.edu/organization/strategicplanning/0610brochure.pdf

Kentucky General Assembly. (1997). *Kentucky postsecondary education improvement act of 1997.* Retrieved October 30, 2007, from www.lrc.ky.gov/recarch/97ss/HB1/bill.doc

Labovitz, G., & Rosansky, V. (1997). *The power of alignment: How great companies stay centered and accomplish extraordinary things.* New York: Wiley.

13

Progressive Leadership and Professional Development in the Louisiana Community and Technical College System

Walter G. Bumphus

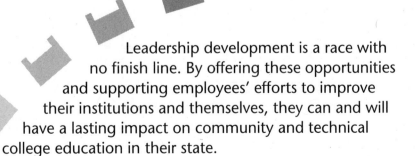

Leadership development is a race with no finish line. By offering these opportunities and supporting employees' efforts to improve their institutions and themselves, they can and will have a lasting impact on community and technical college education in their state.

—*Walter G. Bumphus, The University of Texas at Austin*

Before hurricanes Rita and Katrina, there was another rebuilding effort in Louisiana's recent past. The state began restructuring its community colleges and technical schools in the late 1990s. Combining and aligning these two disparate educational functions took the vision and strong leadership of President Emeritus Walter Bumphus, his staff, and the board. Collectively, this rock-solid leadership team spent years igniting the region's economic vitality with a common vision to educate and train residents of the state.

Relationships between college leaders and key political figures were built and strengthened across the state, from its top office to the local parish park—a difficult task when all of higher education was experiencing a leadership exodus because of retirement. Building a future for Louisiana's 2-year colleges took more than changing a name; it took investing in the long-term development of its leaders.

The newly created Louisiana Community and Technical College System established the Leadership Development Institute to grow its own corps of future administrators—now the rising vanguard of community college leaders. The trust, expertise, and commitment of those leaders miraculously enabled them and their colleagues to maintain operational education environments through one of the nation's worst natural disasters.

Author's Note. The author wishes to acknowledge Angel M. Royal, who served as executive assistant to the president and as vice president of external relations, for her significant contributions to this chapter and for her leadership and support of the Leadership Development Institute during my tenure as president of LCTCS.

CREATED IN 1999, THE LOUISIANA Community and Technical College System (LCTCS) was the newest state 2-year community and technical college system in the country—consisting of 7 community colleges, 2 technical community colleges, and 40 technical college campuses, organized into eight regions. These institutions were created to serve virtually every parish in the state. Before the creation of LCTCS, Bossier Parish, Delgado, South Louisiana, and Elaine P. Nunez Community Colleges, which were being transitioned to LCTCS, were managed by the University of Louisiana System. Baton Rouge Community College, which was created out of the desegregation settlement (1981 consent decree), was managed jointly by the Louisiana State University and Southern University Systems. The 40 technical campuses were managed previously by the State Board of Elementary and Secondary Education; and Louisiana Delta Community College was created after the formal enactment of the system. In 2003, the LCTCS board designated two technical college campuses as technical community colleges, creating the Sowela and the L.E. Fletcher Technical Community Colleges. The 4-year institutions in those areas were moving toward selective admissions; had this system not been created, many of Louisiana's citizens would have been denied higher education opportunities—the result of the impending gap in the 2-year college services. This consolidation of 2-year institutions into one system that could coordinate their activities for the advancement of the state as a whole was difficult yet necessary to ensure that all Louisiana's citizens had access to market-driven, high-quality educational programs and services.

Governor Murphy J. "Mike" Foster, Jr. created the system to provide educational opportunities to citizens who might not be interested in pursuing a 4-year degree. In creating the Board of Supervisors of Community and Technical Colleges, he proposed a vision. Rather than the board focusing on the "old way" of conducting business, he challenged its members to focus on the "new way" of serving Louisiana (see Table 13.1).

Further, Governor Foster established a "charge to the board," designed to govern operations. First, he charged the board to function as a corporate body, in the interests of citizens, employees, workforce, economic development, and cultural enhancement. His main focus was to ensure that although board members represented specific areas of the state, they did not function to protect only the institutions within their district but to think as a global body with responsibility across the state. Second, he charged that a process of the continuous evaluation of the effectiveness of the system and campus CEOs or the programs offered by the campuses be established. Governor Foster wanted to be assured that board members were not micromanaging the institutions for which they were responsible but rather would establish a framework to measure the effectiveness of the

Table 13.1 Governor Foster's Vision for LCTCS

The Old Way	The New Way
Local direction and control: A campus CEO directly responded to requests of local members of management boards and local legislators.	Statewide direction and control: Each campus CEO works to fulfill the new board's mission through the board's CEO and staff.
Local sense of responsibility: A campus CEO was committed to what was best for his or her campus.	Statewide sense of responsibility: Each campus CEO is committed to the best ways to fulfill his or her part of statewide mission of LCTC System.
Independent view of service: A campus CEO offered as many courses and programs as possible using the resources assigned to his or her campus.	Cooperative view of service: Each campus CEO works to ensure that local needs are met in the best possible way, regardless of which campus' resources, credits, or program are involved.
Decisions on hiring, promotion, reward, release of faculty and staff were based on political or local pressure: Staffing decisions were made for local, personal, or political reasons.	Decisions on hiring, promotion, reward, release of faculty and staff are based on experience and need for specialized services: Staffing decisions are made based on need for and value of services offered.
Mission followed money: State funding was based on credit or clock hour production or number of people employed.	Money follows mission: State funding is based on performance, value of services rendered, and effectiveness of interinstitutional cooperation.
Employee-centered programming: Programs were offered at times and in modes convenient for faculty.	Student- and employer-centered programming: Programming is offered at times and in modes convenient for students and employers.
Focus on campus development: Plans, programs, and reward systems were based on the best interests of campus.	Focus on workforce, economic development, and cultural enhancement: Plans, programs, and reward systems are based on responsiveness to workforce needs, positive impact on economic development, and cultural enhancement.
Campus CEO as politician with knowledge of education: A campus CEO directly responds to requests of local members of management boards and local legislators.	Campus CEO as educational leader/manager with awareness of political interests: Each campus CEO works to fulfill the new board's mission through the board's CEO and staff.

institutional and system leadership, focused on accountability. Third, he charged the system CEO to possess proper vision and leadership abilities, and the board to exercise the power necessary to supervise and manage institutions of postsecondary education under its control in accordance with the responsibilities outlined in the Constitution of the State of Louisiana.

A 17-member board of supervisors, constitutionally required to be representative of the state's population by race and gender to ensure diversity, oversees the system. Fifteen of the members are appointed by the governor, with consent of the senate, and serve overlapping 6-year terms. Two students serve on the board. Not only did the inaugural board of supervisors have to bring together institutions that had been administered previously by other entities, they also had to address the fact that several institutions had operated previously under a traditional 4-year university model and truly did not understand the role, scope, and mission of 2-year colleges.

I arrived in the second year of operation of the system. Significant progress had been made in combining the technical colleges and other institutions into a single system—clearly, a major challenge to create a culture where community colleges and technical college campuses would work together for the benefit of all citizens loomed large. Florida, California, Texas, and Georgia provided effective examples of successful implementation, consolidation, and successes and informed some of the decision making and infrastructure established by LCTCS.

In 1999, many community and technical college employees in the state had a limited understanding of effective national models of 2-year college education. Most of those 2-year college employees had worked in 4-year or secondary institutions and were accustomed to the traditional agrarian schedule and operations. In addition, like many other states that had "vo-techs" or technical colleges, there was a long history of serving the whims of local politics rather than following standard college practices. With the creation of a new system, there was a need and opportunity to provide experiences that immersed these employees in innovation as it related to curriculum and program planning, responsiveness to business and industry, and workforce education.

In 2001, members of the Board of Supervisors of Community and Technical Colleges charged the system president with designing a comprehensive program, focused on leadership development to include best practices of 2-year institutions, as well as components centering on personal and professional development. The board, system president, and system staff devoted considerable time to exploring and debating the critical characteristics and competencies that the board desired in its future leaders, job descriptions, searches, and evaluations. In essence, the board felt strongly that leadership would affect significantly the likelihood that the desired world-class status could be achieved.

After a thorough assessment of the system's needs and a review of the research of leadership and professional development offerings, five initiatives were identified as lynchpins for the comprehensive statewide professional development program. Those initiatives together encompass leadership development for all levels within the institution. In 2001, LCTCS initiated a comprehensive program to develop and foster leadership development on a statewide level. The program included the following: (a) an orientation for new college chancellors, (b) a comprehensive growing-our-own program for midlevel managers, (c) professional development initiatives for senior-level leaders (Senior Leadership Academy), (d) a workshop for newly appointed division deans and department chairs, and (e) a statewide conference and leadership development day for all employees (the LCTCS Conference and Leadership Development Day).

Ultimately, this program included the board's and president's vision for the Leadership Development Institute (LDI) and related professional development programs that were planned and implemented to create a world-class system of community and technical colleges. The leadership strongly believed that with a new system there was a unique opportunity to invest in human capital to make LCTCS the best in the country—to that end, to develop a program grounded in leadership theory and best practices in educational and workforce training programs, and professional development for faculty and administrative leaders in community and technical colleges already well-regarded on the national level. The vision was that as the programs were implemented, the system could strive to bring in leaders with a record of success with fresh ideas and grow our own as well. Inaugural searches for chancellors and vice chancellors brought in leaders from established community and technical colleges from across the country. However, the hope was that as more staff within the system gained additional professional experience and participation in leadership training, a cadre of leaders would be developed that would be competitive in the national searches the system undertook for its chancellor and vice chancellor positions.

ORIENTATION FOR NEW COLLEGE CHANCELLORS

Regardless of the position classification (entry level, mid-management, or senior level), solid orientation programs should be available to ensure that all employees are successful in the new positions they assume—especially critical for newly appointed presidents and chancellors. Although these people may have been well-prepared for the positions they are assuming, fundamental operational and cultural issues may become problematic. Early exposure to these issues can help avoid early missteps or setbacks.

Under the leadership of the system president, LCTCS developed an orientation program for newly hired chancellors to provide them with a comprehensive overview of the organization and the board process. The chancellors participated in meetings with top governmental officials. New chancellors spend extensive time in meeting with the commissioner of higher education and other board of regents staff, the secretaries of the Louisiana departments of labor and economic development, representatives from the state department of education, and members of the governor's staff. The information gleaned in these meetings, coupled with the information provided by staff, assists leaders in understanding the budget and capital outlay processes, facility planning issues and legislative issues, as well as how the board process works for approval of college agenda items.

In addition to the meetings with external partners and stakeholders, each new chancellor was scheduled to meet monthly with the system president for ongoing orientation, advice, and counsel. These meetings provided an opportunity for the new leaders to discuss and understand the culture of the state, as well as campus and system operations. New CEOs also met routinely with board members and system staff to get a holistic view of the organization and its operations, and to receive ongoing support in their campus CEO roles. The meetings with the system president and staff educated the new leaders on the system's priorities of student access, student success, and student engagement and allowed time for collaboration on new system initiatives to support these priorities. However, several chancellors observed that opportunities to reflect on the first few critical months in a leadership position and address questions one-on-one with the president were the most valuable aspects of the program.

THE LEADERSHIP DEVELOPMENT INSTITUTE

In the developmental stages of LDI, the goal was to provide participants with exposure to situations that would lead to increased understanding of the role of 2-year colleges in the communities that they served. As the program evolved, the goal was to emphasize the components for successful leadership and pay special attention to the self as a leader. Although the system's focus is on shoring up the pipeline, it had become increasingly important to encourage leadership from all vantage points in the organization. Not everyone wanted to pursue positions in senior leadership; some preferred to lead from the middle.

From the onset, the system leadership acknowledged that there is no cookie-cutter approach to the development of a comprehensive program for leadership development. Successful leadership programs need to address not only the key competencies as identified by the collective work of professionals but also the unique needs of the organization. The following questions should be asked through the assessment process: What is the ultimate goal of the program? How much time must be allocated for the program to provide a holistic view of leadership in the 2-year college? Are all of the components that the organization believes are essential to effective leadership included in the curriculum? How will the organization know that the goals have been met?

Answers to these questions provided the initial framework for LDI. The LDI program was developed as a yearlong program for emerging leaders in middle-management positions who aspired to acquire the skills necessary to move toward senior-level positions. The program is open to full-time employees, including faculty (on at least 60% release time for the duration of the program), professional staff, and administrators. The current maximum class size is 21. Each community college and technical college region may nominate one individual, and four slots are reserved for the system. Although employees in the system are eligible to complete the LDI application and apply directly to the system for the at-large slots, they must have the support of their campus CEO to be considered. Class members must represent ethnicity and gender diversity, with the system president reserving the right to work with campus leaders to make any modifications necessary to reflect the diversity of the system in the program participants.

Components included in the LDI were selected to ensure that there is ongoing dialogue and engagement between system leaders, the program coordinator, and the participants. LDI includes the following:

- Emergenetics® assessment and team-building activities
- Completion of an individual leadership plan
- Five on-site meetings at the system office
- Written feedback reports after four of the five on-site meetings
- Mentoring and the completion of mentor feedback reports
- Reading assignments and the completion of book reports
- A reflection paper completed at the conclusion of the institute
- Completion of an internship away from the participant's home campus

LDI includes two components: a college component and a traditional personal enrichment component. Participants may enroll in the program for undergraduate or graduate college credit, but they must make this decision before the conclusion of the first on-site meeting. Once made, this decision cannot be reversed or modified.

Because LCTCS is an emerging system with institutions across the state, it was important to start the program at a global level and then move on to more specific programmatic and functional levels. The first meeting exposes the participants to a variety of important elements (e.g., assessment and team building). In previous years, the system used the EQ Map Questionnaire (Cooper, 1997), facilitated by an external college CEO. Currently, LCTCS uses a trained facilitator to administer the Emergenetics survey and provide team-building exercises. This current assessment instrument was determined to be a better match to the goals that the system hopes to achieve. In focusing on the self as a leader, it is important for emerging leaders to understand the ways they think and behave and how these thoughts and behaviors influence their personal and professional lives. As a result, they are better able to see how their colleagues' and other professionals' behaviors may differ from their own. Coaching can help them use this information to improve their own communication skills.

Team-building is important, and it is critical to promote interaction with and communication between the organizations' current and emerging leaders. New LDI participants have opportunities to meet with members of the board of supervisors, the system president, system staff, and current system chancellors. Each chancellor provides participants with feedback on his/her leadership journey and shares information about criteria they use to select leaders. The panel session concludes with a dynamic question-and-answer time during which participants ask current leaders any questions they wish. Presentations by board of regents staff address academic affairs, workforce development, and institutional effectiveness.

In recent years, the program has been revamped to provide ongoing interaction between the system president and LDI participants. This interaction is facilitated by "reflection" sessions, scheduled at the conclusion of each meeting to allow for a review of events that have taken place over the course of the meeting and allow the president and participants to get to know each other better. The reflections are not scripted and provide many teachable moments. All sessions that follow the opening meeting begin on Wednesday afternoon and end at Friday noon. The initial comprehensive session is designed to bring participants up to speed on higher education, the LCTCS board, and system operations. Sessions two and three address global issues and gradually begin to shift to regional issues. Topics presented in the second and third sessions include ethics in leadership, legal issues in higher education, preparation for a promotion, and crisis and conflict management. As the program progresses, the topics become more institutionally focused and address topics such as planning and budgeting, resource development and grant writing, institutional effectiveness, and the politics of education. The fourth meeting addresses the politics of education (e.g., understanding the legislative process, funding higher education, policy development, and hiring practices).

The LDI program was launched in the 2001–2002 academic year, with a class of 35 employees. After assessing the success of the initial program and feedback from the national speakers, we decided to reduce the class size to a number that would afford more meaningful interaction between facilitators and participants. The program now accommodates 22 to 24 employees. At the conclusion of the 2005–2006 academic year, 126 employees had participated in LDI. In April 2007, LCTCS administered a survey to past participants. LCTCS mailed 108 surveys and received 98 responses. The responses have helped the institution move forward with future planning. Eighty-nine percent of respondents believed that LDI provided a holistic picture of leadership in the 2-year college. When asked if the training provided had allowed them to be successful in their current jobs, 85% of respondents answered "yes"; 43% reported that they have moved to other positions and that the training assisted them in those new positions.

Other areas of interest included the participants' attainment of additional education, promotional opportunities and willingness to recommend the program to others. Forty-five percent responded that their participation in the program motivated them to pursue additional higher education (e.g., at the University of New Orleans, The University of Texas at Austin, The University of Texas at Arlington, Lamar University, Oral Roberts University, Walden University, and Louisiana State University). Forty-one percent of respondents indicated that they have received a promotion within LCTCS since their participation in the program, and an additional 6% have received promotions outside of the organization. Of those promoted, past graduates serve within LCTCS as vice presidents, regional directors, and deans—meeting the goal of growing leaders to move into senior-level positions. Of the responses received, 93% indicated that they would recommend the program to current or former colleagues at their institution. This feedback provided by participants to the questions asked, were important. The written comments are affirming. Several comments illustrate the power of an effective leadership and professional development program.

> When I completed LDI, I was asked to assume the role of campus coordinator, an interim leadership position. The fiscal condition of the campus was in peril. Acadian campus has experienced a deficit situation for the past 3 years. Changing the culture of the attitude on campus among faculty and staff was especially challenging. It was truly a long and arduous year. Through hard work, dedication, and a new focus, we managed to overcome the deficit and put the campus back in the black. Looking back, I never would have been able to accomplish this incredible feat without the LDI training. LDI gave me expert advice and training, enabled me to network with other professionals in the LCTCS arena, and gave me the confidence I needed to overcome the deficit situation successfully.—P. Miers (class of 2004–2005)

> LDI provided me with exposure to the various leadership roles and positions in the 2-year college setting. As a newcomer to higher education, I could not have asked for a better experience and opportunity to expand my knowledge of the role of our system within the state's education system.—E. Hill (class of 2004–2005)

LDI is a visionary innovation that should continue. It shows that LCTCS is seriously committed to the professional development of its personnel. We must be both told and shown how to be good leaders. Press on.—M. Baines (class of 2005–2006)

LEADERSHIP DEVELOPMENT FOR DIVISION DEANS AND DEPARTMENT CHAIRS

Division leadership is an important component for the viability of academic programs and services of the institution. With such tremendous responsibility for ensuring the viability of their respective academic departments, it is astonishing that there is usually little or no training for this work. Having previously served in faculty positions only, most newly appointed division deans and department chairs have little or no knowledge of the responsibilities they are asked to assume. In many cases, they lack the basic skills necessary to address the complex human resources, financial, and other administrative issues that they will face. LCTCS recognized the lack of professional development opportunities for new division deans and department chairs early on. In 2002, a plan to develop a training seminar, specifically tailored to the unique needs of people assuming these administrative appointments, was developed and launched.

The system's division deans and department chairs were surveyed to assess their professional development needs and the methods of delivery that were most conducive to delivering the professional development. The results collected from the survey provided the framework for the topics to be covered. Over the course of several days, participants engaged in interactive meetings about performance management and appraisal, other human resource issues, budget management and finance, legal issues in higher education, and fundamentals such as program creation and review.

SENIOR LEADERSHIP ACADEMY

In 2005, the system's technical colleges underwent a major reorganization. Before the reorganization, the 40 campuses of the technical colleges were arranged in districts, with each cluster of campuses reporting to a vice chancellor and provost. The seven vice chancellors and provosts reported to a chancellor, who in turn reported to the president. To establish a process for reorganization, several recommendations were proposed to ensure that there would be no negative impact on the services provided to the students or the institution's partners in the transition.

The recommendation with the most impact was to arrange the technical college campuses into regional technical education centers (R-TEC), a cluster of campuses within a given region, led by a regional director. What made this arrangement different from the previous district model was the amount of autonomy the regional directors would have in making decisions regarding the operation of the campuses within a given region plus the elimination of the technical college chancellor's office. At the conclusion of this transition, the functions performed previously by the Louisiana Technical College chancellor's office would be assigned to the system or to the regions.

With the elimination of the chancellor's position, and more authority to administer the campuses being vested with the regional directors, it was important to ensure that these people received a comprehensive, ongoing program of professional development; many had never had the broad scope of responsibilities that they would now be expected to assume. Lessons learned through LDI and the training for division deans and department chairs assisted the system staff in crafting this program. Much like LDI, the Senior Leadership Academy (SLA) was designed to provide relevant training to new campus regional directors.

SLA consisted of three sessions, the first of which took place over 1 week and coincided with the monthly board of supervisors meeting. During the first meeting, new leaders addressed pending issues that needed to be resolved before the formal transition to the new model campuses (which included but were not limited to budget allocation) as defined by the accrediting agency, and operational responsibilities assigned to the system and region. After review of pending issues, the stage was set to move forward with training and professional development. Members of the LCTCS board of supervisors visited with all new leaders, laid out their expectations, and answered questions. In addition, the president of the system met with participants to communicate his expectations. It was extremely important for all leaders to understand the accountability measures that would be used to evaluate their performance.

In addition to meeting with board members and the president, the newly appointed regional directors received an introduction to the system staff and were provided information about the staff's unique roles within the organization. This component was important—it provided them with information to help make efficient decisions and understand the protocol for getting staff support and gathering advice. However, before spending one-on-one time with each member of the staff, the system introduced an array of issues addressing ethics and internal controls. The system wanted all participants to understand the rules of law that they must follow.

In addition, the system provided interactive discussions on goal setting and planning to meet specific targets—the key to the success of new leaders. Although they must understand the organization's expectations, this understanding alone does not prepare them adequately for success. It is imperative that new leaders are educated about establishing goals, developing plans for goal attainment, evaluating their progress toward goal achievement, and forging collaborations to ensure that comprehensive services are available to the communities that they serve. With limited resources, leaders must understand the importance of leveraging the institution's capital. Many new leaders do not understand the rules of engagement with the different stakeholder groups. Leadership training must address this issue to help the leader and the institution remain responsive to the community.

Eight new leaders participated during the first year of the program. All evaluated the experience as extremely valuable in providing them with a comprehensive picture of the job to be done, as well as the skills to be successful in moving forward. To ensure that these people continue moving forward in a positive manner, board members have requested routine progress reports on the standards of accountability metrics that were established to determine goal achievement.

CONFERENCE AND LEADERSHIP DEVELOPMENT DAY

Formalized programs of leadership development have fulfilled one important need for the organization: to develop a cadre of leaders for the future. However, these programs do not have the ability to provide professional development to a large segment of the system's employees. Conference and Leadership Development Day was designed to celebrate the accomplishments of outstanding faculty and professional support staff and provide networking opportunities for system employees and a venue for sharing state and national best practices. This initiative offers a comprehensive day-and-a-half program for all employees, regardless of their positions within their respective institutions. Sessions are designed for support staff, faculty and professional staff, and senior-level administrators; they are hosted each August, just before the beginning of the fall semester. The system has supported this event financially, with the exceptions of lodging and transportation for participants. The Conference and Leadership Development Day is a themed initiative, with an agenda shaped by the priorities of the system. Conferences hosted after Hurricane Katrina have focused on recovery and resurgence and methods of becoming better and more efficient organizations after natural disasters. Before Hurricanes Katrina and Rita, the organization focused on best practices in academic and student affairs, leadership and professional development, workforce and economic development, and organizational issues.

The Conference and Leadership Development Day is organized around strands, or high-priority areas of interest. At least one or two sessions are offered in each stream for each time slot on the agenda. The system serves as conference central for the event and includes information on the venue, agenda, awards selection criteria from each institution, as well as online registration. All updates are posted on this Web page, in addition to being communicated to all employees through the system's e-News newsletter.

The official conference begins at 3:00 on a Sunday afternoon, but several pre-conference sessions are offered before the opening ceremony for employees arriving early. The opening session's kickoff by a keynote speaker is followed by an awards ceremony. Each institution has developed criteria with which it selects an outstanding professional staff member, outstanding professional support staff member, and an outstanding faculty member for recognition. These criteria are posted on the conference central Web site for review by all employees. In addition, the LCTCS president presents President's Awards for Service Excellence at this meeting. These awards are for people selected solely by the president who have gone above and beyond the call of duty to provide exemplary service.

In previous years, the system has facilitated the meetings of faculty senate groups and other affinity groups immediately at the conclusion of the conference. This strategy allows networking opportunities for those employees who do not have many opportunities to meet, because they are scattered across the state. Employees can maximize the time that they are away from their campuses to handle business associated with their administrative or faculty roles. Vendors interested in showcasing advances in classroom technology may participate in this meeting. LCTCS has developed donor levels. Depending on their donor level, vendors may select their exhibit hall space, host a session for product demonstrations, and attend social events hosted by the board and president. Any funds collected through donor level fees are used to offset conference expenses.

In August 2003, the first conference was hosted in Baton Rouge. Participation was limited to 900 participants because of the size of the venue. In 2004, the conference moved to New Orleans, and approximately 1,200 employees participated. In 2005, approximately 1,000 participated in conference and leadership development day activities. After Hurricanes Katrina and Rita, the system decided that it was important to continue the tradition of the conference, although the meeting was limited to 500 participants. Because of budget uncertainties, administration believed this to be a wise decision. It is expected that participation will climb back to original numbers, because the event is scheduled to be moved back to Baton Rouge.

CONCLUSION

A successful comprehensive institutional leadership development agenda at a college, district, or state level must be grounded in research and an in-depth assessment of the institution's and region's culture and needs. Failure to address either of these key components will lead to a short-sighted initiative that does not achieve the goals for which it was established. The key questions to ask are those we asked early in the process. Institutions must balance solid research against the visible and invisible barriers within the institutional culture and create a plan that works for and will be embraced by that specific institution. Through the establishment of a comprehensive catchall institutional leadership development agenda and the generous funding of the Ford Foundation, LCTCS was able to inform chancellors, other senior-level leaders, and mid-level managers about professional challenges and experiences. This educational effort resulted in the system's quantum leaps in its development in a short period of time.

In addition to building several new campuses with state-of-the-art equipment, LCTCS has developed a cadre of leaders capable of positively embracing change. These employees are prepared to deliver first-rate programs and services within new institutions. This leadership training and professional development has proved extremely useful after Katrina and Rita as LCTCS employees worked to recover, renew, and breathe new life into the devastated areas and respond to student needs under less-than-optimal circumstances. Leadership development is a race with no finish line. There is always the opportunity for continued development and improvement. The system continues to provide personal and professional growth opportunities to its employees. By offering these opportunities and supporting employees' efforts to improve their institutions and themselves, the system ensures that these professionals can and will have a lasting impact on community and technical college education in their state.

REFERENCES

Cooper, R. K. (1997). *EQ Map Questionnaire: An integrated EQ assessment and individual profile*. Kirkland, WA: Q-Metrics.

14

Tallahassee Community College: Responding to the Challenge of the Internet Age

William Law

As much as anything else we must do in fulfillment of our mission, the fundamental realities relating to the empowerment, individualization, and self-determination of the individual should direct and impel the changes in what we teach, how we teach it, and how we prepare our students.

—*William Law, Tallahassee Community College (FL)*

Located in the Florida Big Bend region, Tallahassee Community College serves a unique three-county population that combines poor, isolated rural communities, Florida's historically wealthy agricultural communities, and the Florida state government. President William Law understands well that the global changes of the 21st century influence Tallahassee's historic community.

Tallahassee Community College has adapted to the changes it faces by taking a hard look at data and increasing transparency. Using new technology, the college has created student learning portals that synthesize student data into always-accessible, always-accurate portraits of the students' learning plans, test scores, and course and advising histories. Concurrently, student affairs programs were united, and advising was increased and improved. The result is a synthesized support system that gives students clear direction and empowerment over their own learning paths and provides the college with detailed data for analysis of college programs and student trends.

T O THE EXTENT THAT THE Internet Age is a flex point in history—as is evidenced by increased democratization, the bypassing of old strictures, and the need for new knowledge and skill—the U.S. community college should be positioned ideally to respond. Community colleges are founded on almost the same principles: more access to higher education (democratization), alternatives to residential colleges (bypassing old strictures), and postsecondary certifications and associate degrees (a need for new knowledge). Yet, even these basic advantages are experiencing great stress. The greatest impact of the flat world is that one of the historical strengths of the U.S. community college—its service and value to our society's middle class—is under great duress. Our historical commitment to provide additional opportunities for citizens in a variety of areas is growing in scope and urgency:

- Extensive remediation is needed for underprepared students. Despite decades-long efforts to strengthen K-12 education, our country is able to point to only limited success in some communities. The number of students who drop out of school or who make it to graduation with inadequate basic skills continues to grow.
- Returning adults demonstrate the increasing premium on education and training as more students seek skills and certifications at ages well beyond the traditional 18- to 24-year-old range; those trends will accelerate.
- Bachelor's degree seekers increasingly choose the community college for reasons of cost or classroom ambience and quality.
- For many, bachelor's degrees are losing their luster as the only desirable outcomes of education; connecting students with opportunities requiring less than baccalaureate education is a growing priority of high school (and middle school) advising efforts.
- To put the challenges in perspective, we need to expand our services to those with inadequate preparation, to those previously prepared needing to upgrade their skills, and to those who previously would have sought their postsecondary education from another source.

Like every other challenge, the successful response will require a vision, a plan, and an executable strategy. Each institution will need to respond within its own context, history, resources, and abilities. The response in every quarter will demand that we do things with more focus, efficiency, and attention to results than at any time in the past. The framework for response will require that we find the means for students to bring their energies and resources (beyond tuition and fees) to assist in the solutions. There are far too few faculty and staff, and far too many students to serve, if we do not empower students to serve themselves to fulfill their educational goals. Indeed, our approach to serving students will need to be a part of the enhanced learning process. Just as we must take responsibility for the cognitive preparation of our students, so too must we prepare students with the social, workplace, and personal skills that will be demanded of them in the Internet Age and flat world.

TALLAHASSEE COMMUNITY COLLEGE'S RESPONSE

Structuring, envisioning, and executing a plan work best when there is a consensus about the context and direction of the efforts. At Tallahassee Community College (TCC), we find ourselves returning regularly to three visions that help us adapt our many efforts to the new challenges:

- The definition of student success is that students finish what they start.
- Those of us who do not teach share a common responsibility to help students get to class in the best condition for learning.
- We must act on the realization that access to college changes students' self-perception, but degrees and certificates change students' lives.

These guidelines allow all members of the college community to see that their roles contribute to the overall success of our efforts. No one group or person is charged with fixing the problems or meeting the new challenges. The guidelines also honor the long traditions of community college education that have earned us our deserved respect but at the same time focus on directly addressing the new challenges. Lastly, these guidelines can be communicated in an appropriate form to students to invite their energy and commitment to the response.

The most troubling and often unspoken weakness of our colleges is that far too many students drop out of our institutions before they achieve their desired goals. We celebrate, of course, the many successes of our students, and we highlight the anecdotal stories of our students who have overcome the greatest hurdles. Nevertheless, the analysis of our historical record is that barely one third of the students who enter our institutions persevere to earn an associate degree. At the level of each course, we find that course dropout rates, W grades, make up 15% to 20% of all grades awarded, on the average, and the range escalates to 35% to 40% in some courses on a regular basis.

If we profile our students, we find that the pattern of course dropout is widespread. Too many students take course loads that are unrealistic, given the considerable constraints on their time, the deficiencies of their earlier preparation, or the fragility of their financial resources. As soon as one of these factors comes into play, a student feels the need to drop out of one or more courses in an attempt to bring the stresses under control. This response mechanism, however, is only that—a response. It avoids addressing the underlying weaknesses and invites continued repetition until the student loses heart (or runs out of money) and drops out of school. This dropout pattern is highly detrimental to students beyond the college experience. We do students a grave disservice in preparing them for life beyond our colleges when we abet this dropout process. Clearly, such behaviors will prove detrimental in the workplace, where a premium is placed on reliability and fol-low-through. Overreaching and quitting can translate to serious consequences in personal finance, both in day-to-day living and long-tem financial planning.

Within our colleges, this pattern is an undiagnosed cancer. For the most part, our systems have evolved to a no harm–no foul approach to dropping out of courses. Grades of *W* or *I* often are not counted in a student's GPA. Consequently, students can be in a seriously threatening downward spiral of course completion, while at the same time maintaining average or above-average GPAs. Only a very few colleges have moved to or expanded their academic probation systems to intercede in a student's program on the basis of course completion rates rather than on GPA.

In summary, we have given precious little attention to the actual patterns of success (or lack of success) of those we have committed to educate. Only one third of the students who enter will be awarded a degree eventually, whereas twice as many will find their way out of our college, largely without our knowledge or awareness. Pick your own favorite bromide for the situation of community colleges:

- *Don't drink from a fire hose.* At TCC (and I suspect most others), we have doz-ens of support programs for students. In fact, we have too many programs for any one person to be able to sort through or for any advisor or faculty member to know the best program for any particular student.
- *If you don't know where you're going, you can end up somewhere else.* The earli-est engagement with students is far too unfocused to provide a solid basis on which students can build their college career; we cause students to make choices that are too often uninformed and, indeed, often detrimental to their best interests (e.g., having underprepared students enroll for a full load to remain on their parents' insurance).
- *If it ain't broke, don't fix it.* The widespread lack of data and information on student success allows us to maintain the systems and practices that we have always used—changes in demographics, pedagogy, technology, or student preparation are employed sporadically, if at all.

THE STUDENT PORTAL

At TCC, we have committed proudly to student success, and we have evolved our commitment as we have developed tools and insights. We have adjusted our pace as we have gained confidence and learned from our missteps. We have sought and gained valuable help from many quarters—Achieving the Dream (ATD), Title III, College Board, and several State of Florida initiatives. All of this assistance has energized the college and led us to a commitment that refines and distills our practices.

The college has embarked on a comprehensive effort to ensure—or rather to require—that every student create an electronic portal containing an individualized learning plan. With the portal, we can centralize our many excellent efforts to ensure student success, to assist students in getting to class in the best condition for learning, and to help students maintain demonstrable progress toward a desired goal. Our belief is that the best means for us to serve students individually and for students to get the best support for their unique needs is to establish a single repository for information, communication, and student self-determination.

The Student Portal Framework

In 2002–2003, the college launched its first efforts to provide an online advising tool, Eaglenet. The tool was home grown and provided an excellent first start to supporting student advisement and self-advisement. Students' records and test scores were available, a learning styles self-assessment was incorporated, and multisemester course planning was included, as well. The first efforts, as expected, were not perfect, yet they were well received by both students and faculty members. Primary concerns emerged from the faculty on their ability to advise the wide array of students. Potential university-transfer students without remedial restrictions were easiest to assist; specialized guidance for students seeking workforce degrees and certificates were the most difficult for many faculty.

In addition to Eaglenet, other online tools emerged from both the state level and the college's individual efforts:

- Building on Florida's sophisticated and comprehensive common course numbering system, degree audits and credit-transfer simulations for nearly all Florida university programs were developed. Students were provided the ability to simulate the impact of transferring to any university, as well as the impact of changing majors.
- Within the college, our reaccreditation Quality Enhancement Plan contained a commitment to design and develop an early warning system for students in remedial courses. This system was implemented in the 2005–2006 academic year.

- TCC is one of the community colleges to be selected in the first round of the Lumina Foundation's ATD initiative; our college's implementation plan focused on early student feedback and support for first-time-in-college students.
- Major expansion of Blackboard as a course management tool has taken place over the past 3 years; content delivery and course communications are the norm at the college.
- The commonality of these tools is that they allow students to be proactive in the management of their own success.

The ATD grant focused college efforts on identifying the barriers to success for students of color and transforming institutional processes to bring success rates (degree attainment) for students of color to the level of nonminority students. Fundamental to this process was the refinement and use of accurate and timely data on which to determine differences and to craft and monitor programs to transform the college.

The old saying that "good experience grows out of bad experience" best describes our efforts. Several well-conceived initiatives to address the core problems of student dropout patterns proved ineffective, hard to implement, and not feasible for large-scale implementation. Perseverance, however, led us to rethink the value of student learning plans as the most proactive means for us to help students succeed, while teaching them to channel their own best efforts. As we developed the conceptual framework for engagement and support of ATD students, we realized that the effort should include all students. After 3 or 4 years of high-priority activity focused on student success—finishing what they start—we had made little progress in course completion rates, semester-to-semester perseverance, and graduation rates.

In the fall of 2006, our college leadership team initiated the requirement that students have learning plans on file before registering for the spring 2007 semester.

- The initial requirement covered 6,700 students (of 13,500 total enrollment).
- Those required to have a plan were already within some existing support structure at the college—ATD, honors, assigned to faculty advisors, first-time-in-college support, athletics, international student support, probation, or the like.
- Faculty were responsible for advising a specific number of students, and they received comprehensive advising training.
- The plans are electronic and are the repository of all information the college has pertaining to the student (e.g., test scores, transcripts, advisement

requirements, current enrollments, holds, finance, financial aid–scholarship information, prior notes and advice, self-assessment information).

- The plans are owned by the student and can be changed at any time by the student.
- The plans can be accessed online anywhere, at any time; this is critical for assuring accurate, timely decisions by the student.
- The plans are intended to be the basis for communication with the student. They are tied closely to a much more robust e-mail communication system (e.g., Amazon, Fed Ex, and other online systems that continuously update the status of your order or account).

The Vision of the Student Portal

Students come to our colleges from an ever-widening variety of backgrounds, preparations, and aspirations. The first engagements with students must be sensitive to their differences and not force them into structures that work best for us. At TCC, we begin by assigning a college e-mail address to every student who submits an application. Our cost of adding each new account is miniscule; our message to the student is loud and clear—we will provide an easy means for you to give information to us, get information from us, or hear answers from us to questions you might have.

This early engagement is not just a matter of style. One issue that emerges from student progress analysis is the realization that as many as 10% of the students who go through the initial application and assessment processes fail to register for courses. Our working premise is that providing some modicum of student control and ownership at the earliest date can raise the confidence level of each student. We create a means of encouraging, responding, and supporting students in those initial, sometimes tenuous, moments.

The most important prospect of the learning plans and student portal approach is that it gives the institution a much greater ability to learn about our students' actual behaviors. The centralization of efforts through the learning plans affords an opportunity to do some valuable data analysis on the manner in which students move through the institution on a success path or a path that confounds their success:

- The plans foster multisemester–multiyear course planning; we can observe plans that have nonsuccessful patterns (e.g., discontinuity in math courses, excessive course loads).
- We can discern weak or nonexistent contact with advisors.
- Faculty and advisors can address a lack of response to early-warning alerts.

236

- Course dropout patterns that presage eventual college drop out can be anticipated and modified.
- Lack of coherence in the plan between stated goals and current and future enrollment planning becomes obvious.
- Financial aid matters, including standards of progress concerns that would end financial aid eligibility, can be predicted and avoided.
- Florida's concerns, specifically the potential for having to pay full instructional cost for the third attempt in any course, can be avoided.
- Assessing students' progress toward degree or certificate attainment and adopting proactive communication to guide and encourage students' course choices in fulfillment of requirements can be provided to students as a value-added benefit.
- Enhanced connection to the college's career center is facilitated, when appropriate, to assist students preparing to seek jobs.

The reality that we now face at TCC is that we can be predictive and intercede proactively. Not surprisingly, we find that we have not developed the systems and programs to take full advantage of the new knowledge; our many systems and interventions have been designed to function in a reactive, not proactive, mode. Financial aid standards of progress are the best examples. We can follow through on a timely basis to deny aid after the student falls below the mandated standards of progress. Yet, almost as easily, we can profile and determine in advance which students are approaching that chasm and interact with them to prevent their falling below the standards.

Progress of the Student Portal

The implementation of the requirement for a student portal did not have measurable impact on student enrollment. TCC's growth is among the fastest in the state. A great deal of energy has been devoted to stratifying the advising help inherent in the implementation of the system. Specifically, assignment of students to faculty for advisement is more purposeful. High-need, first-time-in-college students are not assigned to faculty; rather, they are the purview of our professional counselors and advisors. Efforts to pair students in certificate or science degree programs with faculty members from those programs are in progress. A great deal of additional faculty training and support has been created and put into place.

Although the responsibility for advisement was included in salary and workload consultations nearly two decades ago, there is a strong, new energy apparent from within the faculty ranks. An ongoing faculty advisory committee has been instrumental in the work necessary to make the learning portal and the learning plans valuable to students. At key times in the implementation process, this faculty group has counseled us to maintain our commitment and focus. To the credit of the student affairs staff (now renamed student success), the learning portal and learning plan tools have become a centerpiece in our student orientation process. Within the first hours of a student's introduction to TCC, the student is introduced to the learning plan process and assisted in developing his or her individual plan. The knowledge that the tool will be the common factor for all students is allowing the student success staff to rethink and revise how students can and will receive information about college programs and services. Orientation to the college increasingly takes on the flavor of student self-determination—with nearly untold support readily available.

The commitment to have all students use the student portal is opening new avenues for our efforts to communicate better with our students. A comprehensive review of our many communications is under way. What do we send? When do we send it? From which office does it originate? Is it timely? Does it complement other communications? Can students keep track of all the communications? Our commitment is to make the portal valuable to the student as the repository of all interactions with the college.

Because the student portal system has as its base the sharing of information, we can better (and more easily) share information across the divisions of the college. As the student success staff refines and expands its communications to students, we find that the same information is shared easily with the faculty to assist in their advisement responsibilities. Any historical separation between student affairs and the instructional programs is dissolving rapidly. Our academic and student success teams have been proactive with our university partners to whom our students will transfer, most specifically Florida State University. If we had any second thoughts about the need for the learning plans and portals, those misgivings were swept aside when we learned that our principal university partner was implementing a similar requirement for its students. Our excellent, long-standing articulation agreements are available now to students for their own planning.

The development of the student portal has been shared with the college's board of trustees. Nearly every month over the past several years, we shared our baseline information and student progress tracking with the board. In fact, we have created a separate portal for the board of trustees where we archive each month's workshop presentations and share *all* of the data we use to guide our day-to-day decisions. The board has a complete picture of our efforts to improve student success and is aware of our progress and struggles. Everyone in the institution has access to the same data.

TCC has been fortunate to secure a federal Title III grant to fund the next stages of development for the student learning portal. The hard work of the past decade to conceptualize, design, implement, and refine an online outreach to students has delivered the faculty and staff to a sophisticated level of preparation for a break-through in the use of the online portal as the central place for communication and support. Student response has been favorable. Our dialogue with students has been structured in terms of success at the college and later in life—not more mind-less bureaucratic requirements to make life easier for the institution. The portal and learning plan efforts have given new importance to the faculty advisement process, and we receive favorable feedback on that high-touch portion of the over-all effort. We get equally valuable feedback when parts of the system—technical as well as human—do not work as advertised.

The college intends to increase the active plan requirement to cover all stu-dents eventually. Our working plan is to grow the requirement with entering stu-dents. We expect that the plan will allow students to become self-directed learners as they move through the institution. Our need to devote intensive time with stu-dents should diminish generally as they become comfortable with the comprehen-siveness of the student portal. We hope to be able to provide more time and focus to students at the beginning of their TCC experience, allowing them to become more self-directed.

CONCLUSION

The changes in global society wrought by the Internet Age place new demands and stresses on community colleges' traditional roles. These changes require stu-dents to be better prepared academically, more proactive in responding to new changes, more aware of their own growth and development, and more committed to a lifetime of continuous, purposeful self-development. To do our part in pre-paring students for these challenges, TCC has provided a framework that assists students to be better prepared and to learn how to stay better prepared. We have chosen to use the power of ubiquitous, online information to strengthen the means by which we advise, counsel, and support our students. We have chosen to give each student the tools to determine how best to call on our many resources, while at the same time making certain that *every* student is aware and consistently nur-tured in calling on those resources.

Our efforts are reflective of the long-standing service of the college to our dis-trict. Failure to engage the challenges of the Internet Age will diminish what has gone before us. In the long run, our success will be determined by our own perse-verance. As we so often tell our students, we need to finish what we start.

Conclusion

Common Themes Among Creative Community Colleges

John E. Roueche, M. Melissa Richardson,
Phillip W. Neal, and Suanne D. Roueche

WITH GOOD REASON, A NATIONAL discussion is occurring about the poor state of our educational system. However, "the traditional trust the public has placed in education's ability to improve the common good need not be lost" (Roueche, Johnson, & Roueche, 1997, p. 184). Friedman (2004) pointed out that no magic formula can fix today's educational challenges, but passion, curiosity, and "learning to learn" are qualities that have transformational potential (p. 302). The importance of lifelong learning (Gleazer, 1980) and educating for the affective domain (Roueche & Ciez-Volz, 2006) are at the forefront of the community college mission. These traits are found in creative thinking and problem solving, and, increasingly, they are the trademarks of forward-thinking educational institutions. They are the trademarks of institutions that are economically savvy and unafraid of change—willing to track, analyze, and share their endeavors, whether successful or not, keeping their fingers on the pulse of community needs, and putting student success at the forefront of their institutional mission.

Imagination can dream up many creations, but dreaming is only the brainstorming stage in creative transformation. Applied creativity is the goal for colleges responding rapidly to the need for change. As Robinson stated, "innovation is putting that creativity into practice as applied creativity" (cited in Scanlon, 2006). Roueche and Roueche (2000) contended that community colleges need to "make friends with the future" (p. 16). Creative community colleges value the challenges that the future holds. They prepare for it by encouraging innovative processes and by reframing the pressures of the future into transformational tools to build flexible, sustainable, open-door institutions.

CREATIVITY AT WORK

Creativity is not selective; it is not bound by age, ethnicity, gender, nationality, or socioeconomic status. The creative community colleges and college systems we have profiled are of all sizes and located in every region of the country. They face unique local issues but share national and global pressures. Their commonalities offer us insights into the creative choices that are sustaining, growing, and positioning community colleges as indispensable educational institutions in our cities and towns. The educational institutions we have profiled share similar creative visions. Although they implement them in ways tailored to their individual communities, several shared themes emerge.

Reaching Students

These colleges recognize they must nurture and respect the students they have, not the students they had yesterday or that they wish they could have tomorrow. The realities of enrolling young and old, increasingly diverse, U.S. and international students; the low socioeconomic status of many; and a hard look at their skills on entering college combine to create an array of extraordinary challenges that colleges must face. Demographic changes create new challenges for retention, fill developmental education programs to capacity, and put advising staff on alert for emergency intervention. Learning programs for seniors, partnerships with colleges abroad, and college centers in the heart of their urban districts are but a few of the myriad of creative solutions to meeting students' nontraditional problems and pressing needs.

An inspirational partner to these new initiatives is recruitment: colleges actively seek new members for this disparate student body. Through innovative middle and early colleges, they reach out to students before they consider or arrive at the college doors. Through energetic collegewide recruitment initiatives, students see and hear from college advisers and faculty before they graduate from high school—they learn that college is a possible dream. Recruiters and advisers are going out into businesses and industrial manufacturing plants, urging potential students toward additional workforce training and skill development and thus contributing to the hum of their local economies, as well as national and global needs.

Technology

Creative colleges have learned to harness the new wave of technology for the good of the college and support of the students. College Web portals become uniting forces between students, faculty, and staff—helping colleges be more transparent, empowering students to know their progress through their learning plans, and providing quick access to student services that otherwise might be frustrated by the layers of bureaucracy or inflexible time constraints. As creative colleges move forward in the nationwide march toward more e-learning, they offer student support services in tandem with online course offerings, recognizing that online student success depends on full commitment to the technology and to the more recent generation's preferred learning styles.

These community colleges are data informed. Advanced analytical data programs do more than house college records. They provide detailed, useful, and immediate assessment about the health of college programs and the reality of students' progress. Technology is a marketing tool to inform the community about the college and to inform college constituents about the community. Organizations such as CCSSE and Achieving the Dream, which help to gather the data and start important conversations about it, are important community college partners.

Reduced to 1s and 0s, technology appears mechanistic. However, today's technological tools are flexible and adaptable. Implementing technology at the broad scale of the community colleges profiled here requires vision before adoption and implementation. It requires decision makers to imagine the experience of those who will use the system. Determining who collects the data, who sees the data, who analyzes the data, who has decision-making discussions about the data, and who acts on the results of these discussions are vital human elements in this technology.

Friendships and Partnerships

Allowing collective imaginations to shape the direction of the college is one way the community colleges profiled here apply their creativity. Partnerships are no longer considered fringe activities. Community colleges are committed to building relationships with many entities. Corporate partnerships aid relationships for workforce development and strategic community development. They help with community awareness of the vital role the community college has in building, maintaining, and growing the economic foundation of local areas. They bring opportunities for fundraising, putting colleges in touch with key community members who can help with creative solutions to funding challenges.

International partnerships are corporate and collegiate, helping to develop talent for a global workforce, sharing knowledge, and building a common culture between U.S. college students and international college students. These partnerships secure the learning of an increasingly international student body and blur the boundaries of local college service districts. Learning at these creative community colleges is a worldwide adventure, a necessity in this flattening global economy.

Community partnerships include strengthening friendships with other educational institutions. P through 16 initiatives and college-transition programs are easing the difficulty of student transitions from institution to institution, securing student confidence in college success, and opening students' eyes to possibilities for education and careers that extend beyond what they see within their own communities. Teamwork with local schools and 4-year institutions has become an integral source of information that identifies where students are dropping out, what critical learning needs to happen for retaining skill development, and the requirements that must be met for transfer.

Several leaders shared their careful media-courting strategies. Just like corporate entities, community colleges benefit from strategic marketing and public information sharing. Deliberate attention to the press counters stiff competition from for-profit institutions—increasing in almost every community—and negative reports about the state of higher education in general. In a reverse marketing strategy, many leaders broadcast news of comparable benchmark institutions to key constituents on campus. None of these colleges exists in isolation anymore. Authors of these chapters counseled patience (e.g., having the patience to create relationships in the right places, with the right people, at the right times, for the right kind of change). Patience, they observed, is the major task for addressing the challenges of today's rapid pace of change.

Facilities Transformation

Many colleges expressed their creativity and efficiency with new building projects. As aging buildings deteriorate and enrollments grow, significant energy, resources, and imagination were dedicated to building new places to gather (e.g., dormitories and student centers, libraries, student success centers, science and technology buildings, and even classrooms combined with retail centers). The buildings' usability and inspirational qualities are considered carefully. If colleges look like learning places, students are more likely to be inspired to achieve, and the community can be proud of its local community college. Most importantly, colleges should function as learning places, taking advantage of extensive research about creative and stimulating learning environments to discuss and develop inviting and successful learning experiences.

Honoring the Arts

Community colleges can be artistic institutions; they provide practical education, by design, and are quite capable of remarkable creative endeavors. Many of the colleges profiled here celebrate their creative spirit. From enhancing theater and music programs to sponsoring community art exhibits and celebrations to providing space for artistic inspiration and reflection, these colleges recognize the value of embedding a culture of the arts on campus.

> *As more community colleges are realizing, embedding the arts and culture in the community, business, and social milieus can be a significant advantage for talented people and lead to the availability of high-quality jobs in the global marketplace, and it can provide the distinguishing features that give a place an identity that can drive economic development. (Rosenfeld, 2006, p. 6)*

Financial Solutions

Every president of every college showcased here addressed the challenges of funding, as community colleges receive less and less support from state budgets and turn more and more to alternative funding sources. Creative adventures are opportunities for colleges to shore up their financial resources; "necessity is the mother of invention." Great creativity occurs in the face of inspiration, and an empty wallet can be very inspirational! Some of the many creative ways community colleges keep their doors open and build a financial base for the future include reaching out to students and building the student body; using technology to track college resources, prevent waste, and make sustainable choices; developing partnerships that lead to stronger foundations and additional opportunities for shared contracts; and spending money that builds the college culture in recognizable ways, such as new facilities and artistic outreach programs that will build an alumni base and attract community support.

Global Philosophy

At no time in the history of the community college has there been more focus on the global impact of education. With the burgeoning of the Internet age, the lines between service districts are no longer restricted to county or state boundaries. Students now have the ability to sample courses from any institution in the world, and professors may instruct from a distance. In addition, services have become as important as the product. Creative community colleges understand this. Creative leaders ensure that their employees realize that if they are not reaching out to students, businesses, and governments throughout the world, someone else will. Forming partnerships with international organizations is as important as articulation agreements with 4-year universities. Creative leaders understand that we must articulate with the global economies as we train a new, skilled workforce that may enter baccalaureate institutions and certainly will enter the global workforce.

CREATIVE LEADERSHIP STRATEGIES

Everyone can be creative, but creativity is not embedded automatically in the fabric of the workplace. According to a recent survey by the Fairfax Economic Development Council, "While a vast majority of American workers (88 percent) consider themselves creative, fewer than 2 in 3 think they are tapping their creative capacities on the job" (Gardner, 2007). However, the leaders in this book are different. Their innovative endeavors are visible evidence that they value and encourage creativity.

Taking Risks

Let there be no confusion about this point: Creative leaders take risks that others may not. Leading a public institution is risky business, and leading creatively is riskier still. Many creative leaders will admit that taking their institutions in the directions they have could have cost them their careers—society was not always ready for such change. When leaders create change to better position their institution before challenges occur, the vision is not always as apparent to others as it is to the leader with his or her unique view of reality. Courage to change despite public opinion, and disciplined decision making despite opposition, help creative leaders mold their future.

Do creative leaders manage the type and amount of risk they take? An expert in risk management recently pondered whether risk management was little more than "astrology or phrenology," trying to predict the future through seemingly unrelated events (Kloman, 2006, p. 1). Creative leaders rely on data collection, evaluation, vision, and other tools to reduce their risk. Years of experience give them common sense. Outstanding staff provide expert advice and leadership of their own. These factors, combined with a solid set of core values (e.g., integrity, belief in self, belief in others, and courageous thought) allow creative leaders to trust their decisions better and reduce risk. Even if they fail, they initiated the effort for what they believed to be the right reasons, and they can live with that. They celebrate success and learn from failure. Creative leaders live inseparably with their values and are willing to die (figuratively speaking) doing the same. At the end of the day, they say, "All you are left with is values, so make them good."

Charting a Different Course: Perceptual Shift

O'Banion (1997) wrote, "The learning college creates and offers as many options for learning as possible" (p. 47). Creative leaders seek, take, and create options but not blindly. Intentional and driven, creative leaders create cultures that support student success in the face of future challenges. Creative community colleges draw strength from challenge; they do not cower in its presence. Leonardo da Vinci claimed, "All our knowledge has its origins in our perceptions" (BrainyQuote, 2008a). If this is true, then viewing a challenge as negative breeds negative knowledge. The opposite is true for creative leaders. They do not see the future as something that happens to them; rather, they see the future as something they can create and shape.

Stealing Power: From Threat to Motivation

It is easy to say that not focusing on a threat decreases its power. However, the world does not appear to work that way. Will the lack of governmental funding disappear if we close our eyes? The time and energy community college leaders use to dwell on negative forces in their colleges can make a significant difference in how entrenched the negatives become.

Creative leaders accept the fact that funding will diminish and that other challenges could affect their colleges negatively. They give these challenges their due diligence and begin mobilizing their forces. They seek partnerships that recreate their funding streams so that federal downturns do not cripple the college but represent only a glancing blow. The college leaders featured here share a competitive spirit. Creative community colleges meet the challenge and as the challenge grows closer, so does their resolve to steal its power. They absorb the challenge's momentum and redirect it to catapult their enthusiasm into building relationships, partnerships, and consortiums that produce the prize the challenge threatens to steal—student success.

At a 1971 meeting at the Xerox Corporation, personal computer pioneer, Alan Kay (1989) said, "The best way to predict the future is to invent it." A few years later, a participant inspired from that meeting—Steve Jobs—looked into the future and invented the first personal computer. These presidents and chancellors are not at the mercy of the future; they are creating it. This philosophy is not new in history, but it is new to community college leadership. These creative leaders—and many more around the globe—are looking into the future and creating a tomorrow that will affect student success in ways we have not imagined yet. Those working from a strong foundation of values will be the ones who have vision and follow-through, the ones who are creative leaders.

THE FOUNDATION: VALUES AND BELIEFS

A common denominator among creative leaders is the foundation that makes effective creativity possible. A solid foundation supports numerous possibilities. It removes fear of instability and replaces it with confidence to venture out. It creates an internal compass and strips challenges of their awful grip. Creative leaders transform mindsets, attitudes, and cultures to welcome change. By understanding these systems, institutionally and individually, they are free to approach opportunities in varied and creative manners. As one of our authors wrote, "In the end, it is all about values."

Becoming crystal clear about what the institution stands for frees creative energy and gives employees focus, purpose, and confidence. Creating a culture supportive of innovative thinking strengthens the resolve of institutions to take risks that may, or may not, pay off. However, the process is the ultimate reward. The community colleges and leaders in this book were invited to share their creative endeavors because of their demonstrated ability to never lose sight of a key group of values and beliefs.

Vision

Creative acts are fleeting if they lack vision. Creative leaders communicate clearly and create conditions in which the direction of the institution is easy to understand. It is the enduring nature of value-based creativity that permeates creative institutional cultures, the essence of a well-designed vision. Institutions with vision understand where they are going. This value is responsible for freeing the creative spirit. Creative leaders channel their passion to breed enthusiasm. Having an "internal compass" helps leaders help the college constituents understand why their work matters. They know their vision. "You don't know what you don't know" is an important adage. Creative leaders help their employees understand what they need to know so that the right change environment can exist. Understanding the logistics of transformation is critical to an effective vision. Presidents or chancellors must know where to start and how to create buy-in, and they must have the patience to see the transformation through—while modeling the qualities they support.

Affective Domain

Creative leaders value the whole person. They understand that education happens on multiple levels—cognitively, behaviorally, emotionally, socially, and now virtually. It is important to reach out to people and to facilitate the ability for people to reach back. Creative community colleges thrive by creating and supporting connections. Connections promote love for learning. Students who are engaged by faculty or staff form valuable relationships that transcend the grade. In his research of social intelligence, Goleman (2006) found that meaningful, positive connections infused the needed ingredient to overcome the worst social evils such as poverty, crime, and drug use; and transcended "race, ethnic background, or family structure" (p. 291). Creative leaders know that relationships between those within the college are most crucial to student success.

With this atmosphere on college campuses, people enjoy learning. They appreciate the process of learning, and they understand that it is more than a book and computer. Learning reaches a new level when the process, as much as the course material, is appreciated. Creative community colleges do not simply celebrate milestones or victories. They celebrate the process and path they took together; they celebrate learning. Without relationships, there is no institutional heart. Connecting on a human level requires a mutual understanding that both parties are invested in the relationship; both are equally vulnerable. As one of our creative leaders wrote, "Be genuine, and reveal some vulnerability or convey an honest sense of one's self—all good ways to gain confidence and build trust within an organization." Some would argue that revealing leaders' vulnerabilities weakens their ability to lead. We contend that it makes them human.

Integrity

Creative leaders in this book insist that integrity means leading with honesty and encouraging a free and safe exchange of ideas. A culture of trust is built by dissolving hidden agendas, and institutional and personal energies can focus on the matter at hand rather than worrying about whether in-house power struggles are occurring. When employees can work without fear of reprimand for sharing creative ideas, innovation occurs naturally. However, with honesty comes the expectation or requirement that difficult issues be confronted. Living with integrity means embracing tough decisions (e.g., eliminating a position or program). Few enjoy this process, but maintaining a healthy vision for the college requires serious reflection on issues, both good and bad.

Conducting business with integrity has become even more important now that community colleges have entered the age of accountability. Striving to reach goals is only the first step. Evaluating progress and effectiveness allows colleges to make accurate decisions. Data turn on the headlights as we drive down the sometimes hazy road into the future. Creative community college leaders inspect what they expect, not because they lack trust in their employees, but because they know that by reviewing all aspects of institutional behavior, nothing is left to guesswork or hidden.

Public colleges must conduct business transparently. As Thomas Jefferson observed, "Whenever you do a thing, act as if the whole world were watching" (BrainyQuote, 2008b). Donors, the government, and the public watch community colleges closely. The altruistic reasons around which educators created their careers disappear during audits. Creative community college leaders understand that everything they do is for the public good. Displaying their operations, decisions, and behaviors demonstrates they are good stewards of the public's trust, money, and children. Ultimately, creative community colleges believe that through demonstrating their work to the public, they earn the community's trust—and there is nothing more important to the long-term sustainability of a community college.

Courage to Change

Change involves the unknown. It is risky and even dangerous. Nevertheless, creative leaders and community colleges know that with good vision, values, and people, the institution will reach new plateaus. They have the courage to believe in their own potential and to go with it. Employees at creative community colleges know that some of their efforts will not reach the desired outcomes, but they also know they have administrative support that allows them to try new ideas without fear of retribution. When employees know that someone believes in them, that their supervisors will be there to support them regardless of the outcome, they will give of themselves beyond imagination. Creative leaders get this, too. Creative leadership celebrates the journey—not just reaching the destination. They understand that the outcome is important to reaching the college's goals, but the journey employees take to reach that goal is a tremendous investment of effort. This effort is celebrated at creative community colleges. Celebration rejuvenates the spirit when goals are reached, and repairs worn souls when they are not.

Developing a trust and belief in those you employ means knowing when to loosen the reigns. Creative leaders surround themselves with the most qualified personnel available, develop trust and vision together, and then let the employees do their jobs without interference. These leaders believe in their employees' abilities. They provide the support, confidence, and encouragement so that people can think outside the box. With that foundation of trust, courageous commitments begin to spark. When creative sparks fly, there is no stopping a creative community college.

Relationships

Relationships are a nonnegotiable necessity within creative community colleges. Leaders and followers alike understand that education takes a village and that no one can be successful in these environments in isolation. Relationships make our lives outside of education meaningful. It is no different within the walls of a college. Through relationships, we create a vision for the future, we test our integrity, and we act courageously. We are social creatures by nature, and *social,* by definition, means community.

Creative leaders understand the importance of relationships because their jobs focus on creating them. Each year, a growing percentage of presidents' workdays reportedly are spent on making connections with business, industry, and potential donors. They realize that creating partnerships allows the creative community college to acquire resources that might otherwise be unavailable. As Carl Kuttler, president of St. Petersburg College, once warned, "No partners, no prosperity" (Roueche, Tabor, & Roueche, 1995, p. 131). Leaders also realize they cannot do it all themselves. Building relationships outside the college walls is the responsibility of everyone in the college. Building community trust and providing testimony to the impact the college is having requires a belief in relationships that is pervasive throughout the ranks of faculty, staff, and students.

The stereotype of external leader and internal followers is outdated. Relationships between departments prevent the silo effect. Faculty in creative community colleges realize that for students to understand how job skills transfer across multiple work environments, a requirement in today's labor market, the faculty must be the first to bridge the departmental iron wall and encourage working together. Learning communities are an invention of creative thought and abound in creative community colleges.

Disciplined Decision Making

With creative leaders' value-based foundations in place, they are able to make disciplined decisions. By never losing sight of their core values and beliefs, they can wade through the difficult times when unpopular tasks must be completed. It is not easy in today's world to release an employee for the right reasons, particularly tenured faculty. It is even more difficult in union environments. However, we think creative leaders are better able to make the right decisions because they stick to what they know is right; they remain steadfast to their values. Values allow the creative leader to master fear and doubt, so that their creative energies can rise to the occasion.

Creative leaders are disciplined, intentional, and focused on their values. They can focus on strengths and become the best at their craft; simply being good is not good enough. As Collins (2001) wrote in his best-selling book on leadership, "Good is the enemy of great" (p. 1). There are no guarantees in life, but leaders can be certain that without values, all creative efforts will wander aimlessly without direction, be void of the appreciation for others, and lack the genuineness to last.

THE FUTURE

Our world excites and frightens. Changes often happen before we see them coming and formulate a response. How are some colleges able to survive, and even thrive, in this environment? They are getting better at anticipating the future.

> *The excellent companies are learning organizations. They don't wait around for the marketplace to do them in; they create their own internal marketplace. … Intriguingly, the top companies have developed a whole host of devices and management routines to stave off calcification. They experiment more, encourage more tries, and permit small failures. (Peters & Waterman, 2004, p. 110)*

How can community colleges—entrenched in tradition for 90 years—rise to meet these challenges, stay true to their roots, and meet the changing demands of their students and the global economy? This type, pace, and amount of change occurring now have never been among the challenges of our community college world. For some, change will happen to them. For others, change will become a comfortable, yet exciting, tool with which to create new opportunities for student success. Now, community colleges will be faced with several notable realities:

- The lines between K–12, community college, and baccalaureate institutions will disappear. The community college educational mission will absorb the others, to propel these colleges into become the largest segment of higher education.
- Student enrollments will increase four-fold, on some campuses, in a span of 20 years.
- Changing demographics will require colleges to provide developmental education, orientation, and first-generation student services for the largest at-risk student body ever seen on our campuses.
- Community colleges should not expect the already-reduced federal and state funding to return but rather raise funds to become more self-sustaining.
- Managing community colleges is big business; some already have more students and personnel than the largest of universities and corporations.

- *Community* will never have the same connotation it had when community colleges were first being built or that it has today.
- By 2010, this century's first decade will have seen three of every four community college presidents retired and replaced. New leadership styles will accompany new leaders to their posts.
- Technology will enable and significantly improve faculty/student engagement. Soon, teachers and learning objects will virtually appear in three-dimensions wherever and whenever students need. Education will continue to be increasingly mobile.

In pursuit of understanding how some colleges survive these challenges, we found a growing number with creative cultures, repositioning themselves to become immune to the more dramatic demands on their facilities and services. Many more creative leaders and colleges exist beyond this book. You may be lucky enough to call one "home." Home, a relative term, is a favorite descriptor used by employees of creative community colleges. These colleges know where they are going and why they are there; and they are enjoying the journey.

Now that we have looked at creative community colleges and their transformational leaders, we feel more secure than ever in believing in our collective future, whatever it may hold. We trust that it will be full of success stories. The messages here showcase the reality that education will require more creativity and commitment than ever before. Collectively, creative community colleges are rising to the occasion. The lessons learned from their leaders illustrate the importance of creating the futures we envision, not the futures we inherit.

REFERENCES

BrainyQuote. (2008a). [Leonardo Da Vinci quote]. Retrieved from www.brainyquote.com/quotes/authors/l/leonardo_da_vinci.html

BrainyQuote. (2008b). [Thomas Jefferson quote]. Retrieved from www.brainyquote.com/quotes/authors/t/thomas_jefferson.html

Collins, J. (2001). *Good to great.* New York: HarperCollins.

Friedman, T. (2004) *The world is flat: A brief history of the twenty-first century.* New York: Farrar, Straus, and Giroux.

Gardner, M. (2007, October 15). How companies can encourage innovation. *The Christian Science Monitor.* Retrieved October 20, 2007, from www.csmonitor.com/2007/1015/p13s01-wmgn.html

Gleazer, E. J. (1980). *The community college: Values, vision, & vitality.* Washington, DC: American Association of Community and Junior Colleges.

Goleman, D. (2006). *Social intelligence: The science of human relationships.* New York: Bantam Dell.

Kloman, H. (2006). The future of risk management, again. *Risk Management Reports, 33*(10). Retrieved February 11, 2008, from www.riskreports.com/protected/archive/rmr1006.html

O'Banion, T. (1997). *The learning college.* Phoenix, AZ: ACE/Oryx Press.

Peters, T., & Waterman, R. (2004). *In search of excellence: Lessons from America's best-run companies.* New York: HarperCollins.

Rosenfeld, S. (2006). *Cool community colleges: Creative approaches to economic development.* Washington, DC: Community College Press.

Roueche, J. E., & Ciez-Volz, K. (2006). *Teaching and learning with heart: The affective domain in the community college. Celebrations.* Austin, TX: National Institute for Staff and Organizational Development.

Roueche, J. E., Johnson, L. F., Roueche, S. D., & associates. (1997). *Embracing the tiger: The effectiveness debate and the community college.* Washington DC: Community College Press.

Roueche, J. E., & Roueche, S. D. (2000, May/June). Facing the new millennium: Making friends with the future. *Community College Journal, 70*(5), 16–22.

Roueche, J. E., Tabor, L., & Roueche, S. D. (1995). *The company we keep.* Washington, DC: Community College Press.

Scanlon, J. (2006, February 23). Reading, writing, and creativity. *Business Week Online.* Retrieved October 1, 2007, from www.businessweek.com/innovate/content/feb2006/id20060223_167340.htm

Index

About the Contributors

George R. Boggs is president and CEO of the American Association of Community Colleges (AACC), based in Washington, DC. AACC represents more than 1,100 associate degree–granting institutions and more than 11 million students. Boggs previously served as faculty member, division chair, and associate dean of instruction at Butte College in California; for 15 years he served as the superintendent and president of Palomar College in California. He served as a member of the Committee on Undergraduate Science Education of the National Research Council and on several National Science Foundation panels and committees. He holds a bachelor's degree in chemistry from Ohio State University, a master's degree in chemistry from the University of California at Santa Barbara, and a doctor of philosophy degree in educational administration from The University of Texas at Austin.

Walter G. Bumphus is a professor in the Community College Leadership Program at The University of Texas at Austin. Before this position, he served as president of the Louisiana Community and Technical College System (LCTCS). During his tenure, LCTCS governed seven community colleges, two technical community colleges and one technical college with 40 campuses across the state, serving 51,000 students. After his departure, the LCTCS board conferred on Bumphus the title of President Emeritus of the Louisiana Community and Technical College System. Bumphus holds the distinction of being one of the few educational leaders to have received the National CEO of the Year Award and to have chaired AACC's board of directors (1997); he has also served as a member of the board of directors of the American Council on Education. Bumphus was selected as the ACCT Marie Y. Martin CEO of the Year for the 2005–2006 academic year. Bumphus holds a BA in speech communications and an MA in guidance and counseling from Murray State University (KY). He earned his PhD in higher education administration from the Community College Leadership Program at The University of Texas at Austin.

Donald W. Cameron was appointed president of Guilford Technical Community College (NC) in 1991, a position he still holds. He had served as executive vice president from 1981 to 1990. He began a 34-year career in education as a high school teacher and coach and served in a variety of faculty and administrative positions at universities and community colleges in North and South Carolina. Cameron holds an associate, a bachelor's, a master's, and a doctoral degree. Cameron is involved in numerous civic activities and is in demand as a speaker on education's role in economic development, leadership development, and succession planning. He has been recognized with numerous awards from Outstanding Teacher of the Year, 1968, to the North Carolina State Board of Community Colleges President of the Year Award, 2001. Cameron has demonstrated his commitment to workforce preparedness in serving community colleges for more than three decades. His outstanding leadership in developing partnerships with business and industry has truly served the Greensboro community well.

Richard Carpenter became the president of the North Harris Montgomery Community College District (TX) in 2007. Before his arrival in Houston, he was the 10th permanent president of the College of Southern Nevada, beginning in 2004. With 25 years of experience as an administrator and faculty member in higher education, he leads one of the largest multicampus 2-year college districts, which enrolls 47,000 students. At the College of Southern Nevada, he managed an annual operating budget exceeding $100 million and directed a staff of 2,800, possessing a service area the size of Virginia. For 2½ years before heading to the College of Southern Nevada, Carpenter served as president and state director for the nationally prominent Wisconsin Technical College System with 16 colleges, 440,000 students, 19,000 employees, and a $1 billion annual operating budget. During the 20 years before Wisconsin, he headed community colleges in Minnesota, California, and Alabama; his first presidency was at Kentucky's Somerset Community College at the age of 29. Holding a PhD in community college leadership from North Carolina State University, the native of Louisiana maintains a nationwide reputation as a leader in higher education. His current national service includes the presidency of the National Board of Directors for Community Colleges for Innovative Technology Transfer, and membership in the U.S. Space and Rocket Center Foundation, its board of trustees, and AACC. Throughout his career, Carpenter has received numerous state and national awards and recognitions for achievements in higher education, economic development, and community leadership.

Christine Johnson, a native New Mexican, has served in a variety of education roles in Colorado in a career that spans more than 30 years. A first-generation college student, Johnson is known for championing access and equity in public and higher education. She earned her bachelor's degree from New Mexico State University, and master's and doctoral degrees from the University of Colorado at Boulder. Johnson's first 15 years were in the public education sector in the Denver Public Schools. Her years in public schools included high school teaching, middle and high school principalships, and 2 years as an assistant superintendent in a suburban district. Her national education perspective was provided by 5 years of working with states on their education reform agendas with the Education Commission of the States. She spent 10 years in the community college sector, including 3½ years as the chief academic officer for the Colorado Community College System, and the last 6½ years as president of the Community College of Denver—the nationally recognized urban, multi-campus community college. Johnson has served on local, state, and national boards, including those of the National Assessment Governing Board, the Fund for the Improvement of Postsecondary Education, U.S. Department of Defense Workforce Development Taskforce, National Commission on Study of the 12th grade, College Board National Commission on Community Colleges, the Colorado Commission on Higher Education Lumina Foundation Policy Advisory Board, and Coca Cola's School/Business Partnership Board. Among Johnson's accomplishments are opening doors of opportunity for low-income and first-generation students; leading the Community College of Denver to higher levels of student retention, graduation, and transfer; and forging strong community and business relationships that helped generate 45% of the college's budget during the toughest funding cuts in Colorado's state's history.

Marie Kane is superintendent and president emeritus of Chaffey College (CA), where she served for almost 7 years. Before that, she was president of Phoenix College for 8 years. Other positions include provost, Norco Campus, Riverside Community College, and dean of instruction, San Joaquin Delta College. She holds a PhD from Arizona State University in mathematics education, an MS in mathematics from Lamar University, and a BA in mathematics from The University of Texas at Austin. Kane has written and spoken on topics including leadership and governance at state and national levels. She was named the Pacific Region CEO of the Year in 2004 by the Association of Community College Trustees.

Brent Knight serves as president of Morton College in Cicero, Illinois. He has been a community college president at Pierce College in Tacoma, Washington; Austin Community College in Texas; and Triton College in River Grove, Illinois.

As a vice president, Knight served in one of the largest privately held corporations in the nation for 7 years. He earned a doctorate in educational leadership from Western Michigan University and completed his postdoctoral study at the University of Michigan. His accomplishments include major capital construction and remodeling campus and business projects throughout the United States. His expertise in strategic planning makes him a sought-after speaker. He is a visiting scholar at the University of Michigan. Knight's civic involvement includes board-level positions in the Michigan Botanic Gardens, Greater Lakes Mental Health, Westlake Community Hospital Board, and the Illinois Council of Community College Presidents. He has been published in numerous books and higher education journals.

William Law has served as the president of Tallahassee Community College since May 2002. He is now in his 20th year as a community college president, having served previously in Texas and Illinois. Law began his community college career as vice president at St. Petersburg Junior College in 1981, moving from the position of staff director for the Committee on Higher Education in the Florida House of Representatives. Law holds an MS and a PhD in higher education administration from Florida State University. He earned a BA in English from LeMoyne College in Syracuse, New York. Throughout his career, Law's primary focus has been on improving student performance and retention and strengthening workforce education in the communities where he has served. The artful use of technology by students, faculty, and institutions has characterized his leadership. Law served as a member of the Florida Council of 100, chairman of the local Economic Development Council, chairman of the Florida Council of Presidents, and member of the Board of the Mary Brogan Museum of Art and Science.

Michael B. McCall is the founding president and CEO of the Kentucky Community and Technical College System, where he oversees a system that has an annual operating budget of approximately $633 million and an additional $228 million capital construction projects to operate a seamless complex system of 16 colleges with more than 65 campuses, touching the lives of more than 300,000 citizens. McCall has served more than 37 years in community and technical colleges. Before his appointment as the founding president of KCTCS, McCall served as president of South Carolina's comprehensive technical college system and provided leadership for South Carolina's economic development training programs. Earlier in his career, he served as president of Florence Darlington Technical College (SC), president of Paul D. Camp Community College (VA), and as dean and faculty member at community and technical colleges in Virginia. McCall received a BS in physics and mathematics from the University of North Carolina at Wilmington and MS and EdD in physics from Virginia Polytechnic Institute and State University. He has been recognized for his advanced collaborative partnerships, economic development, innovative use of technology, and team-oriented management. McCall received the 2005 National Council for Continuing Education and Training's National Leadership Award–Inside the Field. The National Institute for Staff and Organizational Development honored McCall with its 2005 International Leadership Award. In 2004, he received the prestigious honor from *Kentucky Monthly Magazine* as the 2004 Kentuckian of the Year. In 2006, McCall completed his tenure as AACC's board chair and has served on boards and commissions including the Business Higher Education Forum; United Way of the Bluegrass; Southern Growth Policies Board; the editorial board of the *Community College Journal of Research and Practice*; the advisory board of the Center for the Integration of Research; Teaching, and Learning; and the National Council of State Directors of Community Colleges.

Stephen K. Mittelstet is president of Richland College of the Dallas County Community College District (TX), where he has served on the humanities faculty since the college opened in 1972. Mittelstet has been president at Richland College since 1979 and was recognized by the 79th Texas Legislature for his 25 years of outstanding service to Texas. Mittelstet is the 2007 recipient of both the national Educational Testing Service's O'Banion Prize for "inspiring significant change to teaching and learning" and the National Institute for Staff and Organizational Development International Leadership Award. Under Mittelstet's leadership, Richland College is the first community college to be recognized by the White House and the U.S. Department of Commerce as a recipient of the 2005 Malcolm Baldrige National Quality Award. He also serves as the superintendent of schools for the newly chartered Richland Collegiate High School for Mathematics, Science, and Engineering. Mittelstet earned his BA summa cum laude in English, French, and history/religion from McMurray College (KY) and his PhD in higher education administration and English from the Community College Leadership Program at The University of Texas at Austin. Mittelstet has earned numerous honors and awards such as the 2006 Texas Association for Black Personnel in Higher Education Community Award for Educational Advancement, and the 1994 American Council of Teachers of Foreign Languages Outstanding Foreign Language Educator.

Phillip W. Neal is a doctoral student in the Community College Leadership Program at The University of Texas at Austin. He serves as a psychology faculty member and the coordinator of student services and counseling at Laramie County Community College–Albany County Campus (LCCC) in Laramie, Wyoming. Neal has held numerous instructional and student support positions, including on the Faculty Senate, the Distance Education Advisory Committee, the Student Services Leadership Team, and the Albany County Campus Facilities Design Team. He displays his passion for leadership development by serving as a faculty mentor and conducting workshops with high school students, community college student leaders, and business leaders. During his career, Neal was honored with the LCCC Faculty Excellence award and is a University of Texas at Austin Roueche Senior Research Fellow.

Bob Paxton has been the president of Iowa Central Community College in Fort Dodge since 1995. Before this position, he served as a vice president of instruction and dean of student services at Cowley County Community College and Area Vocational-Technical School in Arkansas City, Kansas, and the director of admissions at Colby Community College in Kansas. He earned his bachelor's degree in ministry and counseling from Nebraska Christian College, his master's degree in guidance and counseling from Fort Hays State University, and his doctoral degree from the Community College Leadership Program at The University of Texas at Austin. Paxton has been involved in numerous local and state organizations including the Fort Dodge Mayor Leadership Team, Fort Dodge Correctional Facility Advisory Board, Iowa Coordinating Council for Post-High School Education, Iowa Association of College and University Presidents, Webster County Economic Development Executive Team, Trinity Regional Hospital Board of Directors, and a board member and coach for the Fort Dodge Youth Soccer Association. In addition to his professional positions and affiliations, he has been recognized as a 2000 International Leadership Award recipient by the National Institute for Staff and Organizational Development, he was selected as the 1998 Iowa Community College Administrator of the Year by the Iowa Association of Community College Trustees, and he is the 1997 Community College Leadership Program Distinguished Graduate.

Richard M. Rhodes became president of El Paso Community College (TX) in 2001. Before being named president, he served as the vice president of business services at Salt Lake Community College in Salt Lake City (UT) for 8 years. From 1983 to 1994, Rhodes served as the vice president of financial and administrative services and interim president at El Paso Community College (TX), and before that he was the comptroller and accountant at New Mexico State University from 1975 to 1983. A native of Alamogordo, New Mexico, Rhodes received a bachelor's degree in business administration in accounting and an MA in educational management and development (higher education) from New Mexico State University. He earned his PhD from the Community College Leadership Program at The University of Texas at Austin. Rhodes is active in the El Paso community serving on the executive board of the Greater El Paso Chamber of Commerce and several other El Paso civic boards. In addition to his local commitments, Rhodes serves on the Executive Board of the Texas Association of Community Colleges and the Formula Funding Advisory Committee for the Texas Higher Education Coordinating Board. Rhodes is chair of the Texas Association of Community College Trustees and Administrators; in 2007, Governor Rick Perry appointed Rhodes to serve on the Commission for a College Ready Texas. Rhodes received the Distinguished Graduate Award from the Community College Leadership Program at The University of Texas at Austin, the Minority Small Business Advocate of the Year, Services Award from the U.S. Small Business Administration, and the Vision of Excellence award from the El Paso Hispanic Chamber of Commerce, and he was inducted into the El Paso Business Hall of Fame in 2006.

M. Melissa Richardson is a doctoral student in the Community College Leadership Program at The University of Texas at Austin. A Senior Roueche Fellow, a Jesse Jones Scholar, and an editor for NISOD, she recently transitioned from a position of English professor at Central Texas College in Killeen, a position she held since 1999. In her tenure at Central Texas College, Richardson held leadership roles on the Southern Association of Colleges and Schools Accreditation Compliance Team, the Professional Development Committee, and the Faculty Senate. Richardson has published several short stories and book reviews and has presented at regional and national conferences.

John E. Roueche is a nationally recognized authority in community college education and the author of 35 books and more than 150 chapters and articles. He has spoken to more than 1,300 community colleges and universities since 1970. A 1981 study at Florida State University named him outstanding living author in the field of community college education. He received the 1988 B. Lamar Johnson National Distinguished Leadership Award from the League for Innovation in the Community College; the 1986 Distinguished Leadership Award from the American Association of Community Colleges; the 1986 Distinguished Research Publication Award from the National Association of Developmental Education; the 1985 Outstanding Learned Article Award from the United States Press Association; the 1984 Golden Key Distinguished Research Award from The University of Texas; the 1982 Teaching Excellence Award from The University of Texas; and the 1977, 1992, 1993, and 1996 Outstanding Research Awards from the Council of Universities and Colleges. He was selected by The University of Texas at Austin faculty to receive the 1994 Dean's Distinguished Faculty Award. In 1998, he was honored by his colleagues with The University of Texas Career Research Excellence Award.

Suanne D. Roueche is the author of 13 books and more than 35 articles and chapters. She is also editor of *Innovation Abstracts* for the National Institute for Staff and Organizational Development. Roueche is the 1997 National Leadership Award recipient from the AACC. She received the 1984 Outstanding Research Publication Award from the Council of Universities and Colleges, as well as the 1987–1988

Distinguished Research/Writing Award from the National Council of Staff and Program Development. She conceptualized and developed the Community College Teaching Internship Program in the Department of Curriculum and Instruction at The University of Texas at Austin, and she organized and developed the first comprehensive developmental studies program at El Centro College (Dallas), where she taught for 10 years before joining the staff at The University of Texas.

Jerry Sue Thornton is president of Cuyahoga Community College, the largest community college in Ohio, whose mission is to provide high-quality, accessible, and affordable educational opportunities and services—including university transfer, technical, and lifelong learning programs—that promote individual development and improve the overall quality of life in a multicultural community. Thornton manages a budget of $140 million, oversees three campuses and two learning centers, and directs 1,596 full and part-time faculty and 800 support and administrative staff. The college serves approximately 26,000 credit and 32,000 noncredit students annually through 77 degree programs and unique services for special-population segments. Thornton began her career as a junior high school teacher in Earlington, Kentucky, moved on to Murray High School, then to Triton College in River Grove, Illinois, where she became dean of arts and sciences. In 1985, she became president of Lakewood Community College in White Bear Lake, Minnesota, and continued in that position until coming to Cuyahoga Community College (OH). Her educational background includes a PhD from The University of Texas at Austin, attendance at The Institute for the Management of Lifelong Education at the Harvard Graduate School of Education, an honorary doctorate of Humane Letters from the College of St. Catherine in St. Paul, Minnesota, and a master's and bachelor's degree from Murray State University.

Steven Wallace became Florida Community College at Jacksonville's fourth president in 1997. His résumé includes professional service in Minnesota, Ohio, and California. In all, Wallace has spent 30 years working in community colleges, starting with his alma mater, Chaffey Community College (CA). He has served as an instructor and administrator during his career. He began as an adjunct faculty member at Chaffey and, in 1975, became a full-time faculty member in the college's innovative Learning Center. In 1977, Wallace became Chaffey's district director of learning disabilities and later the director of marketing and legislative affairs. Wallace left Chaffey in 1981 for Lakeland Community College (OH). There he served as vice president for administrative services for 9 years. While at Lakeland, he administered a wide range of college functions, including finance, facilities, computer services, human resources, strategic planning, admissions and registration, legislative and legal affairs, and the Center for the Fine and Performing Arts. Wallace has held two previous college presidencies, both in

Minnesota: first at Austin Community College (1990–1992) and then at Inver Hills Community College (1992–1997). He also had statewide responsibilities concerning faculty professional development, academic and administrative computing, labor relations, and distance learning. He is recognized nationally for his leadership in community economic development, student success initiatives, academic technology, and the emerging community college baccalaureate. Wallace earned an associate in arts degree in 1972 from Chaffey Community College, followed by bachelor's and master's degrees in psychology from California State University at San Bernardino, and he received a doctorate in higher education administration in 1989 from Claremont Graduate University in California. Since arriving at Florida Community College at Jacksonville, Wallace has been involved in the community serving on numerous local boards such as the Jacksonville Regional Chamber of Commerce, Take Stock in Children, United Way, Enterprise North Florida, and the Schultz Center for Teaching and Leadership. His statewide leadership roles have included chair of the Florida Community College Council of Presidents, and the Council's Economic Development Committee. At the national level, he was vice chair of the Community College Baccalaureate Association.